"To use the word *timely* for a book abou~~t~~ may seem inappropriate. But in this case the adjective is exactly right. Many of us have wanted to spread the word that Herman Bavinck's theological perspective can contribute much to a renewal of the church's life and mission today. Now in this book John Bolt has made the case in a concise and convincing manner!"

Richard J. Mouw, Former President, Professor of Faith and Public Life, Fuller Theological Seminary

"This obvious labor of love explores an important but insufficiently highlighted aspect of Bavinck's thought. Leaving virtually no pertinent stone unturned throughout his life and published works, Bolt provides both a full presentation of Bavinck's views and his own understanding of their continuing relevance for Christian discipleship today. Here is valuable instruction in Bavinck's thought presented in a way that will also stimulate the reader's own thinking on the issues raised."

Richard B. Gaffin Jr., Professor of Biblical and Systematic Theology, Emeritus, Westminster Theological Seminary

"Trinitarian, Christ-centered, and culturally engaged, Herman Bavinck immerses us into a vivid vision of the gospel of Jesus Christ. Bavinck's rich theological imagination provides a compelling alternative to the many vapid, pragmatic approaches to faith today. John Bolt provides an accessible and illuminating guide to Bavinck's theology of the Christian life in the most expansive sense: the Christian life of fellowship with God and others, in family, work, and politics. Bolt skillfully navigates these waters in order to open up the treasures of Bavinck for today's church."

J. Todd Billings, Gordon H. Girod Research Professor of Reformed Theology, Western Theological Seminary

"Perhaps every generation in the church age could claim a need for Bavinck's perspective on the Christian life. We can't let our salt lose its saltiness and our light lose its brilliance—*not now*. Bavinck encourages us in this regard even as we are in the world, not of the world, and sent into the world. In one seamless volume, Bolt shows how Bavinck's contributions help correct our nearsightedness as we become tethered to his conviction that the Word of God is ever living and ever active in every day."

Gloria Furman, author, *Glimpses of Grace* and *Treasuring Christ When Your Hands Are Full*

"Never before have I read such a fine and stimulating overview of Herman Bavinck's life and theology. John Bolt shows clearly why the study of Bavinck is growing worldwide and why this theology is a great help for today's Christians. Bavinck and Bolt are a great team!"

Herman Selderhuis, Professor of Church History, Theological University of Apeldoorn; Director, Refo500, The Netherlands

"Not one square inch of nature, work, culture, or history escaped the reach of Herman Bavinck's expansive Christ-centered worldview. Of the great Reformed theologians, Bavinck is the generous giant, with a heart as wide as his axiom 'grace restores nature.' Bavinck's vision of a sovereign Savior at work in the world, carefully grounded in the gospel, suits him to speak authoritatively on the Christian's place in this world. This book is a masterpiece from John Bolt, a man who knows Bavinck's mind as well as anyone."

Tony Reinke, Staff Writer and Researcher, desiringGod.org; administrator, hermanbavinck.org; author, *Lit!: A Christian Guide to Reading Books*

"Bolt's portrait of Bavinck and his theology captures the man himself: clear, elegant, biblically saturated, theologically rich, philosophically nuanced, irenic, and aimed at the Christian life. Drawing on a diversity of sources, Bolt not only brings the riches of Bavinck's mature theology into conversation with current theological concerns, but also applies it to the most practical elements of faith, marriage, family, work, and culture. He ably introduces readers to Bavinck's vision of the Christian life as part of God's movement of grace restoring nature and a cosmic redemption aimed at restoring and elevating creation to its intended goal. Most of all, it is a vision of following Jesus out into the world as the Father conforms his children into the image of the Son in the power of the Spirit for the sake of his glorious name."

Derek Rishmawy, Director of College and Young Adult Ministries, Trinity United Presbyterian Church, Santa Ana, California

BAVINCK

on the Christian Life

THEOLOGIANS ON THE CHRISTIAN LIFE

EDITED BY STEPHEN J. NICHOLS AND JUSTIN TAYLOR

BAVINCK

on the Christian Life

FOLLOWING JESUS IN FAITHFUL SERVICE

JOHN BOLT

CROSSWAY

WHEATON, ILLINOIS

Bavinck on the Christian Life: Following Jesus in Faithful Service

Copyright © 2015 by John Bolt

Published by Crossway
    1300 Crescent Street
    Wheaton, Illinois 60187

Cover design: Josh Dennis

Cover image: Richard Solomon Artists, Mark Summers

First printing 2015

Printed in the United States of America

Trade paperback ISBN: 978-1-4335-4074-5
ePub ISBN: 978-1-4335-4077-6
PDF ISBN: 978-1-4335-4075-2
Mobipocket ISBN: 978-1-4335-4076-9

Library of Congress Cataloging-in-Publication Data

Bolt, John, 1947–
   Bavinck on the Christian life : following Jesus in faithful service / John Bolt.
      pages cm.—(Theologians on the Christian life)
    Includes bibliographical references and index.
    ISBN 978-1-4335-4074-5 (tp)
   1. Christian life. 2. Bavinck, Herman, 1854–1921.
I. Title.
BV4501.3.B6555   2015
248.4'842—dc23   2015000576

For my children,

Michelle
David (and Kim)
Justin (and Lori)

and grandchildren,

Adrianna, Michaela
Caden, Evan, Charlotte
Jordan, Emily, Olivia, Annika

whose being is one of the great joys of my life
and
whose life of flourishing Christian discipleship is my daily prayer

CONTENTS

SERIES PREFACE

Some might call us spoiled. We live in an era of significant and substantial resources for Christians on living the Christian life. We have ready access to books, DVD series, online material, seminars—all in the interest of encouraging us in our daily walk with Christ. The laity, the people in the pew, have access to more information than scholars dreamed of having in previous centuries.

Yet for all our abundance of resources, we also lack something. We tend to lack the perspectives from the past, perspectives from a different time and place than our own. To put the matter differently, we have so many riches in our current horizon that we tend not to look to the horizons of the past.

That is unfortunate, especially when it comes to learning about and practicing discipleship. It's like owning a mansion and choosing to live in only one room. This series invites you to explore the other rooms.

As we go exploring, we will visit places and times different from our own. We will see different models, approaches, and emphases. This series does not intend for these models to be copied uncritically, and it certainly does not intend to put these figures from the past high upon a pedestal like some race of super-Christians. This series intends, however, to help us in the present listen to the past. We believe there is wisdom in the past twenty centuries of the church, wisdom for living the Christian life.

Stephen J. Nichols and Justin Taylor

ABBREVIATIONS

Analysis	Bolt, John. *A Theological Analysis of Herman Bavinck's Two Essays on the* Imitatio Christi. Lewiston, NY: Edwin Mellen, 2013.
"Catholicity"	Bavinck, Herman. "The Catholicity of Christianity and the Church." Translated by John Bolt. *Calvin Theological Journal* 27 (1992): 220–51.
Certainty	Bavinck, Herman. *The Certainty of Faith.* Translated by Harry der Nederlanden. St. Catharines, ON: Paideia, 1980.
"Com. Grace"	Bavinck, Herman. "Common Grace." Translated by Raymond C. Van Leeuwen, *Calvin Theological Journal* 24 (1989): 38–65.
Dogmaticus	Bremmer, R. H. *Herman Bavinck als dogmaticus.* Kampen: Kok, 1961.
Dosker	Dosker, Henry Elias. "Herman Bavinck: A Eulogy by Henry Elias Dosker." In Herman Bavinck, *Essays on Religion, Science and Society,* edited by John Bolt, translated by Harry Boonstra and Gerrit Sheeres, 13–24. Grand Rapids: Baker, 2008. Originally published in the *Princeton Theological Review* 20 (1922): 448–64.
ERSS	Bavinck, Herman. *Essays on Religion, Science, and Society.* Edited by John Bolt. Translated by Harry Boonstra and Gerrit Sheeres. Grand Rapids: Baker, 2008.
Family	Bavinck, Herman. *The Christian Family.* Translated by Nelson D. Kloosterman. Grand Rapids: Christian's Library, 2012.
"Gen. Prin."	Bavinck, Herman. "General Biblical Principles and the Relevance of Concrete Mosaic Law for the Social Question Today (1891)." Translated by John Bolt. *Journal of Markets and Morality* 13, no. 2 (Fall 2010): 437–46.

Gleason   Gleason, Ron. *Herman Bavinck: Pastor, Churchman, States-
                 man, and Theologian.* Phillipsburg, NJ: P&R, 2010.

Handboekje   Bavinck, Herman. *Handboekje ten dienste der Gerefor-
                 meerde Kerken in Nederland voor het jaar 1894.* Middleburg:
                 Le Cointre, 1893.

Hepp   Hepp, V(alentijn). *Dr. Herman Bavinck.* Amsterdam: W. Ten
                 Have, 1921.

"Imit. I"   Bavinck, Herman. "The Imitation of Christ" [1885–1886]
                 ("De navolging van Christus, I, II, III, IV," *De vrije kerk* 11
                 (1885): 101–13, 203–13; 12 (1886): 321–33. ET in *Analysis*,
                 "Appendix A," 372–401. Page numbers provided in square
                 brackets [ ] in the notes refer to the pagination in *Analysis*.

"Imit. II"   Bavinck, Herman. "The Imitation of Christ and Life in the
                 Modern World" [1918] ("De navolging van Christus en het
                 moderne leven"). In *Kennis en leven: Opstellen en artikelen uit
                 vroegere jaren*, 115–45. Kampen: Kok, 1918. ET in *Analysis*,
                 "Appendix B," 402–40. Page numbers provided in square
                 brackets [ ] in the notes refer to the pagination in *Analysis*.

Landwehr   Landwehr, J. H. *In Memorian: Prof. Dr. H. Bavinck.* Kampen:
                 Kok, 1921.

"Moral Infl."   Bavinck, Herman. "The Influence of the Protestant Reforma-
                 tion on the Moral and Religious Condition of Communities
                 and Nations." In *Alliance of the Reformed Churches Holding the
                 Presbyterian System*, 48–55. Proceedings of the Fifth General
                 Council, Toronto, 1892. London: Publication Committee of
                 the Presbyterian Church of England, 1892.

PofR   Bavinck, Herman. *The Philosophy of Revelation: The Stone
                 Lectures for 1908–1909, Princeton Theological Seminary.* New
                 York: Longmans, Green, and Co., 1909.

RD, 1–4   Bavinck, Herman. *Reformed Dogmatics.* Edited by John Bolt.
                 Translated by John Vriend. 4 vols. Grand Rapids: Baker,
                 2003–2008.

Saved   Bavinck, Herman. *Saved by Grace: The Holy Spirit's Work in
                 Calling and Regeneration.* Edited by J. Mark Beach. Trans-
                 lated by Nelson D. Kloosterman. Grand Rapids: Reformation
                 Heritage, 2008.

Tijdg.   Bremmer, R. H. *Herman Bavinck en zijn tijdgenoten.* Kampen:
                 Kok, 1966.

Wereldb.   Bavinck, Herman. *Christelijke wereldbeschouwing.* 2nd ed.
                 Kampen: Kok, 1913.

PREFACE

Why do people resist the Christian gospel? Is it because Christian claims are unreasonable and a stumbling block for really smart people? Intellectual objections against the faith have been raised since the days of second-century antagonists such as the Greek philosopher Celsus. Christian apologists such as Justin Martyr then, and C. S. Lewis more recently, have responded with thoughtful rebuttals. A good, intellectually honest case can be made for the truth of Christianity. Its doctrines are not irrational.

Our faith seems more vulnerable, however, in the practice of Christian living. Believers and non-Christians are frequently united in denouncing hypocrisy in the church. In the words attributed widely to Benjamin Franklin, "How many observe Christ's Birth-day! How few, his Precepts!"[1] Christian talk is lofty, the complaint goes, but Christian walk is weak. When Christian lives don't measure up to the high standards set by the gospel, we might well wonder whether those standards are even possible. Friedrich Nietzsche put it very bluntly: "In truth, there was only one Christian and he died on the cross."[2] Christians who might dismiss Nietzsche as a despiser of Christianity cannot, however, dismiss Dietrich Bonhoeffer's warnings about "cheap grace" and his call for "costly discipleship."[3] In contexts where Christians are a majority, it may be too easy to be a Christian. When "others" live decent and respectable lives, the more radical demands of Christian discipleship—"deny [your]self and take up [your] cross and follow me" (Matt. 16:24)—may strike even the most evangelical and orthodox Christian as extreme or fanatic.

---

[1] This statement is often quoted and can be found on multiple Internet sites, some citing *Poor Richard's Almanack* (1743). See, for example, http://en.wikiquote.org/wiki/Poor_Richard%27s_Almanack#1743.

[2] F. W. Nietzsche, *The Antichrist*, trans. H. L. Mencken (New York: Knopf, 1918), 111–12 (sec. 39).

[3] Dietrich Bonhoeffer, *The Cost of Discipleship*, vol. 4 of *Dietrich Bonheoffer Works*, ed. Geffrey B. Kelly and John D. Godsey, trans. Barbara Green and Reinhard Krause (Minneapolis: Fortress, 2001), 37–198.

Under those circumstances, it becomes easy to rationalize "cheap discipleship" by appealing to good, biblical—and particularly Reformed—staples such as total depravity: we all "fall short of the glory of God" (Rom. 3:23); "I do not do the good I want to" (Rom. 7:19). Not only does this fail the critical test of Scripture itself—"you therefore must be perfect, as your heavenly Father is perfect" (Matt. 5:48)—it also gravely injures Christian testimony and witness. How the Christian gospel is viewed by non-Christians is directly tied to what they see of Christian conduct. Our Lord himself taught us that his followers would be known by their "fruit" (Matt. 7:20). The challenge cannot be avoided or evaded. Even allowing for overstatement, the following claim by American singer and songwriter Kevin Max ought to disturb all Christians: "The greatest single cause of atheism in the world today is Christians: who acknowledge Jesus with their lips, walk out the door, and deny Him by their lifestyle. That is what an unbelieving world simply finds unbelievable."[4]

If there is any truth to this claim, it represents a major departure from the witness of the early church. A second-century work, "The Letter to Diognetus," describes Christians with these words:

> They dwell in their own countries simply as sojourners . . . . They are in the flesh, but they do not live after the flesh. They pass their days on earth, but they are citizens of heaven. They obey the prescribed laws, and at the same time, they surpass the laws by their lives. They love all men but are persecuted by all. They are unknown and condemned. They are put to death, but [will be] restored to life. They are poor, yet they make many rich. They possess few things; yet, they abound in all. They are dishonored, but in their very dishonor are glorified. . . . And those who hate them are unable to give any reason for their hatred.[5]

The church father Tertullian reported that the Romans declared about Christians, "See how they love one another."[6] Christian conduct is essential to Christian witness; our walk must match our words.

Aware of this, Christians articulate the need for head and heart and hands to be in sync. The additional wrinkle here is the concern that our

---

[4] *Goodreads*, accessed October 10, 2012, http://www.goodreads.com/author/quotes/739520.Kevin_Max.
[5] "Epistle of Mathetes to Diognetus," in *Ante-Nicene Fathers*, ed. Alexander Roberts and James Donaldson, 10 vols. (New York: Christian Literature, 1885–1896; repr., Grand Rapids: Eerdmans, 1950–1951), 1:23–30.
[6] Tertullian, "The Apology," in *Ante-Nicene Fathers*, ed. Alexander Roberts and James Donaldson, 10 vols. (New York: Christian Literature, 1885–1896; repr., Grand Rapids: Eerdmans, 1950–1951), 3:46 (chap. 39).

words might demonstrate a merely intellectual grasp of Christian truth that does not touch our hearts and is not reflected in the work of our hands. Cerebral Christianity is tied to cold hearts and unwilling hands. This is a complaint most often directed at a Christian tradition like the Reformed, known and respected for its doctrinal rigor, sound theology, and philosophical accomplishments.

When my Calvin Seminary colleague John Cooper and I were graduate students living in Toronto, Canada, in the late 1970s, one evening while riding the streetcar we became involved in a deep philosophical-theological discussion about the soul. In the midst of our animated conversation, a young man sitting in the seat behind us tapped us on the shoulders and said, "If you had the love of Jesus in your heart you wouldn't have to mess up your heads with all that philosophy." We thanked him for his concern and tried to point out in the brief time we had that philosophy was one of the ways in which we could honor the lordship of Jesus Christ. The apostle Paul told the Romans to be transformed not "by the *removal* of your mind" but by their mind's *renewal* (Rom. 12:1).

Our young brother's concern, however, is not to be despised. Intellectualism is a real threat to full-orbed Christian discipleship. Nineteenth-century Southern Presbyterian theologian James Henley Thornwell (1812–1862) clearly recognized this when he wrote the following about a certain kind of theology:

> It gave no scope to the play of Christian feeling; it never turned aside to reverence, to worship, or to adore. It exhibited truth, nakedly and baldly, in its objective reality, without any reference to the subjective conditions, which under the influence of the Spirit, that truth was calculated to produce. It was a dry digest of theses and propositions—perfect in form, but as cold and lifeless as a skeleton.[7]

A generation later, Herman Bavinck echoed Thornwell's concern and explicitly expressed judgment on his fellow Dutch Reformed churchmen. After his death in 1921, one of Bavinck's contemporaries indicated that Bavinck was particularly annoyed by church leaders who constantly shouted "Reformed, Reformed," while their life and conduct stood in sharp contrast to basic Christian morality.[8] Shortly after World War I, Bavinck

---

[7] *The Collected Writings of James Henley Thornwell*, 4 vols. (Richmond: Presbyterian Committee of Publication, 1871–1873), 4:34.
[8] Landwehr, 72.

concluded one of his last essays with sharp criticism of significant economic sins among his fellow Dutch Reformed Church members, sins that
"not even the most stringent orthodoxy can make good."[9] That he had in
mind some of the "world-transforming" followers of Abraham Kuyper
(1837–1920) is clear from a revealing passage in his classic work *The Certainty of Faith* where he singles them out for their penchant to criticize
more "pietist" and "other-worldly" members of the Reformed communion:

> While these nineteenth century Christians [pietists] forgot the world for
> themselves, we run the danger of losing ourselves in the world. Nowadays
> we are out to convert the whole world, *to conquer all areas of life for Christ.*
> But we often neglect to ask whether we ourselves are truly converted and
> whether we belong to Christ in life and in death. For this is indeed what
> life boils down to. We may not banish this question from our personal or
> church life under the label of pietism or methodism. What does it profit
> a man if he gains the whole world, *even for Christian principles*, if he loses
> his own soul?[10]

The question I want to pose at the very beginning of a volume on Herman Bavinck's understanding of the Christian life is whether this great
Reformed theologian, broadly celebrated for his erudition and theological genius, practiced what he preached and taught. How does his theology
relate to his ethics? In other words, was his great mind combined with a
warm heart for the Lord and a commitment to a life of Christian service?
Does his life stand up to the scrutiny of his own theology?

It is my honor and pleasure in the pages that follow to provide the evidence for a positive answer to these queries. The opening chapter is an exploration of Bavinck's own desire, frequently expressed during the years he
was a student at the University of Leiden, "to be a worthy follower of Jesus."[11]
Part 1 explores the basis of Bavinck's theology of Christian discipleship,
which can be summarized especially under the rubrics of creation/law and
union with Christ. The three chapters of this foundational section are followed by two chapters describing the shape of Christian discipleship in
terms of the imitation of Christ and sketching out the contours of Bavinck's

---

[9] *Analysis*, 440.
[10] *Certainty*, 94. The italicized phrases, which are my emphasis, are thinly veiled references to the neo-
Calvinist followers of Abraham Kuyper.
[11] According to Bavinck biographer R. H. Bremmer, this sentiment appears often in Bavinck's journal
during his student days (*Tijdg.*, 32).

worldview. The remaining four chapters apply this vision concretely in marriage and family, work and vocation, culture and education, and finally, civil society. The volume concludes with Bavinck's only published sermon—on 1 John 5:4b—as a summary statement of triumphant Christian discipleship. My translation of this sermon into English was prepared specifically for this volume. Taken together, the chapters of this volume serve as an introduction to and brief primer of Herman Bavinck's thought.

A few words are in order about the method I used to set forth Bavinck's understanding of the Christian life and the content of both parts of this volume. My method in each chapter might best be described as eclectic. That is to say, I have gathered together a large number of key quotations from Bavinck's large corpus of writings into what I trust will be a coherent narrative. The supporting structural narrative is mine, but it is my desire to let Bavinck's own voice be dominant. Stylistically, this meant using numerous large block quotations, even within single paragraphs. I sought to make the whole, quotations and narrative, as seamless as possible, and if readers occasionally find themselves unsure whether the words they are reading are Bavinck's or mine, I will not be unhappy to cede credit to him. My own thinking has been so profoundly shaped by his that I often find myself repeating his words as my own. Both of us would remind the reader that all glory finally needs to be given to God, whose creation is good and magnificent, whose work of redemption is overwhelmingly gracious, whose revealed truth is glorious, and whose love beyond our wildest expectations. It is the joy of the gospel, the truth of the Word of God, that both he and I appeal to for our own life, work, and words.

The structure of this book is built on an architectural model with part 1 serving as the foundation, part 2 the building's superstructure, and part 3 the various rooms of the building. This structure has Trinitarian analogues. Being created in the image of the triune God is the foundation of the life of Christian discipleship. The building itself, however, is Christocentric; conformity to our Lord and Savior, Jesus Christ, is the shape of all genuine discipleship. In a Reformed Christian worldview, discipleship is comprehensive and occupies the full range of human experience: marriage and family, work and vocation, culture and education, and civil society.

When the editors of this series, Stephen Nichols and Justin Taylor, invited me to prepare this volume, I was immediately inclined to accept because the material that follows in this book has been a major part of my life ever since my graduate-student days at the University of St. Michael's College, Toronto. My dissertation addressed the role of the imitation-of-Christ theme in Herman Bavinck's cultural-ethical ideal,[12] and the person, theology, and continuing relevance of Bavinck for the church today has been my constant preoccupation to this day. Making this available beyond the academy and for the benefit of the broader church and Christians who desire to grow in their faith and Christian walk is something I *had* to do. Herewith, my deepest thanks to the editors and to Crossway for making it possible. Stephen and Justin, along with the competent editorial staff at Crossway, notably senior editor Thom Notaro, also made numerous suggestions for improving my prose, deleting unnecessary details, and clarifying important ideas. All writers should be blessed with such editors. Thank you all.

---

[12] *Analysis* (see table of abbreviations) is an updated and slightly revised version of my original (1982) dissertation completed at the University of St. Michael's College in Toronto, Ontario.

CHAPTER I

INTRODUCING BAVINCK: "A WORTHY FOLLOWER OF JESUS"

Photographs of Herman Bavinck—whether the best-known formal head-shot or the less familiar pose of the scholar sitting at a desk in his study—portray a serious, perhaps even stern, man. Making allowances for the conventions of Victorian-era portraiture, the impression given by these photographs is clearly still that of a dedicated, determined, focused, no-nonsense man, one not likely given to frivolity or even leisure.

"Serious" is the right word. One might even be forgiven for perpetuating a stereotypical image by describing him as a somber-looking "Puritan." Familiarity with the secessionist Christian Reformed[1] community his father, Jan, served as a minister and in which young Herman was nurtured would seem to confirm this judgment; it was a community that had separated itself from the National Dutch Reformed Church[2] out of a double concern for doctrinal orthodoxy and proper worship. Like the Puritans, these devoted Jesus followers were passionate about purity of doctrine and holiness of life. Consequently, they were members of a marginalized community characterized by a certain level of flight from the world.

[1] The official name of this church was *Christelijk Gereformeerde Kerken in Nederland*. This church was formed from a significant secession from the National Dutch Reformed Church in 1834.
[2] Official name in Dutch was *Nederlandse Hervormde Kerk*.

One biographer of Bavinck used the term *Kulturfeindlichkeit* (a posture of hostility toward culture) to describe the character of the Bavinck home.[3] Bavinck's childhood and lifelong friend Henry Dosker, who immigrated to the United States and eventually became a professor at the Presbyterian Seminary of Kentucky in Louisville, shares this assessment in the following description of Herman's parents:

> I knew both the parents of Dr. Bavinck intimately. They were typical of their environment and cherished all the puritanical and often provincial ideas and ideals of the early Church of the Separation. Simple, almost austere in their mode of life, exhibiting something of what the Germans call *Kulturfeindlichkeit*, pious to the core, teaching their children more by example than by precept, the mother uncommonly clear-visioned in her ideas and never afraid to express them, the father diffident, aroused only with difficulty, but then evincing rare power. Such were the parents of Dr. Herman Bavinck.[4]

The Bavinck Home

In recent years, other biographers have disputed the claim that the Bavinck home was largely characterized by a separatist hostility to culture.[5] These biographers appeal to the description of the family home given by one of Bavinck's own students, J. H. Landwehr, shortly after Bavinck's death in 1921. Landwehr took special note to defend the family from all accusations of legalism and moralism.

> A truly Christian spirit dominated in the house of the old pastor. One did not find there command upon command and rule upon rule; but, being bound to the Word of the Lord, there was a Christian freedom that was pleasing to behold. This was the rule in the Bavinck home: simplicity is the hallmark of that which is true.[6]

Another biographer surmises that Valentijn Hepp may have confused this simplicity for cultural hostility and "failed to see it as the way [those who are] genuinely civilized from within express themselves."[7]

 The questions that face us here—What was the Bavinck home really

---

[3] Hepp, 14.
[4] Dosker, 15.
[5] Gleason, 27; *Tijdg.*, 15.
[6] Landwehr, 7–8.
[7] *Tijdg.*, 15.

like? Did its simplicity indicate hostility to all culture or only to certain aspects of Dutch nineteenth-century culture? Did the absence of all legalism suggest a degree of openness to the good aspects of culture?—all these questions and more need not, and likely cannot, be answered with a simple yes or no. Bavinck's close friend Dosker finds him to be something of a riddle: "I will admit at once that in some respects, viewed from the standpoint of his parentage, Dr. Bavinck is a conundrum. He was so like and yet so absolutely unlike his parents."[8] As Dosker proceeds with a brief description of the elder Bavinck, however, it appears that the father also exhibited characteristics that give evidence of his own ambivalence on the matters of piety and culture.

Jan Bavinck (1826–1909) came from the little German village of Bentheim, near the Dutch border, and was a member of the German *Alt-Reformierten Kirche* (Old Reformed Church), a group known for its piety and strong adherence to the traditions of the Reformed faith as set forth at the Synod of Dort.[9] Jan was only three years old when his father died, and he was brought up by a courageous and devout Christian widow who "raised her [six] children to love God, to exhibit a Christian character, and to possess biblical honor and integrity as she faithfully instructed her children at home and in the school."[10] In his autobiography, Jan recounted that his upbringing had been rather formal and lacked "the internal life of Christian faith."[11] This all changed for him at the age of sixteen when his uncle Harm took him to hear an open-air preacher, Jan Berend Sundag.

As a young man Sundag had become disillusioned by what he deemed the spiritual deterioration of church life in Germany and developed a relationship with Secession leader Hendrick de Cock, who mentored him in the study of theology. Returning to Germany after his studies with De Cock were completed, Sundag tried to rouse the leaders of the church for revival but was rebuffed. Sundag began preaching outdoors and gathered a small following, including Jan Bavinck, who was deeply impressed and eventually led to leave the National Dutch Reformed Church. His childhood longing to become a minister of the Word returned with that step; however, owing to a lack of finances, the path to that goal seemed remote.[12]

The story of Jan Bavinck's path to ministry in the Secession Christian

---

[8] Dosker, 14.
[9] Gleason, 2–4.
[10] Gleason, 5.
[11] Gleason, 6.
[12] Gleason, 10–12.

Reformed Church provides an important window into the man and his community. In this denomination, the regional authority is known as the *classis*, equivalent to the presbytery in Presbyterian church government. The classis was evenly divided concerning a request from Sundag for assistance in his heavy workload. Sundag had asked for "a candidate from the churches to receive instruction in theology with a view to preparation for service in pastoral ministry." To break the tie vote, the assembly "knelt in prayer and asked the Lord's guidance in casting a lot to decide the matter."[13] Five candidates had expressed interest in pursuing the study for ministry, and after the lot in favor of proceeding was cast, the group was eventually pared down to two, with Jan Bavinck as one of the two men left standing. Once again, the vote between them was a tie, and a young woman who was working in the kitchen to help prepare the meals pulled out a slip of paper with the lot-determined answer. The answer had been "for" the first time; the name "Bavinck" was chosen the second time.[14] This would not be the last time that Jan Bavinck's "fate" was determined by "lot," and the procedure reflects a profound sense of and submission to God's providential leading in the Seceder community. Humility, even undue modesty, was to characterize both father Jan and son Herman Bavinck throughout their lives and ministries.

By all accounts, Jan was "a dedicated and precocious student."[15] According to Dosker, "he must have been a phenomenal student, and must also have enjoyed considerable earlier advantages, for in the small theological seminary at Hoogeveen, where he went, he took over the classes in Latin, Greek and Hebrew." Later, he assisted in the training of ministerial candidates for the Christian Reformed Church, and when the church decided to establish its own theological school at Kampen in 1854, "the elder Bavinck was the first to be nominated by the General Synod, as one of the professors." Uncertain what to do, Jan once again "made the lot settle the matter and declined the call." Why? Dosker also wonders: "Was it his innate modesty, his underestimate of his own powers, that pessimistic view of things, which ever sees lions in the way, of which his illustrious son also had a share?"[16]

The portrait we have drawn thus far shows us a deeply pious man, con-

---

[13] Gleason, 11; Hepp, 11.
[14] Gleason, 12.
[15] Gleason, 12.
[16] Dosker, 14–15.

cerned about the welfare of the National Reformed Church, attracted to revivalist preaching, and profoundly submissive to God's leading. We also see someone who is himself well educated and committed to teaching for an educated ministry. Furthermore, though he shared the pietistic sympathies of his Christian Reformed colleagues in ministry, and his preaching included the typical emphases on introspection and warnings about God's judgment, his son C. B. Bavinck (1866–1941) reported that his "father's clarity of mind preserved him from sickly excesses."[17]

In short, Jan Bavinck was a man characterized by a healthy piety and openness to the best of human learning and culture. We find confirmation of this openness in the elder Bavinck's response to Herman's declared intention in 1874 to study theology at the modernist University of Leiden rather than at the Christian Reformed Church's theological school at Kampen, a move that scandalized the church: young Herman's father and mother both finally supported this move. In response to criticism, father Jan confessed, "I trust in God's grace which is powerful enough to protect my child," adding that "the best church teachers had often obtained their learning from pagan schools while they were upheld by the prayers of godly parents."[18] Bavinck's biographer R. H. Bremmer characterizes the mother as "definitely not narrow."[19]

Bavinck's Secession Roots

Our portrait of the Bavinck home thus far places it decidedly within the circle of the theologically conservative and culturally marginalized Christian Reformed Church community that had seceded from the National Dutch Reformed Church in 1834. Since Herman Bavinck's piety and commitments cannot be understood apart from his upbringing in this community, we need to take a longer look at it. The *Afscheiding* or Secession of 1834 was an ecclesiastical protest against King William I's reorganization of the National Dutch Reformed Church in 1815–1816 and the perceived indifference by the national church to the Reformed orthodoxy established at the Synod of Dort (1618–1619). As the locus of ecclesiastical authority moved away from the local congregation to ecclesiastical boards appointed by the king and overseen by a State Department of Religion, protesters and

---

[17] Hepp, 22; *Tijdg.*, 15.
[18] Landwehr, 9.
[19] *Tijdg.*, 15.

dissenters led by the Rev. Hendrik de Cock, Reformed minister at Ulrum, Groningen, came to the conclusion that "Separation and Return"[20]— separation from the National Church and a return to the teaching and polity of Dort—were necessary. The opening sentence of their declaration reads as follows:

> We, the undersigned Overseers and members of the Reformed Congregation of Jesus Christ at Ulrum, have for a considerable time noticed the corruption in the Netherlands Reformed Church, in the mutilation or denial of the doctrine of our fathers founded on God's Word, as well as in the degeneration of the administration of the Holy Sacraments according to the ordinance of Christ in his Word, and in the near complete absence of church discipline, all of which are marks of the true church according to our Reformed Confession, Article 29.

When the Ulrum church's pastor was suspended by the state church boards for what the declaration describes as "his public testimony against false doctrine and polluted public worship services," the church's consistory appealed to classical, provincial, and synodical boards of the church, but to no avail. Requests to have their case heard and adjudicated were routinely denied, and instead the church was called to repent and to submit without qualification to the National Church authorities.[21]

What especially led the protesters to the conclusion that "the Netherlands Reformed Church is not the true but the false Church, according to God's Word and Article 29 of our confession" was the persecution of the dissenters by the civil authorities.[22] Ministers were forbidden to preach and were arrested; the Seceders were forbidden to gather in public for worship, and they had their goods confiscated and soldiers billeted in their homes. Not until 1869 did the civil authorities grant the Christian Reformed Church full legal status.

Even this brief overview suggests the appropriateness of the characterization given in the opening paragraphs of this chapter, including the term "Puritan." The Christian Reformed Church community of the nineteenth century was a dissenting community that had separated itself from the Na-

---

[20] The official declaration of separation was given the title "The Act of Secession or Return." An English translation is available online at http://www.gcc-opc.org/docs/DeCock.dir/scaneva.htm.
[21] All this is spelled out in the "The Act of Secession or Return."
[22] Article 29 of the Belgic Confession provides the following characteristic of the "false church" that the Seceders understandably applied to their own situation: "[The false church] persecutes those who live holy lives according to the Word of God and who rebuke it for its faults, greed, and idolatry."

tional Church, was preoccupied with purity of doctrine and holiness of life, insisted upon church discipline and a biblically based polity, and occupied a marginalized position out of step with the mainstream of Dutch culture and society. Thanks to the prominent role played by father Jan Bavinck in this church, Professor Hepp's judgment that the Bavinck home shared the characteristic Christian Reformed hostile attitude to culture (*Kultur-feindlichkeit*) seems very plausible at first sight. Nonetheless, two important qualifications temper this impression—the first about the Bavinck home and the second about the character of the Secession itself. We have already considered the first one; now we shall examine the second.

The Secession was not a unique or brand-new phenomenon in the Dutch Reformed Church but shared important commitments with a long history of pious ecclesiastical dissent. Neither concern for theological and confessional orthodoxy nor opposition to the polity arising from a close alliance between the civil and ecclesiastical authorities was born in the nineteenth century. Dissatisfaction with the dominant Dutch Reformed Church can be traced back much farther.

The Reformed Church became the preferred religious body in the Netherlands in the seventeenth century, a major shift from the time of the very first Synod of the Reformed Churches in the Netherlands at Emden in 1571, when the persecuted Reformed Christians constituted themselves as "Reformed Churches under the cross" (*kruiskerken*). From the outset, the Protestant Reformation faced severe opposition in the Low Countries from the civil and ecclesiastical authorities under control of Roman Catholic Spain. As the religious struggle for freedom of worship and conscience merged with a civil struggle for political freedom from the autocratic rules of Charles V, and especially Phillip II (1566–1648), it was the Calvinists who provided the backbone of support for the revolt led by William of Orange. Calvinist preachers provided the ideological perspective that considered the Netherlands the New Israel led by God out of the bondage houses of Spain and Rome.

Though the civil authorities welcomed the support and assistance of the Calvinists in this struggle and accepted the "establishment" of the Reformed faith, they also protected heterodoxy within the church and dissent outside of it by careful civil control of the church. The triumph of orthodox Calvinism over the Arminian Remonstrant party at the Synod of Dort proved to be a shallow and short-lived victory. The new church order adopted by the synod gave civil authorities key roles in approving or rejecting minister's calls to churches, provided for state funds to pay minister's salaries, controlled the theological education in the state universities, and required consultation with civil authorities before national synods could be called. Even at that, neither the National Estates General nor the majority of the provinces approved the Dort Church Order because they were not satisfied with their influence in ecclesiastical matters. The precious little autonomy the Dutch Reformed Church enjoyed was still too much for the authorities.

The Dutch Reformed Church of the seventeenth century, usually described as the Dutch "Golden Age," had acquired freedom from religious persecution and been granted legitimacy and power by the civil authorities, but this acceptance was not accompanied by great spiritual renewal and vigor. On the contrary! Complaints by preachers about worldliness and moral turpitude—drunkenness, licentiousness, blasphemy, profanation of the Sabbath, and so forth—abound in the literature of the seventeenth century. To make matters worse, there was a perception of a cold and dead orthodoxy in those churches that were still concerned about sound doctrine. Rationalism and intellectualism ran roughshod over piety and religious experience. Conditions were ripe for a pietistic reform movement that eventually came in the revival known as the *Nadere Reformatie*: "Further Reformation" or "Second Reformation."

This Dutch revival and reform movement was influenced by English Puritanism and German pietism. The Second Reformation's roots, however, ran earlier and deeper in the religious life of the Low Countries in such figures as Jan van Ruysbroeck (1293–1381) and Thomas à Kempis (1380–1471), author of *The Imitation of Christ*. The spirituality of the Second Reformation was strongly centered on the person of Christ, emphasized the need for a "new birth" or regeneration, and stressed the morality of following Christ. The term "Second Reformation" is closely linked with the famous Reformation slogan *ecclesia reformata semper reformanda est* (the Reformed Church must always be reforming). Behind this slogan was the desire—similar to that of the Anabaptists—that the Reformation be carried to its logical conclusion. A correct *understanding* of Scripture, the church, the sacraments, and so forth, was essential, but it was not enough. The Holy Spirit's power for a new and holy life—in the individual and the community—had to be included in a true reformation. The Second Reformation was about rebirth, but above all, about sanctification and holy living.

For this reason, the conventional caricature of Puritanism in general, and pietism more particularly—namely, that it represents an individualistic, ascetic, otherworldly, and anticultural Christianity—is definitely not applicable to the Second Reformation. The emphasis upon repentance, conversion, a living, active faith and the practice of piety, and the progressive reformation of the life of individuals was matched by a concern for the progressive reformation of the church and of society. The writers of the Second Reformation—commonly called *de oude schrijvers* (the old writers)—were not only familiar to the Dutch Seceders of the nineteenth century; they were also much read and well loved. Bavinck himself expressed appreciation for the best of this tradition of spirituality, especially the strong emphasis on sin and grace. In an illuminating foreword to a volume introducing the Scottish preachers Ralph and Ebenezer Erskine to a Dutch audience, Bavinck writes favorably about the deeply religious and practical character of the Scottish preaching, reflected in its emphasis upon personal conversion. Here is how he characterizes it:

> It constantly moves between the two poles of sin and grace, law and gospel. It descends, on the one hand to the depths of the human heart, unsparingly removes all covers and pretenses used by men to insulate themselves from the holiness of God, and exposes them in his poverty and lowliness before the face of God. On the other hand, it also comes to those men, thus made contrite in spirit, with the promises of the Gospel, unfolding its riches from all sides and applying them to all circumstances of life.

He then adds a brief lament about the devotional literature of his own day:

> [In current literature] the spiritual understanding of the soul is missing. It seems that we no longer know what sin and grace, guilt and forgiveness, regeneration and conversion are. In theory we know them well, but we no longer know them in the majestic reality of life. For this reason the devotional literature of previous times always leaves a different impression than that of the present. Because, although we stand at some distance from it and its form is antiquated, it is and remains natural, in the true sense of the word, while that of the present, when it deals with the soul, seems unnatural and artificial. We feel, when we read the old writers, that we are offered a piece of life; it is reality itself, that we are privileged to view.[23]

---

[23] Herman Bavinck, introduction to *Levensgeschiedenis en werken van Ralph en Ebenezer Erskine*, by R. Erskine and E. Erskine (Doesburg: J. C. van Schenk Brill, n.d. [1905–1906]), 5.

Bavinck clearly appreciated the old writers, but he found fault with those in his community whose otherworldly mysticism had led to a withdrawal from society. Bavinck articulated his concerns in a magisterial address on the catholicity of the Christian church and the gospel, where he chided such folk, including those who fled the Netherlands to avoid persecution and oppression:

> Satisfied with the ability to worship God in their own houses of worship, or to engage in evangelism, many left nation, state and society, art and science to their own devices. Many withdrew completely from life, literally separated themselves from everything, and, in some cases, what was even worse, shipped off to America, abandoning the Fatherland as lost to unbelief.[24]

Bavinck's address then indicates that he understands and even appreciates the strong desire to be faithful to Jesus's call to discipleship, but he still complains that otherworldly mysticism "is missing the full truth of Christianity. It is a denial of the truth that God loves the world. It is dedicated to conflict with and even rejection of the world but not to 'the victory that overcomes it' in faith."[25]

Here we see Bavinck distancing himself from some in his communion who responded to the social and cultural upheavals of the day by withdrawing from the conflict. He, by contrast, was committed to engagement, as is evident from his stated reason for studying theology at Leiden: "I had completed my studying at the gymnasium [preparatory school for university] and harbored a strong desire to further my studies at Leiden in order to become acquainted firsthand with modern theology."[26] Because his parents had just moved to Kampen, they pleaded with him to study for one year at the theological school there. Bavinck acquiesced, but his "desire to obtain a more scholarly training than the Theological School was able to provide" remained, and, evidently with parental approval, he entered Leiden in September 1874.[27] This sets the stage for the Leiden period, a time in Bavinck's life worthy of an extended look.

---

[24] "Catholicity," 246. Here Bavinck is referring to the 1840s emigration of the Secession ministers, Rev. Albertus Van Raalte and Rev. Hendrik Scholte, to Holland, Michigan, and Pella, Iowa, respectively. These emigrations led to the founding of the Christian Reformed Church in North America.
[25] "Catholicity," 246–47.
[26] *Tijdg.*, 20.
[27] *Tijdg.*, 20, 22.

Bavinck's Leiden Struggles

As Bavinck took leave of his parents on September 23, 1874, he was aware that the journey he was beginning would challenge his faith. He had publicly professed faith a year earlier, on March 30, 1873, in the Christian Reformed Church of Zwolle, the city where he received his gymnasium education. Biographers speak of his active participation in the life of the Zwolle congregation.[28] Now, as he departed for Leiden, he expressed his own anxieties in his diary: "Shall I remain standing [in the faith]? May God grant it."[29]

At the time Bavinck enrolled at Leiden, its theological faculty was internationally renowned for its scholarship and its decidedly modernist orientation. The anchors of this faculty were Johannes Henricus Scholten (1811–1885) in dogmatic theology and Abraham Kuenen (1828–1891) in Old Testament, but Cornelis P. Tiele (1830–1902) in the academic studies of religions and the philosophers Lodewijk W. E. Rauwenhoff (1828–1902) and Jan P. N. Land (1834–1897) provided a solid complement. The modernist theology that Bavinck faced was empiricist and decidedly antisupernaturalist but, at the same time, committed to a new synthesis between modernity and the Christian religion. Scholten attempted this by creating a new theological system in which the classic Reformed emphasis on God's sovereignty was recast into a monistic and panentheistic determinism. God was thought of as the all-determining power present in all things. Scholten still identified true religion with the spirit and principles of Jesus, who is our example because he is the one man who was completely controlled by the spirit of God.

I have briefly sketched the salient characteristics of the 1834 Secession and its affinities with the history of Dutch pietism and introduced the modernist theology taught at the University of Leiden because they are the two constitutive influences on Bavinck's life. Jan Veenhof, for example, speaks of these two factors as the two poles that dominate Bavinck's life.[30] A. Anema, one of Bavinck's colleagues at the Free University, once characterized Bavinck as a "Secession preacher and a representative of modern culture," concluding:

> That was a striking characteristic. In that duality is found Bavinck's significance. That duality is also a reflection of the tension—at times the

[28] *Tijdg.*, 19.

[29] *Tijdg.*, 22.

[30] Jan Veenhof, *Revelatie en inspiratie* (Amsterdam: Buijten & Schipperheijn, 1968), 108.

crisis—in Bavinck's life. In many respects it is a simple matter to be a preacher in the Secession Church, and, in a certain sense, it is also not that difficult to be a modern person. But in no way is it a simple matter to be the one as well as the other.[31]

Others who knew Bavinck well made similar observations.

Of utmost importance in this matter is the virtually unanimous testimony of witnesses that Bavinck remained true to his Seceder and pietist roots even though the pressure from the teaching he received at Leiden must have been great. His contemporary Abraham Kuyper, who also studied at Leiden from 1855 to 1862 and sat under the same professors as Bavinck, reports in his autobiographical essay "Confidentially" that he and a class of Leiden students once broke into wild applause when a professor denied the bodily resurrection of Christ. Not only is there no record of similar behavior on Bavinck's part; it is simply unimaginable. In fact, Bavinck firmly defended his community and the legitimacy of its ecclesiastical dissent at the time of his doctoral examination at Leiden on June 10, 1880. Before the liberal "establishment" of the Dutch Reformed Church and the chief representatives of modernist theology, Bavinck defended the following proposition: "Measured by the standard of Reformed principles (art. 38 and 39 [sic!] of the Belgic Confession), the Secession of 1834 was both justified and necessary."[32]

Bavinck meant articles 28 and 29, which define the marks of the true church in distinction from the false church. Though his time at Leiden was in many respects a difficult struggle, Bavinck's own prayer was answered: he remained standing and his church community was greatly relieved. This relief is palpable in a written review of his Leiden dissertation published in the Christian Reformed journal, *De vrije kerk*. The author recalls Bavinck's decision to study at Leiden as a risky venture and expresses gratitude that it turned out well.

> We are grateful to God that this wager—for that is indeed what it always is—turned out so well. So many young people from Christian homes when placed in such an environment are literally lost morally and religiously, later becoming skeptics and even enemies of God's people and opponents of God's truth. With Dr. Bavinck, thanks be to God, that was not the case.

---

[31] Ibid.
[32] H. Bavinck, *De ethiek van Ulrich Zwingli* (Kampen: Zalsman, 1880), 182.

We have it on good authority: All those years he was in Leiden, his conduct was irreproachable and his study habits were exemplary. What is even more important, he remained true to Reformed principles and faithful to his church communion.[33]

After he completed his study period at Leiden in 1880, Bavinck candidly acknowledged his struggles and even spiritual impoverishment as a cost of his time at Leiden: "Leiden has benefitted me in many ways: I hope always to acknowledge that gratefully. But it has also greatly impoverished me, robbed me, not only of much ballast (for which I am happy), but also much that I recently, especially when I preach, recognize as vital for my own spiritual life."[34] Bavinck, nonetheless, retained his close ties with the Christian Reformed Church by preaching frequently in its congregations. His first student sermon, delivered on July 21, 1878, had 1 John 5:4b as its text: "This is the victory that overcomes the world—our faith." Bavinck loved to preach on this text, and it was the text of his only published sermon, preached on June 20, 1901, in Kampen, with South Africa's president Paul Kruger in the audience.[35]

Although it is evident that Bavinck retained his orthodox Calvinist piety and theology while at Leiden, its professors did influence him, especially in matters of method and approach. The scrupulously careful, historical-empirical approach of J. H. Scholten and, especially, Abraham Kuenen had a lasting effect on him. Bavinck's well-documented genial and fair-minded approach to opponents may have been influenced by personal qualities but was also strengthened, if not learned, at Leiden. "If I have one thing for which to be thankful to Leiden," he wrote his friend Snouck Hurgronje, "it is this: to attempt to understand the opponent."[36]

Bavinck as Churchman and Professor

Jan Veenhof contends that Bavinck never distanced himself from his ecclesiastical and spiritual background, but always considered himself a "son of the Secession."[37] Veenhof speaks of Bavinck's "life-long attachment to the spiritual climate of the older separated churches, marked by a deeply

---

[33] Hepp, 84.
[34] Hepp, 84.
[35] *Tijdg.*, 34n66; the translated text of this sermon is reproduced as the conclusion of this book.
[36] Hepp, 84.
[37] Veenhof, *Revelatie en inspiratie*, 95.

existential and, occasionally one-sided pietistic self-examination, but nonetheless truly Reformed experience of the great realities of sin and grace."[38] Further support that Bavinck remained a true son of the Secession is his tireless devotion and labor for the Christian Reformed Church. Upon completing his doctoral studies he accepted the call to the Christian Reformed congregation in Franeker, Friesland, a charge he served from 1880 to 1882. Though brief, Bavinck's pastoral work at Franeker was memorable. The church's immediate history under its two previous ministers was troubled and characterized by division; under Bavinck's care, the congregation experienced healing and flourished. After reviewing the minutes of the church's consistory, as well as those of the supervising classis, Bremmer notes that they bear consistent witness that "under Bavinck's ministry the congregation of Franeker noticeably experienced God's blessing."[39]

As one example of Bavinck's pastoral heart, Bremmer passes on the story of someone who experienced it firsthand as a young man. After Bavinck's death in 1921, the man recalled Bavinck's compassion for those who had physical and developmental disabilities. Bavinck visited the home of an

> elderly woman whose two daughters were practically crippled, spoke with difficulty, and lived in circumstances of poverty; the mother was also not very neat. The two sisters expressed a desire to become members of the congregation and after a conversation with the consistory were gladly welcomed to the Table of the Covenant.

Even when hindered from coming to church for Sunday services because of indisposition, "they were brought to the church by ambulance and sat near the pulpit where they listened attentively and gladly." Recalling this time of his youth forty years earlier, the man reported that this "small tableau" made a significant impression on the young people of the church. He adds that "it was precisely here, with and by means of these simple people whom the world despised as 'of no account,'" that Bavinck called on his congregation "to refashion themselves in the salvation that is found in Jesus."[40] Viewed from the vantage point of our thankfully more compassionate treatment of persons with disabilities today, one cannot help

---

[38] Ibid., 94.
[39] *Tijdg.*, 42.
[40] *Tijdg.*, 38.

thinking that this must have been rare in Bavinck's day. By the standards of any age it provides a wonderful window into Bavinck's Christian and pastoral heart.

Bavinck's short time at Franeker is also noteworthy for two decisions he did *not* make. We have just noted that he was a faithful and effective pastor. At the same time, he also missed the academy and lamented the busyness of pastoral life that got in the way of his passion for studying. In a letter to his Leiden friend Snouck Hurgronje, Bavinck comments on his busy workload but also acknowledges that he "wastes considerable time" and does not understand why. Even when he manages to carve out some time for study, he complains that he "doesn't feel like it," and that his passion for studying was diminishing.[41] At the risk of doing diagnosis from a distance, this sounds like a clear case of mild depression arising from the tension between his pastoral calling and his frustrated sense of calling to be a theologian.

Under those circumstances, a call in February 1882 from a large Christian Reformed congregation in Amsterdam, at double the salary he was receiving in Franeker, would have been a powerful attraction. Keeping in mind that Abraham Kuyper had just founded the Free University of Amsterdam in 1880, a move to Amsterdam would have given Bavinck ample opportunity to refuel his passion for studying and exercise his academic skills. And still, Bavinck took only two weeks to decline the call; he did not feel free to leave.[42]

During the same month he also received an inquiry from the Board of the Free University of Amsterdam about the possibility of an appointment to a faculty position in hermeneutics and New Testament exegesis. This was the second time Kuyper's school beckoned him; prior to its official opening in October 1880, Bavinck had been invited to become one of the charter faculty as a professor of Old Testament and Semitic literature. He had declined then, writing in his diary, "If I had accepted, I would have only done it for Kuyper's sake and attachment to his glory." The second time around he expressed his willingness to consider the offer but also indicated that his deep love for the Christian Reformed Church and concern for the well-being of its theological school gave him pause, particularly because the church herself desired improvement in the theological education of

---

[41] *Tijdg.*, 40.
[42] *Tijdg.*, 38–39.

its pastors. In his response to the president of the Free University's Board, he wrote, "I love my church and would prefer laboring to build it up. The flourishing of her Theological School is close to my heart; there is much there that calls urgently for improvement." Bavinck then observed that the synod of the Christian Reformed Church was committed to such improvement; he also noted that at the upcoming synod meeting (August 1882), he anticipated receiving an appointment to teach at the theological school. Tellingly he added, "There is not much about the place that is attractive but I am drawn to it out of concern for the well-being of the church I serve." Acknowledging that he might end up being disappointed, Bavinck declined the Free University offer until it became clear what his place would be in the Kampen theological school.[43]

The synodical appointment did come on August 24, 1882, and was accepted. In the light of our earlier glance at the life of Herman's father, the following notes from the elder Bavinck's autobiography are a noteworthy postscript. He observed that he (in 1854) and his son (in 1882) were both twenty-eight years old when appointed by the synod of their church—in each case meeting in the Dutch city of Zwolle, near Kampen—to teach at the theological school of the Christian Reformed Church in Kampen. "I gave thanks to God," he wrote, "that my son—not as my successor but as my substitute—took the place that I had not dared to accept because of my lack of faith."[44]

Bavinck remained at Kampen for twenty years, eventually hearkening to the call of the Free University to come as a replacement for Kuyper, who at this time was occupied as prime minister of the Netherlands. Bavinck's departure was not a matter of diminishing concern for his church; if anything it reflected the opposite. The Christian Reformed Church came into being thanks to a secession from the National Dutch Reformed Church in 1834. Fifty years later, in 1886, Kuyper led another dissenting group out of the *Nederlandse Hervormde Kerk*, a group known as the *Doleantie* (from the Dutch verb *doleren*, "to mourn"). Though both groups dissented from the national church because of perceived doctrinal and practical departures from the tradition of Reformed confessional orthodoxy, there were significant theological and ecclesiastical differences between the two groups. For our purposes, we need to shine the spotlight on the theological education

---

[43] *Tijdg.*, 34.
[44] *Tijdg.*, 34.

of ministers. Kuyper and his followers wanted a "scientific" theological education provided at a Christian university such as the Free University of Amsterdam. The Christian Reformed Church, however, had established its own theological school or seminary at Kampen and regarded theological education as the responsibility of the church.

None of this would have mattered much if the two groups had simply gone their separate ways. But in 1892, a major church union took place between a large part of the 1834 Secession church and the 1886 *Doleantie* church, forming a new denomination, the *Gereformeerde Kerken in Neder-land*. Now the question of theological education and ministerial training became an urgent practical matter. To make a long story short, despite Bavinck's important mediatorial role, the two groups were unable to come to an agreement. Instead of joining the two faculties of Kampen and Amsterdam into one institution as Bavinck desired and had worked hard to accomplish, the two schools would continue, business as usual.

For our purposes here it is important to note that Bavinck's proposal faced opposition from both sides of the church: Christian Reformed leaders who wanted at all costs to preserve theological education under the wing of the church, and *Doleantie* leaders such as Kuyper who insisted on a scientific theology situated in the university. Over against the leaders of his own church, Bavinck insisted that theology as the study of God must be related to other areas of human knowledge and that a university is thus a fitting place for a theological faculty. In the years that the two groups were "courting" prior to union, Bavinck emphasized the latter point to his own community. After the union of 1892, however, having been stung by the ferocity with which Kuyper and his lieutenants rejected his proposals for a unified theological education, Bavinck began to highlight the important role of the church in theological education. In the midst of the heated debate taking place in the Union Church in the late 1890s, Bavinck wrote an important, eighty-page brochure, *Het recht der kerken en de vrijheid der wetenschap* ("The right of the churches and the freedom of science/scholarship"). Here's how he framed his own understanding of the debate: "In 1896 it had to do with the right and freedom of the discipline of theological science. Now in 1899 it appears to me that it has to do with the right and freedom of the churches."[45]

It is undoubtedly true that Bavinck's move to Amsterdam provided

---

[45] Gleason, 256.

significant personal and professional benefits and his subsequent labor at the Free University was enormously productive. At the same time, we would not do the man justice if we did not take into account that he also made the move for the benefit of the church. Committed as he was to a solidly academic theological education, he went to the Free University as one who insisted that theology serve the church and be framed by the church. That was a note he believed needed to be included and played, perhaps even fortissimo, in the score of Kuyperian higher education. Good theology, not to mention good theologians, needs the church. In the foreword to the first edition of the *Reformed Dogmatics* (1895), Bavinck put it this way:

> The dogmatic theologian no less than the ordinary believer is obliged to confess the communion of the saints. How wide and long, how high and deep the love of Christ is. A love that surpasses all knowledge can only be grasped with all the saints in communion. It is first of all in and by means of their fellowship that a theologian learns to understand the dogmas of the church that articulate the Christian faith. Above everything else, the communion of the saints provides empowering strength and superb comfort.

On that note we conclude our biographical sketch. Bavinck was a man of deep piety and great learning who faced head-on the challenges posed to Reformed orthodoxy by modernity without forsaking his devout, pietist roots. We will have occasion to consider additional biographical details in the next five chapters, including his career as a theologian and his involvement in Dutch politics, as we explore the range of his theology and foundational ideas about the Christian life. Biographical details about Bavinck's political involvement will be included in chapter 6.

PART I

FOUNDATIONS FOR CHRISTIAN LIVING

CHAPTER 2

CREATED IN GOD'S IMAGE

The Roman playwright Terence (195/185–159 BC) famously said, "I am a man, I consider nothing human alien to me" (*Homo sum, humani nihil a me alienum puto*).[1] Though it is said to have been the favorite maxim of Karl Marx and is also frequently associated with the American poet Maya Angelou, the sentiment is also appropriately linked to Herman Bavinck and is a key to his understanding of the Christian life. We are Christian to be human. The redemption that comes to us through the person and work of Christ does not make us anything other than whole and healthy human beings; it takes away the sin that hinders us from being the image bearers of God we were created to be. As numerous interpreters of Bavinck have noted, the notion that "grace restores nature" is fundamental to his theology. In the power of the Holy Spirit, Christ restores fallen human beings to fellowship with God and enables them to live once again as the image bearers they were created to be.

A Trinitarian Perspective of the Image

Because God is a Trinity—Father, Son, and Holy Spirit—the image of God in which we were created is a triune image. Bavinck describes an image bearer as "a human being in a full and true sense," as "a child of God, God's own offspring, living in communion with him by the Holy Spirit." Originally, "before the fall, a human being was the dwelling place of the entire, Holy

---

[1] In his play *Heauton Timorumenos* (*The Self-Tormentor*).

Trinity, a most splendid temple of the Holy Spirit."[2] According to Bavinck, creation as a whole reflects the very Trinitarian being of God, granting that "there is much truth to the belief that creation everywhere displays to us vestiges of the Trinity. And because these vestiges are most clearly evident in 'humanity,' so that 'human beings' may even be called 'the image of the Trinity,' 'humanity' is driven from within to search out those vestiges."[3]

However, we live in a fallen world, and our understanding of Christian discipleship must take the reality of sin as well as God's grace in Christ into consideration when we ask what it means for us to image the triune God. A Christian person who wants to be a disciple of Jesus must therefore consider the Christian life from a threefold perspective: (1) Who were we created to be, and for what purpose? (the doctrine of creation); (2) Who are we now? (the doctrines of sin and redemption); (3) Who will we become in glory? (the doctrine of eschatology). We also need to ask how these three relate to each other. Does the eschatological goal of glory also determine our understanding of creation? Should we think backward, beginning at the end with what God has revealed to us about our eternal destiny and use that to understand the original human creation? And since we are asking about *Christian* living, how does Jesus Christ relate to each of these vantage points?

Human beings were created to have fellowship with God. Bavinck puts it this way: "As God's image bearers, human beings have a calling rightly to know God our creator, love him with all their heart and live with him in eternity."[4] It is important to recognize here that though Adam was created a good image bearer of God, a yet greater destiny awaited him upon his obedience.

> Although Adam was created in God's image, he was not that image immediately in the full sense, nor was he that image by himself alone. The image of God will only present itself to us in all of its many-splendored richness when man's destiny, both for this life and the life to come, is included in it.[5]

Bavinck bases this claim on 1 Corinthians 15 and the parallels and contrasts drawn by the apostle Paul between Adam and Christ.

---

[2] *RD*, 2:558–59.
[3] *RD*, 2:333.
[4] "Gen. Prin.," 437.
[5] *RD*, 2:564; the quotations that follow in this paragraph and the next are all found on this page.

In 1 Corinthians 15:45–49 Paul contrasts the two covenant heads, Adam and Christ, with each other and compares them, not so much (as in Rom. 5:12–21 and 1 Cor. 15:22) in terms of what they did as in terms of their nature and person. The comparison here reaches its greatest depth and penetrates to the root of the distinction between them. The whole Adam, both before and after the fall, is contrasted to the whole Christ, after as well as before the resurrection.

Bavinck summarizes the difference by noting that Adam, even in the state of integrity, "did not have a glorified spiritual body" because "his natural body had not yet fully become an instrument of the spirit." He follows this up with a lengthy set of contrasts:

As such, Adam, by comparison to Christ, stood on a lower level. Adam was the first; Christ the second and the last. Christ presupposes Adam and succeeds him. Adam is the lesser and inferior entity; Christ the greater and higher being. Hence, Adam pointed to Christ; already before the fall he was the type of Christ. In Adam's creation Christ was already in view. . . . The natural came first, the spiritual second.

Though he begins with 1 Corinthians 15, Bavinck argues that this vision of human destiny is found already in Genesis 1–2. The creation itself must be understood eschatologically, that is, in terms of God's purposes for its glorious destiny. Though given the "breath of life" and having "a paradise as his dwelling place," Adam was also given "a command for guidance" and "a threat of punishment in case of transgression." In Reformed theology, this is known as the "covenant of works," which is a divinely imposed relationship between God and humanity, a relationship under sanctions: obedience leads to blessing; disobedience results in death. Comments Bavinck: "It is evident from this scenario that the first man, however highly placed, did not yet possess the highest humanity. There is a very great difference between the natural and the pneumatic [spiritual], between the state of integrity and the state of glory." In short: we are Christian in order to become truly human, not the other way around.

This theological insight implies that in a Reformed understanding of Christian discipleship the creational, natural vocation of human beings is basic and primary. It is of course true that in the present dispensation, where sin remains, gospel proclamation and the mission and ministry of the church have priority of *urgency*. Bavinck insisted that our involvement in Christian causes must not lead us to "neglect to ask whether we ourselves are truly converted and whether we belong to Christ in life and in death. For this is indeed what life boils down to." This ultimate question is the truly urgent one. Bavinck goes on to gently rebuke certain Reformed folk who take untoward pride in their confessional identity, and even smugly assure themselves that they are not the equivalent of today's "evangelicals" or perhaps even "fundamentalists." "We may not banish this question from our personal or church life under the label of pietism or methodism. What does it profit a man if he gains the whole world, even for Christian principles, if he loses his own soul?"[6] Christians who share the classic Reformed emphasis on the value of all vocations as "service in the kingdom of God" should never downplay the urgency of our Lord's command to proclaim the gospel to the world and disciple the nations. To repeat Bavinck's words: "For this is indeed what life boils down to."

Does this urgency then trump our earlier affirmation of the primacy of creation and the natural life of humanity, or should we caution ourselves against the danger opposite the one discussed in the previous paragraph? Let me get at this by exploring the challenge to authentic Christian discipleship *in* the "ordinary" vocations of daily life that comes from contemporary calls to "radical discipleship." These calls begin with a sharp critique of North American Christians for living comfortable lives that fit in to the expectations and values of our materialistic and hedonistic culture and end with a call to follow the radical demands of Jesus in the Gospels. From top to bottom, our lives, so it is said, should be countercultural and exemplify the values of the kingdom of God that Jesus proclaimed in the Sermon on the Mount. The gospel creates a wholly different culture. Simplicity of life and even a New Monasticism movement become the defining characteristics of this radical Christianity. Its heroes are people like Dietrich Bonhoeffer, Mother Teresa, and Shane Claiborne.

As we reflect on our own Christian walk, there is much in this emphasis that should challenge us and call us to self-examination. Conformity to the world's values has been a temptation and danger since the days of the New Testament, and the apostles Paul (Rom. 12:1–3) and John (1 John 2:15–17) vigorously warn us against it. At the same time, we should also be concerned about potential unintended consequences of this emphasis on radical discipleship. What about Christians who honorably serve God

---

[6] *Certainty*, 94.

in vocations that are not part of a gospel ministry or other explicitly Christian service and, in addition, have not chosen to participate in intentional communities of radical Christianity but remained in their vocations and in their city or suburban churches? Sharp critiques of such a life, accompanied by calls to be "authentically Christian" by becoming a radical disciple, easily produce guilt, and that guilt, I want to suggest, may not be valid or productive.

From the perspective of radical discipleship, devoting oneself to a vocation in business, law, medicine, or information technology may be legitimate but of a lesser value if not exercised in a radical way. Lawyers and doctors who forsake high-paying positions and devote themselves to working for the poor are then lauded; medical specialists in research hospitals or institutes and corporate lawyers, not to mention Wall Street brokers, not so much. Now, I do not want to leave the impression that I discount the sacrifices made by those who radically alter their lives and lifestyle in order to be more faithful to Jesus. On the contrary! When Jesus calls us, we have no choice but to heed his call. My concern is with Christians who might conclude that one person's call, and one kind of call, is the norm for all; one size fits all. An interpretation of Christian calling where a vision of radical discipleship is the norm for everyone could lead us—and dedicated young people choosing their life's calling in particular—to set up a hierarchy of vocations in which explicit Christian service outranks Christian discipleship *in* the "ordinary" professions of our daily lives. It may also have the unintended consequence of discouraging those for whom the ideal is too much; they cannot see themselves becoming martyrs or even missionaries and conclude—wrongly—that the Christian life itself is impossible.

The (quite unintended) consequence of such a hierarchy reminds us ironically of the manner in which the traditional Roman Catholic distinction between "precepts" (for everyone) and "counsels of perfection" (for the "religious," i.e., the members of religious orders) often led to a devaluing of the Christian laity. It was precisely against such a duality that the Reformation trumpeted the calling and priesthood of all believers. Notions of radical discipleship seem to imply that the only place where we can authentically follow Jesus is within the framework of a substitute counterculture established by the Christian gospel. Bavinck begins from a different perspective by noting that the arena of human culture, "including marriage, family, business, vocation, agriculture, industry, commerce, science, art, politics, and society, is not to be seen as a special product of Christianity." Even the relation between the two Testaments reflects this in Bavinck's view. "On the contrary, the New Testament presupposes the Old Testament, redemption is accomplished on the foundation of creation, the work of the Son is bound to that of the Father, grace follows nature, rebirth can take place only after birth."[7]

We ought not to conclude from this that Bavinck rejects Christians' living their lives within culture and society in distinctly Christian ways, ways that often differ radically from society's values and norms. In fact he strongly believes that Christians who were changed by the gospel and led lives at odds with the prevailing culture did dramatically change it. Bavinck is fond of pairing two metaphors from our Lord's parables of the kingdom—pearl and leaven—to make this point. Above all, the gospel is the "pearl of great price" for which one must be willing to forsake everything. "The significance of the gospel does not depend on its influence on culture, its usefulness for life today; it is a treasure in itself, a pearl of great value, even if it might not be a leaven."[8] He immediately adds, however, that "although the worth of Christianity is certainly not only, not exclusively, and not even in the first place, determined by its influence on civilization, it nevertheless is undeniable that Christianity indeed exerts such influence. The kingdom of heaven is not only a pearl; it is a leaven as well." But even here "Scripture's point of departure is creation, because all relationships are connected with it, and thus can only be known from it."[9] In Bavinck's view, it is a mistake to try and fashion a whole new "radically Christian" culture or counterculture. The norms for culture come from creation, not from the gospel. The gospel does not create a brand-new social or political order but renews people, elevates them to the highest dignity as children of God. The gospel creates a new *spiritual* humanity.

We will consider this in greater detail in chapter 4 and for now focus on one important implication of this vision. It means that Christians who are not called by God to gospel ministry—or to other fields of specifically Christian service—ought not to feel guilty about serving God in other vocations as though these were of lesser value, a less-than-faithful response to the call of our Lord. All legitimate vocations are holy in their own distinct way and even precede the specific calling of gospel ministry. God's act of

---

[7] "Imit. II," 135–36 [429].
[8] *ERSS*, 140.
[9] *ERSS*, 141.

creation and his creational, natural gifts to humanity all precede the redemption begun with the call of Abraham. Bavinck insists that

> all the products of culture, marriage, family, state, etc., are good and perfect gifts which come down from the Father of lights. They are provided by God who in his general goodness makes his sun to shine and the rain to fall on the just and the unjust, and who satisfies the hearts of men with food and gladness.[10]

Christians who serve God by stewarding the use of his "good and perfect gifts"—in the home, in education, in medicine, in law, in business, in government, and so forth—are acting as responsible Christian disciples and should be honored for it. The notion of *Christian* discipleship should not be restricted to service that is explicitly linked to the gospel ministry, Christian witness, or Christian service. We live our Christian lives in the vocations to which God calls us, whatever they may be.

Common Grace?

We may have been created good, but we are now definitely "fallen." I introduced the problem of sin earlier in this chapter but then gingerly sidestepped the question of its consequence for Christian discipleship. How "Christian" can our lives become on this side of our Lord's return and the consummation of all things? Is there a limit to how "good" we can become? This is a particularly vexing question to ask of a Reformed theologian such as Bavinck; after all, don't Reformed people affirm the T in the famous TULIP acronym summarizing the Canons of Dort, namely, "total depravity"? Does this doctrine not place limits on the amount of sanctification we can expect in this life? Was Bavinck's contemporary, Professor Benjamin Warfield of Princeton Seminary, not on target when he devoted a major two-volume theological study to combatting the heresy of perfectionism?

Without entering into all the thorny theological thickets introduced by those questions, let us approach them by considering another important Reformed doctrine, often referred to as "common grace." My own personal view is that the term is badly chosen, results in multiple misunderstandings, and potentially leads to moral missteps such as excusing worldliness among Christians. What proponents of the doctrine have in mind—and

---

[10] "Imit. II," 135–36 [429].

this I heartily affirm—is the confession that God continues to providentially watch over creation and fallen humanity and that this care is not restricted to but extends beyond the elect. One of the classic texts usually appealed to for this doctrine is Matthew 5:45: "He makes his sun rise on the evil and on the good, and sends rain on the just and on the unjust."

When Bavinck considers this doctrine, as he does in an 1894 published "Rectoral Address" for the theological school at Kampen, his main concern is to show that God did not withdraw his presence or revelation to humanity after the fall into sin. Human religion remains a response to revelation. However, the entry of sin changes the nature of the revelation that humanity needs. The change comes because the human condition has changed; the joyful, open fellowship with God—walking together in the garden—deteriorates into fear, and human beings attempt to hide from God's presence.

A religion always requires revelation as its foundation and correlate; there is no religion without revelation. The fall indeed brings change. But this change does not consist in God's beginning or ceasing to reveal himself. Revelation continues and God does not withdraw himself. He again seeks out the man and woman. But they are now afraid of the voice of God and flee from before his face (Gen. 3:8–9). The consciousness of guilt drives them from the presence of God. They know of the penalty of death on the day of transgression (Gen. 2:17).[11]

God continues to be present to his creatures; he continues to reveal himself in the works of his hands as biblical passages such as Psalm 19, Acts 17: 24–28, and Romans 1 and 2 testify. But now we need to distinguish God's presence and revelation in a *general* or *universal* sense from his *particular* or *saving* and *gracious* presence. Bavinck maintains a tradition in Reformed theology that goes back to John Calvin in using the term *grace* to refer to both and distinguishing "common grace" from "special grace." Even if we find fault with the term *common grace*—as I think we should—we do well to consider the reason why Bavinck continues to use the term. When God's revelation comes to sinful people, to people who are guilty and deserving of death, it receives a new element, a note of mercy and compassion.

> Revelation continues, but it changes in character and receives a different
> content. Now revelation comes to guilty man, who merits death, as a rev-

---

[11] "Com. Grace," 40; quotations in the following paragraphs are also from this page.

elation of *grace*. Now when God—in spite of the transgression—calls man, searches him out, and sets enmity in place of the defunct friendship, a totally new element appears in his revelation—namely, his compassion and mercy.

It is this "mercy," in the fact that the creation continues after the fall, that Reformed theologians such as Bavinck accent in their use of the term *common grace*. In addition to the Creator's upholding all things by his powerful hand, the mere fact that the world continues is itself a sign of grace. It does not *have* to continue; God would have been within his rights to destroy the world. Though Bavinck himself does not use the term, it is appropriate to speak of a "double contingency" after the fall, and this double notion would cover all that needs to be covered with the doctrine of common grace. As before, creation as a whole is dependent on God's providential upholding of all things; that which is, *need not be.* This is the first contingency. But, in addition, God's continuing to uphold all things by his power after the fall is a *gracious* upholding; his mercy is the second contingency. "Life, work, food, clothing come to [man] no longer on the basis of an agreement or right granted in the covenant of works but through grace alone. Grace has become the source and fountainhead of all life and every blessing for mankind. It is the overflowing spring of all good (Gen. 3:8, 24)."

This common grace, however, does not save us. Life continues, but it is now under the curse and wrath of God. Something more, something new, is needed. And here comes the crucial distinction: "Yet this grace does not remain single and undivided. It differentiates itself into common and special grace." Bavinck describes both common grace and particular grace in *Trinitarian* terms. The universal presence of God to all people comes from the fact that the Creator God is the source of all that is, all that moves and lives, all that breathes, feels, thinks, speaks, and loves. And this Creator God is triune, Father, Son, and Holy Spirit.

> Every good and perfect gift, also among the nations, comes down from the Father of Lights (James 1:17). The Logos, who created and maintains all things, enlightens each man coming into the world (John 1:9). The Holy Spirit is the author of all life, of every power and every virtue (Gen. 6:17; 7:15; Pss. 33:6; 104:30; 139:2; Job 32:8; Eccles. 3:19).[12]

---

[12] "Com. Grace," 41.

Our salvation too comes from the same triune God. God's redemptive presence and revelation, beginning with Israel and culminating in the Incarnation, is thoroughly Trinitarian. Bavinck explains this by meditating on the two important names for God in the Old Testament, *Elohim* and *YHWH*. The Old Testament reveals God as "Elohim, greatly exalted, dwelling in eternity, holy, removed from every creature and all uncleanness." But the Creator and Sovereign of the universe is also the God who covenantally reaches out to Abraham and promises to be his God and the God of his descendants forever. "He is also Yahweh, the God of the covenant, appearing in the 'Malak Yahweh' [Servant of the Lord], and giving himself to Israel, choosing her by grace, rescuing her from Egypt, and purifying her through her sacrificial offerings." This purifying, sanctifying, and equipping is the work of God the Holy Spirit. "He is also, as Spirit, author of health and blessing, causing Israel to base her life in the covenant and to walk in his ways, and thus sanctifying her to be a kingdom of priests [Ex. 19:5–6]." And finally, "the essence of Israel's faith becomes more manifest as it finds its goal and fulfillment in Christ. He is the ultimate content of the *foedus gratiae* [covenant of grace]. In him all the promises of God are 'Yes and Amen.'"[13]

Properly understood, therefore, the doctrine of common grace is the affirmation that, even after the fall, God the Creator continues providentially and graciously to uphold all things and is present to all creatures. Since objections to the term usually arise from its misuse, it is important to remind ourselves why Reformed theologians professed it. John Calvin stated it succinctly and clearly when he acknowledged that God the Holy Spirit "distributes [gifts] to whomever he wills for the common good of mankind." According to Calvin, "the knowledge of all that is most excellent in human life is said to be communicated to us through the Spirit of God."[14] Why is it important to acknowledge this? "If we regard the Spirit of God as the sole fountain of truth, we shall neither reject the truth itself, nor despise it wherever it shall appear, unless we wish to dishonor the Spirit of God. For by holding the gifts of the Spirit in slight esteem, we contemn and reproach the Spirit himself." And further: "But shall we count anything praiseworthy or noble without recognizing at the same time that it comes from God? Let us be ashamed of such ingratitude."[15]

---

[13] "Com. Grace," 43.
[14] John Calvin, *Institutes of the Christian Religion*, ed. John T. McNeill, trans. Ford Lewis Battles, 2 vols. (Philadelphia: Westminster, 1960), 2.2.16.
[15] Ibid., 2.2.15.

The point of affirming the doctrine of common grace is *gratitude*. The doctrine is misused when our attention to all that is good, noble, true, and beautiful in this world is directed more to these gifts themselves than to the Giver. Augustine captures this distortion in a wonderful sermon on 1 John 2:15, "Let us not love the world, neither the things of this world." He pleads with his hearers to "love what God has made," but, citing Romans 1:25—"They adored and served the creature rather than the creator, who is blessed forever"—he warns them against any love that is inordinate and intemperate. "God doesn't forbid you to love those things, but you mustn't love them in the expectation of blessedness. Rather, you must favor and praise them in such a way that you love the creator." Augustine follows this with an extended bride-and-bridegroom metaphor:

> Brothers, if a bridegroom made a ring for his bride, and she loved the ring that she had received more than her bridegroom . . . . [so that] she said, "this ring is enough for me; now I don't want to see his face again," what sort of person would she be? . . . Who wouldn't convict her of an adulterous mind? You love gold instead of the man, you love a ring instead of your bridegroom. If this is how it is with you, that you love a ring instead of your bridegroom and don't want to see your bridegroom, then he gave this earnest to you not to pledge himself to you but to keep you away from him. A bridegroom gives a pledge for the very purpose that he himself may be loved in his pledge. That is why God gave you all these things, then; love him who made them. There is more that he wants to give you—that is, himself, who made them. But if you love these things, although God made them, and you neglect the creator and love the world, won't your love be considered adulterous?[16]

When we appeal to the doctrine of common grace in such a way as to orient our hearts to the concrete gifts of culture rather than to God in gratitude for his gifts, we risk turning our desire for the "goods" of this world into an idol. Though Augustine affirmed common grace when he spoke of the Israelites' "plundering the gold of the Egyptians," he surely did not have in mind that Christians should use the doctrine to rationalize and justify their preoccupation with what is good about the gold. When we focus only or primarily on elements in unbelieving pagan and secular culture that seem "good" to us, we internalize and send a message that "the world is not

---

[16] Augustine, *Homilies on the First Epistle of John*, in *The Works of Saint Augustine*, ed. Daniel E. Doyle and Thomas Martin, trans. Boniface Ramsey (Hyde Park, NY: New City, 2008), 2.11.

as bad as all that." The doctrine of common grace, we must always remember, is intended not to give us permission to bless and use unbelieving culture but to lift our hearts to God, the giver of "every good and perfect gift."

Created for Work?

Our first concern has been to underscore our fellowship with God as the primary purpose and goal of our creation in his image. Now we need to consider the very mundane and practical aspects of being image bearers in the world God created for his glory and for our use. Bavinck insists that these two are integrally connected with each other.

> This eternal destiny in no way forecloses our earthly vocations. The spiritual does not come first; the natural does. The first man was earthly, from the earth (1 Cor. 15:45–47), and was given a vocation also for this world. Thanks to his body, man is connected to the earth, dependent on it for his existence, and in many respects shares its life. With a view to earth, humans are given a double task, to fill the earth and rule over it (Gen. 1:[26]; 2:15).[17]

Bavinck acknowledges here a distinction, a duality that is not a dualistic separation.

> This earthly calling is distinguished from the eternal destiny of humans, just as the institution of the Sabbath alongside the workweek bears testimony. They, however, are not in conflict and form no contradiction; true fulfillment of our earthly vocation is exactly what prepares us for eternal salvation, and putting our minds on those things that are above equips us for genuine satisfaction of our earthly desires.[18]

It is here, in the duality of our "eternal destiny" and our "earthly vocation," that Bavinck chooses to interpret the meaning of our work.

> It is this dual vocation that sets the responsibility of work before humans. God, who himself is always at work (John 5:17) and calls us to be like him in this, did not create us for idleness and blissful inactivity. He gave us six days, therefore, for all sorts of labor involving our heads and our hands as we subdue the earth; our work is also a divine institution.

---

[17] "Gen. Prin.," 438.
[18] "Gen. Prin.," 438.

At the same time, we are not justified by our work and it does not define us. The Sabbath, the seventh day of rest, is not only an opportunity for rest but above all a reminder that "heaven rather than earth [is] the goal of [our] work." We are created for fellowship with God and we exercise that fellowship in our social relationships and earthly vocations by intentionally following God's law. "God's law—written on human hearts—was given as a rule and guide for our entire existence in its internal and external dimensions, covering our daily walk and our commerce. This law is summarized in the duty to love God and the neighbor."[19] In the words of the first resolution of the 1891 Christian Social Congress in Amsterdam, where Bavinck's report "General Biblical Principles and the Relevance of Concrete Mosaic Law for the Social Question Today" provided the foundation for the congress's most important discussion, "Holy Scripture teaches that human society must not be ordered according to our own preferences but is bound to those laws that God himself has firmly established in Creation and His Word."[20]

The role of the law of God in shaping the life of Christian discipleship will be our concern in the next chapter. To wrap up this chapter I want to add a few final words about the image of God, human dignity, and liberty. Bavinck's celebration of the created, natural life of humanity and his elevation of human vocation to the highest level points to the royal dignity that human beings enjoy as God's image bearers. Bavinck is even willing—within the boundaries of human creatureliness and God's law—to speak of humans as "co-workers" with God.

> The Calvinist, therefore, is not satisfied when he is personally reconciled with God and assured of His salvation. His work begins then in dead earnest, and he becomes a co-worker with God. For the Word of God is not only the fountain of the truth of salvation, but also the norm of the whole life; not only glad tidings of salvation for the soul, but also for the body and for the entire world. The Reformed believer continues therefore, "*ad extra*," that reformation which began with himself and in his own heart.[21]

Bavinck's Reformed vision of the Christian life is a big vision rooted in a high anthropology, or doctrine of humanity. God has given to his image bearers great dignity, responsibility, and liberty. To highlight an important

---

[19] "Gen. Prin.," 438–39.
[20] "Gen. Prin.," 445.
[21] "Moral Infl.," 52.

Reformed theological distinctive, we are God's *covenant* partners. According to Bavinck, God so values us that he gave us liberty, including the freedom to rebel against him. God tolerates evil, says Bavinck, because he "is able to govern it in an absolute holy and sovereign manner." We were not created as puppets, as mere "blocks and stones."[22]

> If God had not allowed [sin and evil] to exist, there would always have been a rationale for the idea that he was not in all his attributes superior to a power whose possibility was inherent in creation itself. For all rational creatures as creatures, as finite, limited, changeable beings, have the possibility of apostasizing.

Nonetheless, God did not forestall the possibility of human rebellion and sin. "But God, because he is God, never feared the way of freedom, the reality of sin, the eruption of wickedness, or the power of Satan." Bavinck then goes on to quote Augustine: "Because he knew he was absolutely able to control sin, 'he deemed it better to bring good out of evil than not to permit any evil to exist at all.'"[23]

We humans are noble and created with liberty; we are also fallen, deeply flawed, and in need of God's law. With that in mind, we turn to our next chapter.

---

[22] Canons of Dort, 3/4.16.
[23] *RD*, 3:64–65.

CHAPTER 3

THE LAW AND THE DUTY
OF CHRISTIAN OBEDIENCE

In the previous chapter we focused on the royal dignity God gave to human beings by creating them in his image and likeness. The first and foremost consequence of this biblical teaching is that we are created for fellowship with God, for Sabbath. It is this covenantal relationship with God that endows our life of work and our life in society and culture with its own high dignity. In a restricted but still real sense, we are "co-workers" with God. What we do in this life has significance for eternity. All that we do, down to the most basic necessary functions for life itself, is to be viewed from this eternal perspective: "So, whether you eat or drink, or whatever you do, do all to the glory of God" (1 Cor. 10:31). Our deeds all have consequences; they follow us into eternity: "And I heard a voice from heaven saying, 'Write this: Blessed are the dead who die in the Lord from now on.' 'Blessed indeed,' says the Spirit, 'that they may rest from their labor, for their deeds follow them!'" (Rev. 14:13). Our lives are given new meaning by our fellowship with God in Christ; they are elevated to a higher purpose *for the Lord*, and in this way we are given strength and confidence for our journey: "Therefore, my beloved brothers, be steadfast, immovable, always abounding in the work of the Lord, knowing that in the Lord your labor is not in vain" (1 Cor. 15:58).

In this chapter we want to pay attention to the *how* of our discipleship. In a life of fellowship with God in Christ, what do we turn to for practical, concrete guidance in shaping our conduct? Bavinck stands firmly within the Reformed tradition when he answers this question by turning to the law of God. This is not the default position of North American evangelicals, who tend instead to turn to the example and teaching of Jesus as the first biblical resource for how to live a Christian life. As we shall see in chapter 5, Bavinck also places a great deal of weight on the imitation of Christ as an ethical ideal, but it is not the place where he starts; he starts with creation and the law.

With this step he follows the traditional emphasis on the law in the Reformed confessions and tradition. The Heidelberg Catechism (1563) emphasizes the Ten Commandments as the first key to grateful Christian living, and this is where Reformed ethics tends to focus in instructing the faithful to be good disciples of Jesus Christ. We also find this emphasis on the law and the Ten Commandments in Bavinck, but a mere exposition of his interpretation of each commandment would not be sufficient. It is important to understand the *why* of this emphasis on the law, and here we need to consider another important Reformed theological notion, the so-called covenant of works.

Covenant of Works

As with the doctrine of common grace, it is important to not get hung up with the term *covenant of works*. The notion of works associated with covenant easily degenerates into the mistaken idea that the human relationship with God is a matter of our working rather than being constituted by God's grace. So, once again, let us try to grasp the inner core of this doctrine and why Reformed theology has placed such a great deal of emphasis on it.

For an initial definition of the covenant of works one can hardly improve on the simplicity and confessional clarity of the Westminster Confession of Faith, 7.2 (1647): "The first covenant made with man was a covenant of works, wherein life was promised to Adam; and in him to his posterity, upon condition of perfect and personal obedience."

When God created man, he placed upon him a condition: Obey me and you shall live; disobey me and you shall die. Our very relationship with God from the beginning was constituted by a command, by law. The biblical "proof" provided by the confession is primarily that of Galatians 3:12: "The law is not of faith, rather 'The one who does them shall live by them.'" The Old Testament passage quoted in this verse is from Leviticus 18:4–5: "You shall follow my rules and keep my statutes and walk in them. I am the LORD your God. You shall therefore keep my statutes and my rules; *if a person does them, he shall live by them*: I am the LORD."

The authors of the confession also cite Romans 10:5, where Paul quotes the same Leviticus passage, and they also mention the important Adam/Christ parallel in Romans 5:12–20. Finally, to remind us that disobedience to law results in curse and judgment, the confession takes note of Galatians 3:10 and the probationary command given in Genesis 2:17.

In addition to the Westminster Confession, "the covenant of works is incorporated in the Irish Articles (1615), . . . the Helvetic Consensus Formula (1675), and the Walcheren Articles (1693)."[1] Bavinck also observes that though "the Reformed Confessions do not mention it in so many words, [m]aterially, however, it is nevertheless embodied in articles 14 and 15 of the Belgic Confession, where we read that man's entire nature was corrupted by Adam's transgression of the command of life." It is also implied "in Lord's Day 3 and 4 of the Heidelberg Catechism (Q. & A. 6–11)," where man's creation in God's image "so that he might live with God in eternal happiness" is accompanied by the description of humanity as "totally corrupted by Adam's fall." Finally, it is also noted in "chapter III/IV of the Canons of Dort [where] it is stated that Adam's corruption spread to all his descendants 'by God's just judgment.'"[2] The covenant of works is a recognizably important doctrine in Reformed theology, and we conclude our brief survey with the definition provided by Wilhelmus à Brakel in his classic, popular work of Dutch Reformed theological piety *Our Reasonable Service*: "The covenant of works was an agreement between God and the human race as represented in Adam, in which God promised eternal life upon condition of obedience, and threatened eternal death upon disobedience. Adam accepted both this promise and this condition."[3]

From this summary evidence, the doctrine's basis and purpose are clear. God's relationship to humanity from the outset was a legal, covenantal relationship in which obedience was demanded and to be rewarded, and disobedience was proscribed and under sanctioned curse and punishment: "Obey and live; disobey and die."

However, not all Reformed theologians and biblical scholars, especially

---

[1] *RD*, 2:566.
[2] *RD*, 2:566–67.
[3] Wilhelmus à Brakel, *Our Reasonable Service*, trans. Bartel Elshout, vol. 1 (Ligonier, PA: Soli Deo Gloria, 1992), 355.

in recent years, affirm the covenant of works as a doctrine.[4] Some object because the biblical word for covenant (*berith*) is absent in Genesis 1 and 2. Others find troubling the very idea that Adam would have achieved a higher destiny *if* he had obeyed; any element of conditionality in God's covenant with his people, they say, undermines God's sure promises and the whole scheme looks like something meritorious. And finally, a fundamental objection is often raised against the view that our relationship with God is something *legal*; covenant, so it is then argued, is not legal but personal and relational.

These are all legitimate questions to which appropriate answers are available, but my concern in this chapter is simply to set forth Bavinck's views, which include a positive affirmation of the covenant of works. I will only point out that much of the opposition to the covenant of works strikes me as unnecessary dancing around the issue. Even the doctrine's critics usually want to affirm that God did make "something like a covenant" with Adam. Adam was the representative head of the human race and was given a "probationary command" to test his obedience. Furthermore, his disobedience to that command brought sin, death, and condemnation into the world. Then, as importantly, Adam was a type of Christ, our second head called "the last Adam" in 1 Corinthians 15:45, through whom we are delivered from the consequences of the first Adam's sin. This is the real reason for affirming the covenant of works: the Adam-as-legal-representative/Christ-as-legal-representative parallel developed by Paul in Romans 5 (and 1 Corinthians 15). With all that in place as essential to good Christian doctrine, the debate about the "covenant of works" strikes me as mostly rhetorical. At any rate, we are interested here in the *substance* of the legal character of our relationship with God from the beginning and the reason why Bavinck affirms it: because it is a *revealed* matter.

It is impossible, he observes, to separate religion from revelation. Even before the fall, God revealed himself to Adam and Eve in a personal manner: "The God-human relation in the state of integrity is depicted as one of personal contact and association. God speaks to human beings (Gen. 1:28–30), gives them a command they could not know by nature (Gen. 2:16), and, as by his own hand, brings to the man a woman to be his helper (Gen. 2:22)."[5]

---

[4] A partial list of objectors includes Herman Hoeksema, John Murray, Anthony Hoekema, and John Stek. For a clear defense of the law as the defining characteristic of human life before the face of God, see Bryan D. Estelle, J. V. Fesko, and David VanDrunen, eds., *The Law Is Not of Faith: Essays on Works and Grace in the Mosaic Covenant* (Phillipsburg, NJ: P&R, 2009).
[5] *RD*, 1:308.

The covenant of works is the product of revelation. "Also the covenant of works (*foedus operum*) is not a covenant of nature (*foedus naturae*) in the sense that it arises from a natural human proclivity but is a fruit of supernatural revelation." Bavinck then summarizes the heart of what the Reformed theological tradition calls the "covenant of works": "The covenant of works is nothing other than the form of religion that fits the human beings created in God's image who had not yet achieved their ultimate destiny." There is no religion without supernatural revelation.

> The supernatural is not at odds with human nature, nor with the nature of creatures; it belongs, so to speak, to humanity's essence. Human beings are images of God and akin to God and by means of religion stand in a direct relation to God. The nature of this relation implies that God can both objectively and subjectively reveal himself to human beings created in his image.[6]

Of course the law of God is explicitly revealed in the Ten Commandments and thus an essential part of Jewish and Christian holy writ.

It is crucial that we take note of the emphasis on the intimately personal character of the God/man relationship described in the previous paragraph. Any religious tradition that emphasizes the law as much as the Reformed does faces the ongoing temptation of moralism and legalism. That is why we need to go beyond simply providing detailed expositions of the Ten Commandments when we consider the shape of the Christian life before God. The Ten Commandments are the *covenant* stipulations of Israel's God who brought them "out of the land of Egypt, out of the house of slavery" (Ex. 20:2). *Covenant* is a relational term, and according to Bavinck, it is even the "form of life" characterizing "all higher life among rational and moral creatures . . . . the usual form in terms of which humans live and work together."[7]

As examples, Bavinck mentions "love, friendship, marriage, as well as all social cooperation in business, industry, science, art, and so forth." And if this is true for our earthly, horizontal relationships, "it should not surprise us, therefore, that also the highest and most richly textured life of human beings, namely, religion, bears this character." In fact, Bavinck believes that "in Scripture 'covenant' is the fixed form in which the relation

---

[6] *RD*, 1:308.
[7] *RD*, 2:568.

of God to his people is depicted and presented." The heart of covenant is present even when the precise terms for covenant are absent. "And even where the word does not occur, we nevertheless always see the two parties, as it were, in dialogue with each other, dealing with each other, with God calling people to conversion, reminding them of their obligations, and obligating himself to provide all that is good." "Reformed scholars," he notes, "were never so narrow as to insist on the word 'covenant' since the matter itself was certain: one may doubt the word, provided the matter is safe (*de vocabulo dubitetur, re salva*)." Furthermore, according to Bavinck, "covenant is the essence of true religion."[8]

When we think of the law of God as the guide to our life of discipleship, therefore, we ought to think less in terms of an external set of rules or a legal code and more in terms of parents lovingly and personally providing guidelines to help children navigate their way through life. God's covenant law is personal, relational, and here we have the heart of true religion. After all, God is the Creator and we humans are mere creatures; there is an infinite distance between us. This distance would seem to forestall any kind of fellowship between us and God. "No fellowship, no religion between the two seems possible; there is only difference, distance, endless distinctness. If God remains elevated above humanity in his sovereign exaltedness and majesty, then no religion is possible, at least no religion in the sense of fellowship." All that we would be left with is the relation of "master" and "servant." If there is to be fellowship between God and humanity, and if that relation is to be the model for all other relations among humans,

> then religion must be the character of a covenant. For then God has to come down from his lofty position, condescend to his creatures, impart, reveal, and give himself away to human beings; then he who inhabits eternity and dwells in a high and holy place must also dwell with those who are of a humble spirit (Isa. 57:15).

But these are the precise conditions that describe covenants. "If religion is called a covenant, it is thereby described as the true and genuine religion." According to Bavinck, this covenantal character of an understanding of the God/humanity relation is a distinctive feature of biblical religion. Other religious traditions either elevate God above the world or lower him down to it.

---

[8] *RD*, 2:569.

This is what no religion has ever understood; all peoples either panthe-
istically pull God down into what is creaturely, or deistically elevate him
endlessly above it. In neither case does one arrive at true fellowship, at
covenant, at genuine religion. But Scripture insists on both: God is infi-
nitely great and condescendingly good; he is Sovereign but also Father;
he is Creator but also Prototype. In a word, he is the God of the covenant.[9]

The law that guides us in life is a personal word from a God who has entered
into covenantal fellowship with us.

There are several key practical consequences of this posture. In the
first place, because God is the one who created us and we "owe our very
existence" to him, we have no "rights" before him. "A creature as such owes
its very existence, all that it is and has, to God; it cannot make any claims
before God, and it cannot boast of anything; it has no rights and can make
no demands of any kind." As contingent and dependent creatures we are
entitled to nothing. Our very existence is a gift. "There is no such thing as
merit in the existence of a creature before God, nor can there be since the
relation between the Creator and a creature radically and once-and-for-all
eliminates any notion of merit."[10] Bavinck cites Luke 17:10: "When we have
done everything we have been instructed to do, we are still unworthy servants (*douloi achreioi*)." This suggests a posture of total submission to God.

Yet, no sooner has Bavinck pointed out that we are entitled to nothing than he underscores the freedom that we have been given by God as
creatures. True biblical religion is covenantal, and in covenant we are in
fellowship *and dialogue* with God. God who created by speaking a word,
made us capable of talking back—for ill as well as for good.

Now, however, the religion of Holy Scripture is such that in it human beings can nevertheless, as it were, assert certain rights before God. For
they have the freedom to come to him with prayer and thanksgiving, to
address him as "Father," to take refuge in him in all circumstances of
distress and death, to desire all good things from him, even to expect
salvation and eternal life from him.

We submit to God's law but we do not *simply* submit or *blindly* submit; our
submission is personal, to the living covenantal God with whom we are

---

[9] *RD*, 2:569–70.
[10] *RD*, 2:570.

in fellowship. "All this is possible solely because God in his condescending goodness gives rights to his creature. Every creaturely right is a given benefit, a gift of grace, undeserved and nonobligatory."[11]

Our capacity to speak back to God—in praise and blessing as well as tragically in curse—reminds us that God created human beings not as puppets or marionettes but as "rational and moral beings."

> That is how God created them, and that therefore is how he treats them. He maintains what he created. God, accordingly, does not coerce human beings, for coercion is inconsistent with the nature of rational creatures. He deals with them, not as irrational creatures, as plants or animals, as blocks of wood, but goes to work with them as rational, moral, self-determining beings. He wants human beings to be free and to serve him in love, freely and willingly (Ps. 100:3f.). Religion is freedom; it is love that does not permit itself to be coerced.[12]

That is why true, biblical religion takes the form of a covenant "in which God acts, not coercively, but with counsel, admonition, warning, invitation, petition, and in which humans serve God, not under duress or violence, but willingly, by their own free consent, moved by love to love in return." The duty we owe God is not blind submission to an external law or will but the privileged service of loving gratitude. Our obedience is "not work by which we bring advantage to God, make a contribution to him, and have a right to reward. It is grace for us to be allowed to serve him. God is never indebted to us, but we are always indebted to him for the good works we do (Belgic Confession, art. 24)." Lest we still draw a wrong conclusion from the term *covenant of works*, Bavinck emphatically tells us that "God was in no way obligated to grant heavenly blessedness and eternal life to those who kept his law and thereby did not do anything other than what they were obligated to do. There *is* no natural connection here between work and reward."[13]

Our dependence on God therefore is quite unlike the negative sort of crippling dependence we all too often experience in our relationships. The developmental goal that parents have for their children is appropriate *independence*. Good parents give their children increasing and age-appropriate responsibilities and duties so that they can mature into adulthood. Parents who, with every good intention in mind, overprovide for their children, re-

---

[11] *RD*, 2:570.
[12] *RD*, 2:570.
[13] *RD*, 2:571.

move negative consequences from their bad behavior, and so forth contribute to their remaining immature. Government welfare that does more than simply serve as a safety net for people who temporarily need assistance often fosters a dependence that robs people of their dignity as responsible human agents. That is not how God treats us. He created us as those who can hear his voice, respond in obedience, and be blessed; but we are also capable of saying no to God's direction and then receiving the consequence of our disobedience. Human freedom and maturity require that our lives be ordered in such a way that our actions have consequences. When, with all the best intentions, we seek to shelter people from the consequences of their acts, we diminish their dignity and rob them of an essential part of the image of God in them.

Our Covenantal Duty of Obedience

How then must we live? We begin with affirming a fundamental religious posture of dependence and humility that leads us to obedience. Our duty of obedience is not that of slaves to their master but of children to their heavenly Father. In addition, there are two consequences of this emphasis on covenant of works and law that may strike us initially as counterintuitive: Christian liberty and responsibility. Yes, this emphasis provides us with the greatest imaginable freedom and calls for the greatest possible personal responsibility. To see why and how this is so, we need to remind ourselves that we are speaking about a *covenantal* duty of obedience.

We noted earlier that thanks to the covenant, "God acts [toward us], not coercively, but with counsel, admonition, warning, invitation, petition." Furthermore, "humans serve God, not under duress or violence, but willingly, by their own free consent, moved by love to love in return."[14] Bavinck even contends—again, somewhat counterintuitively—that Old Testament Israel, though a theocracy, nonetheless enjoyed genuine religious freedom. To begin with, the religious leaders, the priest and Levites, "certainly possessed no hierarchical, conscience binding power." Their job, among others, was "to explain the law and instruct the people." Clearly implied here is the need for informed consent to God's law. When religious disobedience was punished, such as Elijah's order to kill the priests of Baal, these "were isolated incidents, prescribed in most cases by special divine command."

---

[14] *RD*, 2:571.

Bavinck concludes that "Israel, also religiously, enjoyed a great measure of freedom. Unbelief and heresy were not punished; there was no inquisition; restraint of conscience was totally unknown." Ordinarily, God sought to bring his people back to him by means of the prophetic word, by persuasion: "And when the prophets testify against a turning away from God and resist kings and priests, they avail themselves of the word, call for a return to the law, but never insist on using force." Even in Old Testament Israel there was a distinction—though not a separation—between "church" and "state." This distinction applied to "members" as well as to "offices and administrations, institutions and laws." Remarkably, "foreigners could participate in the spiritual privileges of Israel, and thus, so to speak, be members of the church, without being citizens; and lepers, unclean persons, people banished, remained citizens, but they were nevertheless isolated, and taken outside the community."[15]

While words can of course be abusive and manipulative, there is something about interpersonal speech communication that is liberating, that enhances liberty and responsibility. We have to respond to words; we can either affirm them or reject them. Assuming there are no additional external coercive conditions—a gun held to our head, the threat of being fired, and so forth—we don't have to do what someone else asks us to do. In healthy covenant relationships, one does what someone requests *for the sake of the covenant itself.* Ideally, husbands complete "honey do" lists because they share their wives' understanding that a certain job, like cleaning the gutters, *needs* to be done. But in cases where such shared understanding may be absent, a husband will do it *for the sake of the marriage* because he loves his wife. Note that this is both a free act and a responsible act. "Voluntary" should not be confused with indifferent libertarian free will, where one is an autonomous moral agent. In covenant freedom obedience is fueled and bounded by love. It is also a responsible act because a husband can refuse. In that case he will suffer consequences, of course, but that too is the case with God.

And finally, our freedom and responsibility are located in community; we are not alone. According to Bavinck this too follows from the doctrine of the covenant of works.

> Adam was not created *alone.* As a man and by himself he was incomplete.
> He lacked something that no lower creature could make up (Gen. 2:20).

---

[15] *ESSR,* 124–25.

As a man by himself, accordingly, neither was he yet the fully unfolded image of God. The creation of humankind in God's image was only completed on the sixth day, when God created both man and woman in union with each other (cf. *'ōtām* Gen. 1:27), in his image.

But, beyond this initial creation, God began here a "journey with mankind . . . [by] immediately pronouncing [upon them] the blessing of multiplication (Gen. 1:28). Not the man alone, nor the man and woman together, but only the whole of humanity is the fully developed image of God, his children his offspring."[16] Adam is the representative head of the whole human race and the original source of its organic unity, and it is in this organic unity of all humanity that we find the fullness of the image of God.

> Just as the cosmos is a unity and receives its head and master in humankind; and just as the traces of God (*vestigia Dei*) scattered throughout the entire world are bundled and raised up into the image of God of humankind; so also that humanity in turn is to be conceived as an organism that, precisely as such, is finally the only fully developed image of God. Not as a heap of souls on a tract of land, not as a loose aggregate of individuals, but as having been created out of one blood; as one household and one family, humanity is the image and likeness of God.[17]

Bavinck underscores the freedom and responsibility of human beings as covenant partners with God by including history in his understanding of the image of God. "The image of God," he contends,

> can only be displayed in all its dimensions and characteristic features in a humanity whose members exist both successively one after the other and contemporaneously side by side. Belonging to that humanity is also its development, its history, its ever-expanding dominion over the earth, its progress in science and art, its subjugation of all creatures. All these things as well constitute the unfolding of the image and likeness of God in keeping with which humanity was created.[18]

To prevent any misunderstanding at this point, we need to point out that this does not lead us to affirm and bless all cultural developments in human history. Bavinck only wants to point out that the full potential of

---

[16] *RD*, 2:576–77.
[17] *RD*, 2:577.
[18] *RD*, 2:577.

our humanity in our relation to the creation was not present at the beginning; it is in the progress of our *lawful* dominion over the earth that we unfold that potential—in creation and in ourselves. In the same manner that God reveals himself fully not at the beginning but over time, so too our grasp of what it means to be an image bearer of God develops and grows. "Just as God did not reveal himself all at once at the creation, but continues and expands that revelation from day to day and from age to age, so also the image of God is not a static entity but extends and unfolds itself in the forms of space and time." Remarkably, God gives to us humans an important role in the unfolding of that image; human history is of greatest significance: "It is both a gift (*Gabe*) and a mandate (*Aufgabe*). It is an undeserved gift of grace that was given to the first human being immediately at the creation but at the same time is the grounding principle and germ of an altogether rich and glorious development."[19]

Covenantal obedience is possible because of God's gift and is to be exercised in responsible freedom. Covenantal obedience is also *lawful* obedience, and we need to conclude our chapter with a brief look at the covenant and law.

Lawful Covenantal Obedience

The theme of this chapter is the role of the law in Bavinck's understanding of the Christian life. Our concern up to now has been to develop an understanding of God's law that militates as much as possible against all forms of legalism and moralism. A more complete antidote to this perennial Reformed temptation requires that we consider the work of Christ in redemption and the work of the Holy Spirit in sanctification, and I will address both in the next two chapters. What I have done in this chapter is to provide a biblical portrait of the covenantal relation between God and humanity as the proper frame for understanding the law in the first place. We are created in God's image and for fellowship with God in covenant. From the beginning, quite apart from sin, our relationship with God is covenantal and legal. God has not hidden his will from us; he has made known to us the conditions for joyful and blessed fellowship. Whenever we isolate the law from that covenantal fellowship, we turn it into a death-delivering judge. The law is gracious and intended as a guide and norm for commu-

---

[19] *RD*, 2:577.

nion with the living God. Framed in that way, it is an invitation to liberty and responsibility.

I need to conclude this chapter with a few words about the practical implications of this *law-full* perspective for our daily Christian walk. Since we are to be "imitators of God" (Eph. 5:1; see Matt. 5:45), the first and most obvious consequence is that we are always to conduct ourselves in ways that enhance our neighbor's liberty and responsibility. This implies, for example, that parents find age-appropriate ways of encouraging free responsibility in their nurture of children. It also means that churches need to respect the Christian liberty of members as they guide them in their discipleship. And it suggests that Christians evaluate public social policy in terms of the same principles. It also implies, finally, that when it comes to matters of social policy and political actions, Christians have an obligation to respect each other's freedom on matters that either are *adiaphora* (things indifferent) or require application of agreed upon moral principles. The example of poverty and poverty relief comes to mind. The Bible is quite clear about the responsibility of God's children to help those who are poor and needy. Whether or not this commitment to the poor demands support for higher taxes and greater government welfare is quite another matter. It is a mistake for Christians to treat *their* policy preferences as self-evident applications of biblical principle. Christians need to respect the liberty of those who take their Christian responsibilities in directions that are different from their own.

But, now, what about applying the actual law itself, notably the Ten Commandments? We will be paying closer attention to specific commandments in the second half of this volume when we consider the specific social spheres of life: marriage and family, work and vocation, culture and education, and civil society (chap. 7–10). To conclude this chapter I want to provide one example of Bavinck's use of several commandments of the Decalogue in a concrete and practical application. Bavinck's report prepared for and address to the 1891 Christian Social Congress in Amsterdam, "General Biblical Principles and the Relevance of Concrete Mosaic Law for the Social Question Today," concluded with seven propositions or resolutions that were debated and finally adopted by the congress, some with modification. After resolutions affirming the importance of being guided and "bound to those laws that God himself has firmly established in Creation and His Word" (no. 1) and attributing "the origin of all social ills and abuses . . . [to] setting aside these ordinances and laws" (no. 3), the fifth resolution declared that "the important general principle for a solution to the social question is that there be justice (*gerechtigheid*)."[20]

This overview was followed by a sixth resolution, which brought together a number of the themes we have been considering here and in the previous chapter: eternal destiny and earthly calling; Sabbath; human life as created in and for community; redemption in Christ; and the dignity, worth, and responsibility of each person as an image bearer of God. Bavinck and the congress were not content to stay at the level of general principle, but became concrete and specific. I offer the whole sixth resolution here as an exemplary application of the vision set forth in this chapter:[21]

> Therefore, it is entirely in keeping with Holy Scripture to:
>
> a. not only prepare people for their eternal destiny, but also to make it possible for them to fulfill their earthly calling;
> b. in the political arena, uphold the institution of the Sabbath alongside the workweek so as to maintain the unity and distinction of our double calling;
> c. guide all our life's relationships in a new way and restore them to their original shape by the same cross of Christ that proclaims our reconciliation with God. This has special relevance for the social arena where [we should seek to]
>
>   - prevent poverty and misery, especially pauperization;
>   - oppose the accumulation of capital and landed property;
>   - ensure, as much as possible, a "living wage" for every person.

This resolution is rooted in creation, imaginatively and responsibly uses God's law to enhance human dignity in our earthly vocations, and at the same time reminds Christian disciples that "preparing for eternal destiny" is at the heart of our calling. That is the point of the Sabbath reminder; Sabbath is a sign that our earthly calling is not the end. And since we cannot reach our destiny as fallen sinful creations *in Adam*, we need to participate in the life of the second Adam. We need to be united with Jesus Christ. That leads us to our next chapter.

---

[20] "Gen. Prin.," 445.
[21] "Gen. Prin.," 446.

CHAPTER 4

UNION WITH CHRIST

This chapter is the longest and most demanding in the book. It is the heart of part 1 ("Foundations for Christian Living") and the volume as a whole. This chapter comes third in this section because union with Christ *logically* follows creation and the law of God. Recall our earlier maxim: We are human before we are Christian, and we are Christian to be truly human. This fundamental reciprocity of dual identities—being human and being Christian—is the key to Bavinck's understanding of union with Christ. We have seen that Bavinck operates theologically with several key dualities: earthly calling and eternal destiny; general revelation and particular revelation; common grace and saving grace. These dualities are important *distinctions* in Bavinck's thought, but they must not be treated dualistically as *separations* and set over against each other. We must not choose earth over heaven or heaven over earth, world affirmation *or* world flight; we cannot opt for nature *or* for grace. And for our purposes here, we must never separate our humanity from our Christianity. Bavinck knows that in this life one-sidedness characterizes individuals as well as groups of people. Strive as we might for harmony and balance in our lives, "no one in this dispensation achieves a completely harmonious answer. Every person and every movement are guilty of a greater or lesser one-sidedness here."[1]

Bavinck responds to this not with despair but with a careful distinction. No sooner has he said that we are all "guilty of a greater or lesser one-sidedness here," than he adds this crucial qualification: "And yet it

---
[1] "Com. Grace," 56.

makes a great difference whether one conceives of this dualism as absolute or relative."[2] What could Bavinck possibly mean here by the oxymoronic-sounding term *relative dualism*? He is reminding us that some form of dualism is inevitable because we still live "between the times." We have not yet arrived in the fullness of God's eternal rest; our lives are *historically*, that is to say *eschatologically*, conditioned by the reality of sin. We experience tensions in our lives because we cannot avoid being pulled by competing longings that may both be legitimate. All dualism is finally overcome in the consummation of the age, when the triumph of God's grace in Christ will be complete and all the brokenness of creation will be healed. Until then, some dualism remains. We are on earth and called to live in God's creation as his royal, stewardly image bearers. At the same time, we can never feel completely at home in this world; our real home is elsewhere. That tension should never disappear from our Christian existence.

Notwithstanding the tension between duality and dualism, I introduce this chapter with these notions because it is in Bavinck's understanding of union with Christ that he achieves a unity of thought. And as we have seen so many times before, he does it with an important distinction.

Mediator of Union/Mediator of Redemption

Almost all discussions about union with Christ take Christ's redemptive work and the pouring out of the Holy Spirit at Pentecost as their point of departure. And this seems only right. After all, the apostle Paul, who is the great New Testament theologian of union with Christ, makes very little distinction between being "in Christ" and being "in the Spirit." Of the many passages where this is indicated, perhaps none says it as clearly as Romans 8:9–11:

> You, however, are not in the flesh but in the Spirit, if in fact the Spirit of God dwells in you. Anyone who does not have the Spirit of Christ does not belong to him. But if Christ is in you, although the body is dead because of sin, the Spirit is life because of righteousness. If the Spirit of him who raised Jesus from the dead dwells in you, he who raised Christ Jesus from the dead will also give life to your mortal bodies through his Spirit who dwells in you.

---

[2] "Com. Grace," 56.

Bavinck of course disagrees with none of this. His own treatment of Christ's work of redemption and the Holy Spirit's application of Christ's work to the believer is rich in emphasis on union with Christ, and we will consider much of it later on in this chapter, as well as in the next. However, Bavinck does have a broader understanding of union with Christ than only the redemptive, and here again he shows the remarkable consistency and coherence of his theological vision. Bavinck's christological reflection begins with creation because the incarnation is not the beginning of the Son's work. The Son—the second person of the Trinity, the Word, the Logos—is also the Creator. "The Logos who became flesh is the same by whom all things were made. The first-born from the dead is also the first-born of every creature. The Son, whom the Father made heir of all things, is the same by whom he also made the worlds."[3] Bavinck repeatedly speaks of Christ as the *mediator of creation*.

Christ as mediator of creation is also the one through whom we have fellowship with God, and he was the one who made this possible from the beginning. "The Son is not only the mediator of reconciliation (*mediator reconcilationis*) on account of sin, but even apart from sin he is the mediator of union (*mediator unionis*) between God and his creation."[4] Bavinck uses the language of "mediator of union" to describe this role of the Son in bridging the ontological distance between humanity and God. This is a good reminder that for us to have communion with God today, we must overcome two obstacles, one moral and the other metaphysical. The first is obvious; our sin blocks communion because unholy human beings cannot enter into fellowship with a holy God. But there is a metaphysical as well as a moral divide; even apart from sin, God is God and we are mere creatures. Communion requires communication, and how is it even possible for God to speak to human beings? As Bavinck put it, "If God were to speak to us in a divine language, not a creature would understand him."[5]

Scripture teaches that God not only created human beings to whom he could speak; they were also created to be able to talk back to him. This required a gracious condescension on God's part. "But what spells out his grace is the fact that from the moment of creation God stoops down to his creatures, speaking and appearing to them in human fashion."[6] What

---

[3] *PofR*, 27–28.
[4] *RD*, 4:685.
[5] *RD*, 2:100.
[6] *RD*, 2:100.

Bavinck is referring to here is the well-known doctrine of divine *accommodation* for which John Calvin too was famous.[7]

There are two dimensions to this accommodation. As Scripture shows again and again, God "appears" to people by way of "messengers" (i.e., angels), through dreams and visions, and even audible words. These are quite ordinary human phenomena, even though they serve extraordinary purposes. Hearing the voice of God requires a willing heart and spiritual discernment; the priest Eli told the young Samuel to say, when he heard God's call, "Speak, LORD, for your servant hears" (1 Sam. 3:9). But accommodation is also present whenever *we* try to speak about God, when we attempt to describe God or say truthful things about him. Since God is so far above us, how can we find the language to do him justice? God is always so much more than even our most lofty descriptions. Bavinck states the problem this way: "Between him and us there seems to be no such kinship or communication as would enable us to name him truthfully. The distance between God and us is the gulf between the Infinite and the finite, between eternity and time, between being and becoming, between the All and the nothing."[8] Speaking about God, not to mention having fellowship with him, is possible only when God in some way "descends" to us and communicates to us *on our terms*. Then, having received a word from God about him, we can confidently repeat the content of his revelation. We speak about God only because he has first spoken to us *in our language*. Our descriptions of God, too—our "God talk" if you will—can only be expressed in a human language that is accommodated to our creaturely status.

We are of course accustomed to the language of "descent" applied to the incarnation, most memorably in the beloved hymn of Philippians 2. But, as we have seen, for Bavinck the role of the Son as *Mediator* goes back to creation and also incorporates the special revelation of the Old Testament dispensation. In his doctrine of revelation, Bavinck specifically ties divine revelation in the old covenant to the work of the preincarnate Christ. The special appearances of God (theophanies) and the prophetic word come from the Word. "Special revelation in the days of the Old Testament is the

---

[7] See John Calvin, *Institutes of the Christian Religion*, ed. John T. McNeill, trans. Ford Lewis Battles, 2 vols. (Philadelphia: Westminster, 1960), 13.1, where Calvin speaks of God's revelation to humanity in terms of nurses "lisping" to infants. Cf. his *Commentary* on Isa. 6:1, where Calvin asks the rhetorical question "How could Isaiah see God when God cannot be seen by mortal men?" He answers that "when God exhibited himself to the view of the Fathers, he never appeared such as he actually is, but such as the capacity of men could receive" (John Calvin, *Commentary on the Book of the Prophet Isaiah*, trans. William Pringle, 2 vols. (repr., Grand Rapids: Baker, 2003), 1:200.

[8] *RD*, 2:30.

history of the coming Christ. Theophany, prophecy, and miracle point toward him and reach their fulfillment in him. He is the manifestation, the word, and the servant of God."[9] It is especially as the messenger of God that God himself is present to his people, and this "angel of the covenant," this "theophany reaches its climax in Christ, who is the [messenger, glory, image, Word, Son of God], in whom God is fully revealed and fully given (Matt. 11:27; John 1:14; 14:9; Col. 1:15; 2:19; etc.)."[10]

The Word who makes God known to the people of the old covenant is the same Word by whom all things were created. Though Christian theology, reflecting the teaching of the Apostles' Creed, appropriates the work of creation to the Father, creation is a work of the whole Trinity in which the Son plays a significant part. The Son is the *wisdom* and *order* of the world; creation's own logos or order reflects the divine Logos. "He is not only the exemplary cause (*causa exemplaris*) but also the final cause (*causa finalis*) of creation. In the Son the world has its foundation and example, and therefore it has its goal as well. It is created through him and for him as well (Col. 1:16)."[11]

Let's pause to underscore what a remarkable theological accomplishment Bavinck has achieved here. He has brought creation, redemption, and eschatology all into the doctrine of Christ without in any way blurring the distinction between nature and grace or sacrificing the gracious character and preeminence of Christ as our Redeemer. It is easy for Christians to err on the side of emphasizing grace, forgiveness, and eternal life at the expense of a life of discipleship in creation; in reaction, other Christians can fall into the trap of making our life in this world all-important. If the former are accused of "being so heavenly minded, they are no earthly good," the latter run the risk of becoming so worldly that they are unfit for eternity. Bavinck's vision avoids both errors. For him, creation's purpose and goal are found in Christ; he is the glory of the Father, "the head, Lord, and heir of all things. United in the Son, gathered under him as their head, all creatures return to the Father, the fountain of all good."[12] Thus, without in any way undermining or minimizing the gracious character of our union with Christ—we don't deserve it and we do nothing to earn it—there is something altogether fitting about our union with Christ in

---

[9] *RD*, 1:344.
[10] *RD*, 1:329.
[11] *RD*, 4:685.
[12] *RD*, 4:685.

our salvation. In Christ, the second Adam, the true man, we become fully human by participating in his humanity, a humanity that from the beginning was formed after the divine Word.

To sum up: Bavinck understands union with Christ as an integral part of a larger pattern of Trinitarian operation. This is how the triune God works! We were created for Sabbath holiness, to bear the image of God in eternal glory. Sin prevents us from our destiny; it alienates us from our true humanity. It is only in union with Christ, in the power of the Holy Spirit, that we are renewed in the true righteousness and holiness for which we were created. We are Christian to be truly human. Of course, that only underscores the necessity and importance of our redemption.

What Is "Union with Christ"?

All human beings participate in the sin of Adam, our federal head. We are organically united in a common fallen humanity and stand under the sentence of God's just judgment. The gospel offers release from this condition, the promise of restored communion with God, and the hope of becoming part of a different humanity. How do we then become part of this new humanity in Christ, the second Adam? And when we do, what is changed— in us, in our fellowship with God, and in our relations with other human beings? What does it mean to be "united with Christ"? Or alternatively, what do we mean when we use the language of "participation," of being "in Christ," or "Christ in us"?

As we begin to explore the idea of union with Christ in greater detail, we need to be sensitive, as Bavinck was in his day, to the pitfalls and errors that have arisen in the history of Christian piety and that are also present in certain contemporary expressions of spirituality. Conflicting unbiblical views of God lead to a variety of spiritual practices that are often at odds with traditional Christian orthodoxy and piety. In some cases, God becomes distant and far removed from us; he is so qualitatively different and sovereign that he is incomprehensible and unapproachable. The opposite error is to blur the boundary between God and his human creatures. The pendulum swings between the twin errors of elevating humanity to the highest and almost godlike level of potential, on the one hand, and bringing God down to such an involvement in our creaturely existence that we lose all sense of transcendence, on the other. Bavinck attempted to capture this feature of human religious life by regularly calling attention to the way in which our conceptions of God shift back and forth between *deism* and *pantheism*.

When we speak of union with Christ as the key to our fellowship with God, we seek to accomplish two things: (1) make it clear that God is not remote and removed from us, as deists propose; and (2) contrary to all pantheism, maintain a clear ontological distinction between God and humanity. To summarize, we are in genuine communion with God, and we never become gods or divine. Let's consider both of these "outside the bounds" views as they come to expression in our contemporary world of Christian spirituality.

In some respects, deism would seem the least likely temptation for Christians today. After all, isn't an excessively subjective and intensely personal "relationship with Jesus" Christianity the hallmark of contemporary evangelicalism in North America? Perhaps, but we should not dismiss deism too quickly. Sociologists Christian Smith and Melinda Norquist Denton, in their 2005 book *Soul Searching: The Religious and Spiritual Lives of American Teenagers*, based on the Lilly Endowment research project "The National Study of Youth and Religion," concluded that the common belief system of American youth could be described as "moralistic therapeutic deism" (MTD). This belief system is not based on one particular religious faith but is drawn from a number of strands from different traditions, which are then combined into an identifiable pattern. Smith and Denton identify five tenets of MTD:

1. A god exists who created and ordered the world and watches over human life on earth.
2. God wants people to be good, nice, and fair to each other, as taught in the Bible and by most world religions.
3. The central goal of life is to be happy and to feel good about oneself.
4. God does not need to be particularly involved in one's life except when God is needed to resolve a problem.
5. Good people go to heaven when they die.[13]

This belief system is not deistic in the classic eighteenth-century sense, because the God who is distant is also available to help us in emergencies and to take care of our needs. Hence the qualifier "therapeutic";

---

[13] Christian Smith and Melinda Lundquist Denton, *Soul Searching: The Religious and Spiritual Lives of American Teenagers* (New York: Oxford University Press, 2005), 162–63.

God is always available as the cosmic helper whose interest is in making us feel good about ourselves. Of course, one cannot imagine anyone describing him- or herself as a "moralistic therapeutic deist"; the term summarizes a generational ethos and is the creation of researchers. At the same time, the evidence that a significant number of American young people, including those who attend churches, seem to share a faith in a god who is relatively uninvolved in their lives and with whom they have little genuine communion is profoundly troubling, and it is appropriate to highlight it here as a threat to our Christian discipleship.

What Bavinck called pantheism is the opposite error; pantheism blurs the boundaries between God and his creatures. As we noted, this can be done by elevating human beings to godlike status or by bringing God down to earth. In either case genuine transcendence is lost; God's "godness" disappears from sight, and he becomes like one of us. While a deistic view of God is helpfully countered by a strong emphasis on union with Christ that makes genuine fellowship possible between Creator and creature, the same emphasis potentially opens the door to the pantheistic tendency. If we *are united* with God in Christ or "participate in God," how do we honor the proper distance between ourselves and God and resist self-deification? Here we encounter, once again, questions about what exactly we have in mind when we speak of "*union* with Christ" or "*being* in Christ," or of "participation." How does our *being* change when it is brought into union with the "*being* of Christ"? What do we make of being the *body* of Christ? How are we temples of the Holy Spirit?

These questions arise quite naturally from the biblical text. The Bible itself pushes us to ponder the possibility of overcoming the boundary between the human and the divine. There are biblical texts that seem to encourage us to seek participation in the very life of God. No single text forces this question upon us more than 2 Peter 1:4, where the apostle describes his Christian readers as "participants in the divine nature."[14]

This verse is a favorite "proof text" for the Greek Orthodox doctrine of *theosis*, or "divinization," as the goal of human salvation. The doctrine is stated precisely by the church father Athanasius in his work *On the Incarnation of the Word*: "For He was made man that we might be made God; and He manifested Himself by a body that we might receive the idea of the

---

[14] A full exposition of this verse is beyond the scope of this volume. For an interpretation that is intentionally within the Bavinck tradition, see Albert M. Wolters, "'Partners of the Deity': A Covenantal Reading of 2 Peter 1:4," *Calvin Theological Journal* 25 (1990): 28–44.

unseen Father; and He endured the insolence of men that we might inherit immortality."[15] We must emphasize here that Orthodox theology insists that this doctrine does not blur the clear distinction between the Creator and the human creature. We do not become God as he exists in his own essence; we only participate in the *energy* or activity of God. At the same time, the formulation of Athanasius—"he was made man that we might be made God"—does make us sit up and take notice. What does "divinization" mean, and can it be construed in such a way that Western sensibilities are satisfied? The following explanation by Orthodox monk and theologian St. Maximus the Confessor (c. 580–662) might help us out:

> A sure warrant for looking forward with hope to deification of human na-
> ture is provided by the incarnation of God, which makes man god to the
> same degree as God himself became man. . . . Let us become the image of
> the one whole God, bearing nothing earthly in ourselves, so that we may
> consort with God and become gods, receiving from God our existence as
> gods. For it is clear that He who became man without sin (cf. Heb. 4:15)
> will divinize human nature without changing it into the divine nature,
> and will raise it up for his own sake to the same degree as He lowered
> himself for man's sake. This is what St Paul teaches mystically when he
> says, ". . . that in the ages to come he might display the overflowing rich-
> ness of His grace" (Eph. 2:7).[16]

Perhaps this explanation does not fully satisfy us, but we must honor two important nuances and qualifications in this passage: (1) Maximus links deification to "the image of the one whole God," a direct tie to the account of human creation in Genesis and to Colossians 3:10, where Paul describes our redemption in terms of a "new self, which is being renewed in knowledge after the *image of its creator.*" Again, we come face-to-face with language of Scripture itself. (2) Maximus explicitly states that Christ "will divinize human nature *without changing it into the divine nature.*" Divinization is *not* a form of pantheism or panentheism.

Before considering Bavinck's critique of the idea of divinization, we must acknowledge that on one specific point it resonates deeply with Bavinck's own theology. *Theosis* is one important way of affirming that

---

[15] Athanasius, *On the Incarnation of the Word,* vol. 4 in *The Nicene and Post-Nicene Father,* series 2, ed. Philip Schaff, 14 vols. (Edinburgh: T&T Clark: 1886–1889), 54.3.

[16] Quoted in G. E. H. Palmer, Kallistos Ware, and Philip Sherrard, *Philokalia: The Complete Text,* 4 vols. (London: Faber and Faber, 1979–1999), 2:178.

our redemption in Christ does more than simply restore humanity to its pre-fall Adamic state. In Christ we are brought to the fullness of what we were created to be as God's image bearers. The understanding is that in the incarnation a union is effected between God and humanity, making it possible for those who are "new creation[s]" in Christ (2 Cor. 5:17) to be divinized. We achieve this through a process of purification (*katharsis*) and the contemplation of the triune God (*theoria*) until we arrive at sainthood (*theosis*). In the Eastern Church, following the teaching and practice of the Mount Athos monk Gregory Palamas (1296–1359), the deification process involves ascetic prayer (*hesychasm*), in which the goal is to arrive at contemplation of God by blocking out the physical senses through inner focus and repetition of the Jesus Prayer: "Lord Jesus Christ, son of God, have mercy on me, a sinner."

Bavinck follows the Western theologians in generally disapproving this tradition and the notion of divinization or deification. We are less interested here in whether Bavinck is correct in all aspects of his critique than in grasping the basic reason for his opposition. What is it that he objects to, and is his objection still of value for us today? Bavinck sees behind the notion of divinization the specter of neo-Platonism, in which all reality is regarded as a seamless web of being, creation is a descending emanation of divine material, and redemption consists of climbing a "ladder of ascents" out of our physical and material existence and back into spiritual divine being. In this view creation in its physical materiality is considered inferior and even evil, while a nonmaterial spiritual reality is superior and good. Such a notion is of course a direct assault on the biblical doctrine of a good creation. Bavinck also objects to the idea that it is possible for human creatures to contemplate the essence of God because God is incomprehensible and infinite. "Humans, therefore, can never have more than a finite human vision of God." Our final state will be glorious, to be sure, but it will always be human. "Regardless of how high and glorious Reformed theologians conceived the state of glory to be, human beings remained human even there, indeed raised above 'their natural position' but never 'above their own kind' and 'that which is analogous to that.'"[17] Human beings never become gods.

This critique is still important today. An immediate and obvious implication is that Christian eschatology and spirituality are light-years re-

---

[17] *RD*, 2:190–91.

moved from Mormon eschatology and spirituality, where God himself used to be a man and we humans can become gods ourselves. This should not be a surprise to readers, but it is still worth emphasizing. Closer to home, there are versions of Pentecostal and charismatic spirituality, notably the so-called "Word of Faith" or "health and wealth" movement (aka "prosperity gospel"; aka "name it and claim it"), that also look suspiciously like they elevate human power to godlike status. Televangelists Kenneth Copeland and Joel Osteen, among others, teach that complete healing of body, soul, and spirit is included in Christ's atonement, and believers only need to "claim it" to possess guaranteed health and wealth. With our words of faith we create our own worlds, acquire prosperity and good health, and even control tornados and hurricanes. In order to emphasize the real and high dignity of our status as children of God, Word of Faith prosperity preachers even use the language of "little gods." *Suffer the Children*, a 2007 documentary produced by Trevor Glass that is highly critical of the Word of Faith movement, includes a startling and disturbing video clip with Creflo Dollar teaching his Atlanta congregation (World Changers Church International) this "little gods" doctrine:

> DOLLAR: "If horses get together, they produce what?"
> CONGREGATION: "Horses!"

Similar questions and answers follow, substituting "dogs" and "cats." Then comes this startling exchange:

> DOLLAR: "So if the Godhead says, 'Let us make *man* in *our* image,' and everything produces after its own kind, then they produce what?"
> CONGREGATION: "gods!"
> DOLLAr: "gods. Little 'g' gods. You're not human. Only human part of you is this flesh you're wearing."[18]

When we talk about union with Christ, it is important to avoid all similar notions that even hint at acquiring godlike status or powers. Specifically, this means inoculating ourselves against the messages coming from the numerous television ministries of health-and-prosperity preachers like Ken and Gloria Copeland, Benny Hinn, Joyce Meyer, Joel Osteen, and

---

[18] This dialogue is taken from Trevor Glass's documentary "Suffer the Children" (2007), accessed August 12, 2013, https://www.mixturecloud.com/media/LV5ikf. The video clip is also available at http://biblelight.net/Creflo-Dollar.htm.

others. Bruce Wilkinson's best seller *The Prayer of Jabez*, we should note, also proclaims a prosperity gospel, albeit in a muted tone. Any suggestion that union with Christ and participating in the life of God might overcome the ontological divide between us and our Creator must be firmly repudiated. We must clearly and unequivocally insist that our union with Christ does *not* turn us into "little gods." Before we move on to a more pleasant and constructive discussion about the meaning of our union with Christ, there is one additional popular evangelical emphasis that also needs to be singled out: the notion of "incarnational ministry."[19]

It has become popular in North American evangelical circles to speak of Christian ministry in incarnational terms. We are called, so it is then said, to "be Jesus" to people. It is, of course, true that the church is the "body of Christ" on earth now that our Lord has ascended to heaven and his human nature is seated at the right hand of the Father. In its Lord's Day 18, on the ascension of Christ, the Heidelberg Catechism asks the following question:

> Q. 47. But isn't Christ with us until the end of the world as he promised us?

The answer points to the important salvation-historical fact that Christ's human nature is no longer on earth; Jesus has left and gone to the Father:

> A. Christ is true human and true God. In his human nature Christ is not now on earth; but in his divinity, majesty, grace, and Spirit he is never absent from us.

His Spirit dwells in his *body,* the church, and in this way the risen Christ remains among us and is present in the world. But notice that *body of Christ* is a spiritual or *pneumatological* term and not a christological one. The church is the body of Christ through its *spiritual union* with the risen and exalted Christ; it is *not* a repetition of the incarnation. Whenever we think of the person of Christ—second person of the Trinity, eternal Logos—or the work of Christ—incarnation, atonement, resurrection, ascension, session, return—we encounter categories that are completely inapplicable to the church. If we would not say that the church makes atonement for sin, ascends into heaven, sits at God's right hand, and will return again on the

---

[19] For the basic perspective on what follows, I am deeply indebted to J. Todd Billings's wonderful exploration of the theme of this chapter, *Union with Christ: Reframing Theology and Ministry for the Church* (Grand Rapids: Baker, 2011), especially chap. 5.

clouds to judge the living and the dead, we should not use incarnational language for it either. The incarnation of Christ was a unique event, and his work as Mediator is unique. We cannot and should not even think of repeating the incarnation.

Obviously Bavinck did not address the errors of these two emphases directly; they arose after his death. But his historical treatment of the doctrine concerning the person of Christ, particularly the heterodox developments in modern christology,[20] does speak to it indirectly. The orthodox, catholic Christian dogmatic consensus on the person of Christ was established at the Council of Chalcedon in AD 451. Chalcedon confessed that Christ is

> one and the same Son and Lord, the same perfect in Godhead, the same perfect in humanhood, truly God and truly man . . . one and the same Christ, Son, Lord, Only-begotten, made known *in* two natures [according to the original reading; not *out* of two natures], without confusion [ἀσυγχύτως], without change [ἀτρέπτως], without division [ἀδιαιρέτως], without separation [ἀχωρίστως].

This consensus did not satisfy everyone, as Bavinck observes: "But—to put it mildly—not all Christians were comfortable with this confession."[21] An oft-repeated critique—to this very day!—asserts that the doctrine of the two natures represents a Greek philosophical model that is neither biblical nor suitable in the modern context. Consequently, modern thinkers proposed radically revising our understanding of Christ.

A popular revision was initiated by the German philosopher Immanuel Kant (1724–1804). Denying that we could have any true knowledge of supersensible realities (such as the fact that Jesus was the incarnation of the second person of the Trinity), Kant proposed that we think of Christ as "a model of morality and a teacher of virtue," and nothing more. "Beyond this, what Scripture and church tradition say about Christ has only *symbolic* value," Bavinck summarizes. He then adds a clarification showing how Kant turns the meaning of the incarnation upside down. It no longer declares what God himself has done for us in Christ's descent to our humanity; it is now only a *symbol* of our human religious quest: "The Christ of the church is the symbol of a humanity pleasing to God: it is the

---

[20] *RD*, 3:259–74.
[21] *RD*, 3:255, 259.

true, only-begotten, much-beloved Son for whom God created the world. The incarnation of Christ symbolizes the origination of a truly moral life in humans." And, to continue, for Kant, "faith in Christ means that for their salvation people must believe in the idea of a humanity that is pleasing to God."[22]

While in Kant the actual history of Jesus is reduced to his being a moral example, nineteenth-century German idealism took this a step further and discounted the historical altogether. Friedrich W. J. Schelling (1775–1854) understood God as absolute, but as an absolute *becoming* that "comes to manifestation in the world as its logos and son." Orthodox Christian theology is mistaken, so it was argued, when it "believes that Christ is the only begotten incarnate Son of God." Rather, "because God is eternal . . . he cannot have assumed human nature in a specific moment of time. As historical fact, Christianity is of passing significance."[23] If history is passé, what then of Christianity, which is so rooted in history? We see in Schelling and in other nineteenth-century figures such as G. W. F. Hegel (1770–1831) a radical turn away from history to the *idea*.

Reading Bavinck's summary of Schelling's understanding of the incarnation requires an advance warning—Schelling's views are abstract and esoteric, and great patience is required to get through the maze of words: "The idea, however, endures forever: the world is the son of God. The incarnation of God consists in the fact that the absolute, in order to be itself, becomes manifest in a world . . . . The world, accordingly, is God himself in the process of becoming."[24] The incarnation is no longer personal; it has become an impersonal cipher for the world process itself. Genuine transcendence is gone. The technical term for this view is *panentheism*, which does not hold that "everything is God" as pantheism does, but asserts that "everything is *in* God."

Schelling's contemporary and fellow idealist Hegel made similar moves. What theology describes with terms such as *incarnation* is turned by philosophy into *concepts*. The incarnation is therefore not about the eternal Son taking on a human nature, but a theological manner of expressing the *idea* of the union between the divine and the human. Thus, many incarnations become possible. "Christ is not the only divine-human figure; humans are basically one with God." Stated differently, "humanity itself is the incarnate God who was conceived by the Holy Spirit, lives a sin-

[22] *RD*, 3:260.
[23] *RD*, 3:260.
[24] *RD*, 3:260.

less life, rises from the dead, ascends to heaven, and so on."[25] Apart from the bloodless abstraction of this language, this radical reinterpretation of the biblical and ecclesiastical teaching about our Lord's incarnation ought to send shivers up the spines of evangelical believers. Think about it; our messy, broken, and sin-stained history is God himself coming into being? What hope is left? Who can save us?

We have spent some time on the pedigree of this notion that we in some way continue the incarnation not to level accusations at those who use the language today but to raise necessary cautions. My own hunch is that those who use this language do so in relative innocence without intentionally carrying along any of the problematic baggage of modern philosophy and theology. At worst, this language represents a kind of theological carelessness rather than open and deliberate heresy. Speaking of Christian ministry in incarnational terms, furthermore, is not necessary. As we shall see at the conclusion of this chapter, the same point can be made by fully utilizing the doctrine of union with Christ *as a pneumatological notion* rather than a christological one. At the same time, those who have been informed of the mischief generated by the notion should then cease and desist. That was the not-altogether-pleasant task of the preceding. We can now turn to the more enjoyable constructive description of the Christian's union with Christ.

Our Redeemed Humanity in Christ

Lamentably, even our constructive work cannot avoid controversy, although we shall try to keep it at a minimum. Controversy cannot be avoided altogether because when it comes to the most profound mysteries of the Christian faith, we can often do little more than mark boundaries. The incarnation itself is such a mystery. How can we really fathom the union of God and man in the one person of Jesus Christ? Earlier, we observed the orthodox, catholic Christian consensus on the person of Christ as formulated at the Council of Chalcedon in AD 451. Chalcedon confessed that Christ is

> one and the same Son and Lord, the same perfect in Godhead, the same perfect in humanhood, truly God and truly man . . . one and the same Christ, Son, Lord, Only-begotten, made known *in* two natures [according to the original reading; not *out* of two natures], without confusion

---

[25] *RD*, 3:261.

[ἀσυγχύτως], without change [ἀτρέπτως], without division [ἀδιαιρέτως], without separation [ἀχωρίστως].[26]

I call attention here especially to the last four terms, which are translated into English as "without confusion," "without change," "without division," and "without separation." Note that Chalcedon did not attempt to *define* the God-man union; rather, it marked the boundaries of an acceptable understanding. If we "mix" the divine and human (confusion, change), we are outside the fence of Christian orthodoxy; if we tear the divine and human apart (division, separation), we are also heterodox. What is true of the incarnation—and this seems obvious—is equally true for our union with Christ. At its core we are dealing with the most profound of human mysteries—the communion between God and humanity; because precise definition will elude us, we can only set boundaries and limits. In the history of the church, these boundaries and limits are forged in the heat of controversy, and we cannot avoid them here. In the remainder of this chapter, we will examine the Reformation debate about the doctrine of justification, the controversy about free will between Pelagius and Augustine, the post-Reformation conflict between the Reformed churches and the Remonstrants, and finally the intra-family debate in the Dutch Reformed Church of the late nineteenth century about "immediate regeneration."

When the Reformation emphasized "justification by faith alone," it was engaging in a polemic against Roman Catholic sacramental understandings of grace. At the risk of oversimplifying, Roman Catholic soteriology (doctrine of salvation) emphasized union with Christ through sacramental participation. The sacraments were seen as the instruments whereby the grace of God was infused into people and in this way changed them. The Reformers saw this as turning grace into something objective and external to the believer and thus overlooking the subjective dimension of religious experience and leaving personal assurance of salvation in doubt. As they saw it, this extrinsic view of grace as infused through the sacraments undermined the truth and certainty of the gospel message. Over against Roman Catholic sacramentalism and infused grace, the Reformers boldly trumpeted the objective, forensic, and legal dimension of justification. The *word* of the gospel *declares* that the "just live by faith," and in Christ we are *declared* to be righteous.

---

[26] RD, 3:255.

In the heat of the ecclesiastical battle that raged in the sixteenth century, positions were staked out by both sides, views hardened over time, and this resulted in mutual condemnations. Without exploring this in detail, we can nonetheless get a glimpse into the contours of the battle lines by considering a few of the anathemas pronounced by the Roman Catholic Council of Trent (1545–1563) in its Decree on Justification (1547). It needs to be said as a correction to some anti-Catholic prejudices still residing in the Protestant and evangelical world that Trent is clear in affirming human inability to earn our salvation and our utter need for the grace and mercy of God. "If they were not born again in Christ, they never would be justified" (chap. 3). However, there is also an affirmation of God's prevenient grace that enables us to "cooperate" with God's grace and become active agents in our own justification (chap. 4). The anathemas that follow the decree confirm both of these points. Not only is canon 1 unproblematic for Protestants; its affirmation of grace might even surprise some: "If any one says, that man may be justified before God by his own works, whether done through the teaching of human nature, or that of the law, without the grace of God through Jesus Christ; let him be anathema." But then, canon 9 clearly has in mind the Reformation emphasis on the bondage of the will and justification by faith alone:

> If any one says, that by faith alone the impious is justified; in such wise as to mean, that nothing else is required to co-operate in order to the obtaining the grace of Justification, and that it is not in any way necessary, that he be prepared and disposed by the movement of his own will; let him be anathema.

That Trent was worried about "cheap grace" and the problem that arises when we reduce justification to a merely forensic, legal question of status before God becomes clear in canon 11:

> If any one says, that men are justified, either by the sole imputation of the justice of Christ, or by the sole remission of sins, to the exclusion of the grace and the charity which is poured forth in their hearts by the Holy Ghost, and is inherent in them; or even that the grace, whereby we are justified, is only the favour of God; let him be anathema.

The debate between Tridentine Rome and the Reformation can be summarily described as a battle over how to understand the new reality that is created by the grace of God in Christ. Is it a new *status* before God—a change from condemnation of the guilty to vindication of the righteous— or is it newness of *being* through sacramental *participation* in the grace of God? The Reformation emphasized the former; Rome proclaimed the latter. A key difference: in accenting the legal dimension of justification, the Reformation dealt with the *activity* of the new life in Christ under the distinct rubric of sanctification; Rome resisted distinguishing justification and sanctification, fearing that this would lead to devaluing the duty of holiness. Put in simple New Testament terms: Protestants worry that the apostle Paul does not get his due; Roman Catholics worry that James gets set aside. Though faith is not a "work," faith without works is dead.

This Reformation-era debate has been revisited in our day. We will not explore it further here; I introduced it to provide a contrast with Bavinck's emphasis on union with Christ in which the forgiveness of justification and the new life in the Spirit both receive their due.[27] In what follows, I will provide a synopsis of Bavinck's views in response to two fundamental and practical questions: (1) *How* does this new life in Christ come to pass? What is the *process* by which it takes place and how can we describe it? (2) *What* is the *content* of this new life? What is its shape and what are its components? What does the new life in Christ look like? To answer these questions, we shall consider Bavinck's understanding of the order of salvation (*ordo salutis*) and conclude with a few observations about the church.

Becoming United with Christ

It is clear already from the New Testament that the new life in Christ can be described in a variety of ways, using different words and metaphors or images. Our Lord himself, in his conversation with Nicodemus (John 3), said that for someone to see the kingdom of God, it was necessary to be "born again" (or "born from above"). In theological terms, this is usually spoken of as "regeneration." When the focus is human guilt before God and the forgiveness of sin that comes through Christ's atonement, the notion of justification is used. The image is that of a law court where a judge pronounces us "not guilty." The language of the law court is not restricted to the notion of justification; the New Testament also uses the legal language of "adoption." When the apostle Paul speaks of God's election, his choosing us "before

---

[27] I underscore here my indebtedness to J. Todd Billings, *Union with Christ*, for the insights that led to this setup.

the foundation of the world," he continues by saying that God "in love . . . predestined us for adoption as sons through Jesus Christ" (Eph. 1:4–5). The new life in Christ also involves a conscious act of the human will in turning away from sin and toward holy and obedient living before God. This is called "conversion." Though our justification is more of a singular act—we are *declared* to be righteous before God in Christ—our life of obedient, holy living is generally a lifelong process of increasingly dying to sin and living to Christ, a process usually referred to as "sanctification."

Recognizing the richness of the biblical language and being aware of the natural human desire to organize and figure out how these dimensions of our salvation fit together, Reformed theologians over the years have discussed this at length. To use the technical theological term, this is a discussion about the *ordo salutis*. Rather than entering this rich—though not always edifying—territory of theological controversy in any depth, we shall restrict ourselves to the fifth-century debate between Augustine and the Pelagians and the seventeenth-century debate the Reformed churches carried on with the Remonstrants or Arminians. For our purposes I will simplify the history, summarize, and pay special attention to the practical, pastoral dimensions.

The British monk Pelagius (390–418) denied that all humans are mortally wounded by Adam's sin and insisted they retain wills that can do good if they hear the law. There is no "original sin" that corrupts us; we sin by imitating bad examples. We need no divine assistance to do good works. Augustine (354–430) proceeded from the conviction that humanity's moral corruption is total and that we are in ourselves incapable of doing any saving good. Divine assistance and grace are needed, not only the external grace of gospel proclamation and sacraments but an internal grace, a grace of the Holy Spirit that is "a communication of power that enlightens the understanding, bends the will, and creates within us all good."[28] Not only does this grace "precede every good work" and create in us "the capacity and the willing" to do good works; it then acts "as cooperating grace to bring about in us the doing itself." This last point is crucial; without insisting that it is the empowering grace of God the Holy Spirit that enables us to do good, we would be stuck in an unholy tug-of-war between God's sovereign grace and human responsibility. "It supplies us the capacity to believe and to love, but then also makes us actually believe

---

[28] *Saved*, 14.

and love."[29] In this way we do become active in our justification; we must believe, and though Christ died *for us*, *on our behalf* and *in our place*, the Holy Spirit does not believe *for us*. The Holy Spirit is the indispensable and personal indwelling of God who makes our dead hearts alive and *able* to believe. But we ourselves must believe!

Both in his monograph *Calling and Regeneration*[30] and in the *Reformed Dogmatics*, Bavinck scrupulously follows the Augustinian line. However, Augustine's position was seriously challenged in the Dutch Reformed churches of the seventeenth century by the Remonstrants, the followers of James Arminius (1560–1609). Arminius did not deny that grace is needed for salvation; he taught that a "prevenient grace" is conferred by the Holy Spirit on all people, enabling them to believe "if they so will" (or not). The following proposition summarizes what his opponents believed he taught: "The grace sufficient for salvation is conferred on the Elect, and on the Non-elect; that, if they will, they may believe or not believe, may be saved or not be saved."[31] Though Arminius includes this definition in his "Apology," where he defends himself against his opponents, his response makes it clear that the proposition is not an inaccurate rendering of his thought. The teachings of Arminius, summarized by his followers in 1610 in a written *Remonstrance* setting forth five disagreements with the Reformed confessions, led to the Synod of Dort in 1618–1619, and eventually to the third confession adopted by Dutch Reformed churches, the Canons of Dort.

Bavinck treats the controversy addressed by the Synod of Dort in some detail in the fifth chapter of *Calling and Regeneration*. This monograph originated as a series of some forty articles written for the broader church press as an effort to communicate "greater clarity concerning the doctrine of immediate regeneration," which was being vigorously debated in his day. In particular, Abraham Kuyper's idiosyncratic view that *presumed* or *presupposed regeneration* of covenant infants by the Holy Spirit is a ground for their baptism generated considerable opposition in the Christian Reformed Church. To understand this, we need to know that in 1886 Abraham Kuyper also left the National Dutch Reformed Church and took a sizeable number of followers with him. Kuyper and his followers referred to themselves as the "*Dolerenden*," which literally means "the ones who are

---

[29] *Saved*, 14.
[30] See *Saved*, in the table of abbreviations, for the full title of the English translation.
[31] James Arminius, "Apology against Thirty-One Theological Articles," art. 28.8, in *The Works of James Arminius: The London Edition*, trans. James Nichols and William Nichols, 3 vols. (Grand Rapids: Baker, 1986), 2:53.

mourning," and their group was known as the *Doleantie*. This now meant that two seceding groups were present in the Netherlands, and because the two had many concerns in common, there arose numerous pleas for unification. In 1892 a union church, the *Gereformeerde Kerken in Neder-land*, came into being, though not all members of the Secession Christian Reformed Church joined the new denomination. It was here, in the new union church, that the debate I have been summarizing became pastorally important. Some members who came from the Secession church claimed that the Kuyper-inspired preachers frequently presumed that their congregants were already born again and therefore failed to call people to conversion. Bavinck's articles and monograph were his attempt to clarify the issues and propose a way forward in the hope, he wrote in his foreword, that "difference of insight does no injury to the unity of the Confession and to the peace of the churches."[32]

Bavinck sets up the question by contrasting "immediate regeneration" with "mediated regeneration": Does God the Holy Spirit need *means* such as preaching and sacraments to communicate his grace (a *mediated* work of the Holy Spirit), or can and does the Spirit also work *immediately*, that is, without means?[33] This sounds terribly abstract, but there are weighty pastoral issues involved, such as infant baptism and the purpose of preaching. If parents believe, for example, that the sacramental grace of baptism is needed for the salvation of their infant, they may feel undue pressure to "rush a baby to baptism," or become anxious about an ill infant who dies before baptism is administered. In this instance, they risk making baptism a matter of superstition. On the other hand, if one becomes so "spiritual" that one dismisses the importance of *means* of grace and is indifferent to corporate worship, sacraments, and church discipline, one sinfully neglects God's own good gifts meant for our good. These were precisely the issues that led to the great debates of the Reformation era and were revisited in the nineteenth-century Dutch Reformed Church.

The Reformation rejected the view that the external means of sacramental grace are *necessary* for salvation. The Holy Spirit, the Reformers said, can and does work immediately, internally. Though conversion of the sinner *ordinarily* comes by the proclamation of the gospel, God the Spirit can regenerate a person's heart immediately, without an outward hearing

---

[32] *Saved*, v.
[33] See *Saved*, 5–8.

of the gospel. If that was the concern on one side, on the other and over against "spiritual Anabaptists," who opposed infant baptism as well as a preaching "office" in the church, the Reformers insisted that Christ chose to govern his church by his Word and Spirit and that he ordained offices and sacraments as "means of grace." Bavinck summarizes the significance of the doctrine of immediate regeneration this way:

> Of all those truths, the doctrine of immediate regeneration occupies a central place, especially in Reformed theology. In the closest possible connection to this teaching lies the relationship between Word and Spirit, between Scripture and church, between doctrine and life, between mind and heart. This teaching involves the most important question, namely in which way and in which order the Holy Spirit applies the benefits obtained through the suffering and death of Christ.[34]

Let's address this constellation of issues by considering the variety of ways in which the New Testament describes the new life in Christ.

"Mystical Union" and the Order of Salvation

The terms "born again," "turning my life around," and being "chosen and called by God" are valid descriptions of the new life in Christ based firmly in the New Testament. However, these expressions do point to three identifiably distinct dimensions of the new life. "New birth" points to our changed *being*; we have a whole new identity because we *are* different. "Conversion" underscores the important role of our wills; in the power of the Spirit, we have *chosen* a different direction for our lives. And finally, "calling" is an essential reminder that our turning around is a *response* to a prior divine invitation, an invitation we "could not refuse."

It is a challenge to sort out the order in which we ought to discuss all these dimensions of the new life in Christ and how they come to pass. Bavinck follows the order in Reformed confessions such as the Heidelberg Catechism in distinguishing the "objective" work of Christ and its benefits from their application to the believer in a subjective and personal manner. But the objective work of atonement and substitution must never be separated from Christ's work by which, in the power of the Holy Spirit, he makes his own the beneficiaries of his atonement. The roles are distinct but inseparable.

---

[34] *Saved*, 5.

Inasmuch as Christ is not only the atoner but also the redeemer, that is, not only, objectively, had to take away the guilt of sin but also, subjectively, had to break the power of sin, this mystical union between Christ and believers is an essential and indispensable constituent in the work of salvation.[35]

This "mystical union" (in the Spirit) is not the starting point however: "Yet [mystical union] is not the only and the first relation that exists between Christ and his own." Where then do we begin? With Christ as the second Adam, the one who federally represents the new humanity. Bavinck appeals here to the very structure of Paul's letter to the Romans: "In Scripture this relation [mystical union] is built on the federal relation: Romans 6–8 follows Romans 3–5."[36] Bavinck insists on the prior objectivity of Christ's substitutionary atonement and stoutly resists all efforts to make atonement a subjective redemption. "This mystical union in the scriptural sense," he insists, "can only be maintained in conjunction with the objective atonement of Christ's sacrifice, when Christ is first of all viewed as the head of the covenant, who took the place of his own in a federalistic legal sense."[37]

Bavinck thus joins and keeps together the covenantal, legal, and forensic dimensions of justification with the believer's mystical union in Christ, a union frequently cut asunder in our heated contemporary debates about the doctrine.[38] But he probes even deeper. Before we consider Christ's work on our behalf, we need to think of the Trinitarian covenant of grace on which it rests.

The covenant of grace, in fact, is anterior to the person and sacrifice of Christ. That covenant, after all, does not come into effect after Christ has accomplished his work, nor start with the Holy Spirit or with the benefits of regeneration and faith; but Christ himself is *in* that covenant. He is the guarantor and mediator of it (Heb. 7:22; 8:6; 12:24); his blood is blood of the covenant and therefore atoning (Matt. 26:28).[39]

---

[35] *RD*, 3:405.

[36] *RD*, 3:405.

[37] *RD*, 3:405; .

[38] Bavinck's treatment of our Lord's substitutionary atonement remains a valuable resource, even for our contemporary discussions, as, e.g., a rebuttal of the so-called "New Perspective on Paul" associated with scholars such as E. P. Sanders, James D. G. Dunn, and N. T. Wright. The fundamental clash between the traditional Reformation understanding of Paul and the NPP concerns the "works of the law." The traditional view holds that Paul is condemning human efforts to earn one's salvation; for NPP scholars, the expression refers to "badges of covenant membership" and is applied to those Gentiles who marked their identity as Christians via Jewish markers such as circumcision. Not all NPP writers deny the penal-substitutionary character of the atonement, but they definitely minimize it and, in some cases, even vigorously oppose it.

[39] *RD*, 3:405.

And finally, Bavinck takes us beyond time to the intra-Trinitarian "pact of salvation" between Father, Son, and Holy Spirit.

> Even more, the covenant of grace was not first established in time, but has its foundation in eternity, is grounded in the pact of salvation (*pactum salutis*), and is in the first place a covenant among the three persons of the divine being itself. Father and Son and Spirit are all three active in that covenant; it is so far from beginning in time with the activity of the Holy Spirit that it has its existence and certainty rather from eternity in the counsel of the Triune God.[40]

As we now consider the *how* of our mystical union with Christ, it is important that we always keep in mind that our union with Christ is built on the foundation of his accomplished work on our behalf, and that this work is firmly grounded in the sovereign good pleasure and will of the triune God. Our salvation is eternally grounded.

With that established, it should be obvious that our consideration of union with Christ must begin by affirming God's sovereign initiative in grace. Specifically, if conversion is an act of our will in turning away from sin and to God, regeneration by the Holy Spirit cannot *logically* follow conversion. We are not "born again" by an act of our will; we are "born from above" (John 3:3). Similarly, though we are "justified by faith," faith cannot be the *ground* of our justification. And even though no less a theologian than John Calvin begins his discussion of salvation in book 3 of his *Institutes of the Christian Religion* with a discussion of sanctification rather than justification, to think that sanctification must happen *before* we can be justified would also be a serious error because it undermines the divine initiative in grace.

We should also pause to consider another implication of starting with an affirmation of God's sovereign and gracious initiative and linking it so closely to the work of Christ. Without the internal work of the Holy Spirit in the human heart, the gospel would never have found a hearing and acceptance in spiritually dead sinners. But the Holy Spirit is the Spirit of Christ, and we must never divorce our new birth from the person and work of Christ and the proclamation of the gospel. If this indissoluble link is not maintained, says Bavinck, one "might . . . draw the obvious conclusion that actually Christ's person and work are not necessary to salvation, and that

---

[40] *RD*, 3:405.

God may equally well regenerate the sinner aside from Christ by the Holy Spirit alone."[41]

Now we need to press the question *How* does this all take place? Can we specify more clearly the manner of the Spirit's working? The first point to be made is that Word and Spirit belong together; the Word needs the Spirit, and the Spirit makes use of the proclaimed Word. To begin with the former, Bavinck indicates his full agreement with the Augustinian position.

> On the basis of God's Word and in line with Augustine, the Reformed taught that the Word alone was insufficient for regenerating the sinner and bringing the sinner to faith and repentance. The Word had to be accompanied by an internal grace, by an operation of the Holy Spirit, in order to make alive once again the person who is dead in sins and transgressions.[42]

Bavinck's answer is fully in keeping with what the Belgic Confession and Heidelberg Catechism affirm about the seamless efficacy of Word and Spirit together:

> We believe that this true faith,
> produced in us *by the hearing of God's Word*
> and *by the work of the Holy Spirit*,
> regenerates us and makes us new creatures,
> causing us to live a new life
> and freeing us from the slavery of sin.
> (Belgic Confession, art. 24; emphasis added)

Similarly, Lord's Day 25 of the Heidelberg Catechism not only ties the Word to the Spirit but also confesses that sacraments are a "means" of the Spirit:

> Q. 65. It is through faith alone that we share in Christ and all his benefits: where then does that faith come from?

> A. *The Holy Spirit* produces it in our hearts *by the preaching of the holy gospel*, and confirms it *by the use of the holy sacraments*. (emphasis added)

This evidently biblical and reasonable position, however, leaves unanswered a number of practical questions that "inquiring minds" keep

---

[41] *RD*, 4:79.
[42] *Saved*, 33.

asking. These "both–and" affirmations of the Reformed confessions teach us that Word and Spirit are inseparable, but they do not address the many practical pastoral questions that regularly arise among Christian believers: What about people who have never heard the gospel, or children who die in infancy without being baptized? What about those whose developmental disabilities set up challenges to understanding the gospel? When baptized children leave the faith, have they committed the sin that Hebrews 6:4–6 suggests is unpardonable? Does this mean that their baptisms were ineffectual? To these and similar questions, we want answers! But here this great theologian, whose intellectual grasp of Christian doctrine and theology continues to awe us, wants us to pull back and exercise humility before God.

When he begins his discussion of how the Spirit relates to the means of preaching and sacraments, Bavinck refers to what the Canons of Dort say about regeneration. The Canons describe regeneration as "the new creation, the raising from the dead, and the making alive so clearly proclaimed in the Scriptures, which God works in us without our help." Regeneration does not come about "only by outward teaching, by moral persuasion, or by such a way of working that, after God's work is done, it remains in human power whether or not to be reborn or converted." It is God's work and—here we come to the heart of the matter!—it is profoundly mysterious and wonderful.

> Rather, it is an entirely supernatural work, one that is at the same time most powerful and most pleasing, a marvelous, hidden, and inexpressible work, which is not less than or inferior in power to that of creation or of raising the dead, as Scripture (inspired by the author of this work) teaches.[43]

With the miracle of rebirth by the Holy Spirit, we need to acknowledge the limits of our own ability, but instead of this being an obstacle to faith, the Canons consider it a source of great comfort and joy: "In this life believers cannot fully understand the way this work occurs; meanwhile, they rest content with knowing and experiencing that, by this grace of God, they do believe with the heart and love their Savior."[44] To underscore this, Bavinck points to the analogy of food sustaining our bodies. If we do

---

[43] Canons of Dort (3/4.12–13).
[44] Ibid.

not eat, we will die, but our Lord showed us that we "shall not live by bread alone" (Matt. 4:4; Luke 4:4). Even when we know a great deal about the nutrients present in food and understand the mechanism of digestion and conversion of food to the energy we live by, mystery remains. We do not understand it perfectly, and we don't understand how people deprived of food are nevertheless sustained by God (as Jesus was in the wilderness), or how people who are well fed by earthly standards can die because of malnourished souls. As Bavinck put it, "Even in the natural world, life is a mystery in terms of its origin and growth, its decay and deterioration, a mystery we must respect but which we cannot penetrate." And here is the punch line: "If this now is the case in the natural realm, how much more will this apply to the spiritual realm? Who is to say in what way God conveys spiritual life and spiritual power to his elect through the means of grace?"[45]

Though the New Testament tells us a great deal about our union with Christ, in the final analysis there is much more we do not know. We need to suppress our insatiable thirst for knowledge beyond our limitations by respecting this mystery and finding our satisfaction and joy in simply living in union with our Lord. As important as good theology is, it must never trump life. To those of us who tend to get caught up in and dwell on secondary and tertiary theological issues, sometimes even turning them into matters of orthodoxy and excommunication, it is worth remembering that this great Reformed theologian, Herman Bavinck, always insisted on honoring the mystery of God's ways with us. There is much about God and his ways that we can know; through the Christian ages, theology has provided us with a rich treasury of knowledge. But full comprehension always eludes us: "Christian theology always has to do with mysteries that it knows and marvels at but does not fully comprehend and fathom."[46] Similarly, for all who wrestle with painful pastoral concerns: God is big enough to handle all our questions, doubts, complaints, and laments. In the end, like the laments of the psalmist, all we can do is turn it over to our heavenly Father, who "is able to [handle our troubles] because he is almighty God," and "desires to do this because he is a faithful Father."[47]

---

[45] *Saved*, 135.
[46] *RD*, 1:619.
[47] Heidelberg Catechism, Lord's Day 9.

Living in the Body of Christ

We have covered a good deal of church history and theology thus far in this chapter. While it is true that probing analysis and making careful distinctions is a worthwhile exercise in its own right—and, for some of us, quite enjoyable—the payoff comes in practical pastoral application. The joy and peace of being united with Christ, of belonging to his body, is the truly important thing. Our reflections on regeneration and the work of the Holy Spirit point us to the experience of Christ's benefits for us. In this last section of the chapter we will take a closer look at two important dimensions of our salvation: justification and sanctification. My concern is primarily pastoral. What is needed for believers to flourish and grow as disciples of Jesus Christ? And, considering all the benefits of union with Christ, where do we begin?

In view of the expansive answer we have seen Bavinck give to the question What is union with Christ? his answer to the last question may surprise some. "Of all these benefits," Bavinck claims, "first place is due to justification, for by it we understand that gracious judicial act of God by which he acquits humans of all the guilt and punishment of sin and confers on them the right to eternal life."[48] He repeats this a few pages later: "Now among all the spiritual and material benefits that God will give to his people in the future by virtue of this righteousness, the forgiveness of sins occupies a place of primary importance."[49] Bavinck's concern is pastoral: what is essential to enjoy the consolation and joy of the gospel? Certainly there can be no peace of mind and conscience, no joy in one's heart, no buoyant moral activity, and no blessed life and death—there can be none of these—before the guilt of sin is removed, all fear of punishment has been completely eradicated, and the certainty of eternal life in communion with God fills one's consciousness with its consolation and power.[50] Forgiveness is neither simple nor a small matter. In fact, "this benefit—the complete forgiveness of sin—is so immense that the natural human intellect cannot grasp and believe it."[51]

Justification can be misunderstood. The Reformation doctrine asserts that we are justified by having Christ's perfect righteousness *imputed* to us. In other words, we are not righteous in ourselves, but because we are united

---

[48] RD, 4:179.
[49] RD, 4:182.
[50] RD, 4:179.
[51] RD, 4:179.

to Christ, God the Judge reckons us as righteous. Justification is thus a legal or forensic category; though we sinners stand condemned by the law of God, "in the gospel God brought to light a righteousness apart from the law (Rom. 1:17–18; 3:20ff.)." Christ comes to stand in our place and God regards us "in him." Though God "had to condemn us according to the law, yet in Christ [he] has had different thoughts about us, generously forgives all our sins without charging us with anything, and accords to us divine compassion and fatherly sympathy in place of wrath and punishment."[52] As the popular Sunday school definition of justification puts it, "God looks at me 'just as if I'd never sinned.'"

This is precisely the point at which critics object to the doctrine as classically stated. It is, they say, only a "legal fiction" because it attributes an "alien justice" or "alien righteousness" to believers. When we speak of "our righteousness," we are describing something external to us that we just accept by faith. God simply transfers Christ's righteousness to us as an accounting trick; there is no real change in those who are justified. Furthermore, God can hardly be said to be acting justly when he condemns someone else—in this case, Jesus—for sins he did not commit and lets us off the hook for the sins we did and do commit. One of the pastoral consequences of this line of thinking, it is then said, is that we are prepared to accept innocent people dying for guilty ones, a truly troubling application. Those who object to seeing justification as a forensic matter usually try to turn it into an *ethical* reality in which God's grace actually makes someone righteous so that God's forgiveness seems just.

Bavinck will have none of it. God, he insists, acts *justly* when he "acquits those who have faith in Jesus." Not only has Christ "become our righteousness" (1 Cor. 1:30; 2 Cor. 5:21; Phil. 3:9); "only those who trust in God's grace in Christ [and have] a personal relationship and personal communion with Christ (Rom. 10:9; 1 Cor. 6:17; 2 Cor. 13:5; Gal. 2:20; Eph. 3:17)" are justified. In the same way that we are "*in Adam*" as sinful human beings, so too those who are *in Christ* are truly in communion with God.

> That communion with God is a mystical union. It far exceeds our understanding. It is a most intimate union with God by the Holy Spirit, a union of persons, an unbreakable and eternal covenant between God and ourselves . . . . It is so close that it transforms humans in the divine image

---

[52] *RD*, 4:206.

and makes them participants in the divine nature (2 Cor. 3:18; Gal. 2:20; 2 Pet. 1:4).[53]

Here Bavinck appeals to the mystery of the incarnation: "When this communion with God and humankind is truly—not as a fiction but as true reality—understood, its kinship with and analogy to the incarnation leap out at us."[54] Communion between humanity and God would be impossible were it not for the incarnation. "For if the incarnation is impossible either from the side of God or from the side of humankind, then neither can religion truly consist in communion between God and human creatures."[55] "To make his communion with humankind a reality," God "united himself with it in Christ as its head. Christ, accordingly, is not an individual beside other individuals, but the head and representative of humanity, the second and last Adam, the mediator between God and humanity."[56]

So then, justification is not a "legal fiction" and our righteousness as justified sinners is not an "alien righteousness." God did not just arbitrarily impute Christ's righteousness to sinners. In the incarnation the divine Word did not "adopt" an individual human person, Jesus of Nazareth; the divine Word assumed and was joined to "an impersonal human nature."[57] Christ was not simply "an individual beside others. His work did not consist in bringing back to communion with God the one individual person with whom he united himself; on the contrary, his assignment was to assume the seed of Abraham, to be head of a new humanity and the firstborn of many brothers."[58] To use different language, also familiar to Bavinck, we are *organically* united to Christ in his humanity just as we are to Adam in our sinful humanity. When God justifies us in *Christ*, he acts justly; we *are* righteous.

Practically, this means that believers are

freed from all dread and fear. They have peace with God (Rom. 5:1). They are no longer under the law (Rom. 7:4; Gal. 2:19; 4:5, 21ff.) but under grace (Rom. 6:15), and they stand in freedom (Gal. 5:1). They are no longer servants but children, having the spirit of adoption and therefore also being heirs of God (Rom. 8:15–17; Gal. 4:5–7), awaiting with great assur-

---

[53] *RD*, 3:304.
[54] *RD*, 3:304.
[55] *RD*, 3:305.
[56] *RD*, 3:305.
[57] *RD*, 3:305.
[58] *RD*, 3:305.

ance the completion of their adoption as children (Rom. 8:23) and the hope of righteousness (Gal. 5:5), for if God justifies, who is to condemn? (Rom. 8:31–39).[59]

To be justified *by faith* means to believe that God's declaration about us is just and true.

Delivered from the bondage and slavery of sin and guilt, no longer servants but adopted children, those who are in Christ are *free* to love and to live holy lives. It is in this liberty that we then speak about our sanctification and the so-called means of grace: preaching and sacraments. The first point is that just as in our justification, so too in our sanctification: we are not alone. Sanctification is *in Christ*.

> To understand the benefit of sanctification correctly, we must proceed from the idea that Christ is our holiness in the same sense in which he is our righteousness. He is a complete and all-sufficient Savior. He does not accomplish his work halfway but saves us really and completely. He does not rest until, after pronouncing his acquittal in our conscience, he has also imparted full holiness and glory to us.[60]

Bavinck sees sanctification both as a *passive gift* of God the Holy Spirit and as an *active responsibility.* "In the first place it is a work and gift of God (Phil. 1:[6]; 1 Thess. 5:23), a process in which humans are passive just as they are in regeneration, of which it is the continuation." In Christ, we *are* holy.

> But based on this work of God in humans, it acquires, in the second place, an active meaning, and people themselves are called and equipped to sanctify themselves and devote their whole life to God (Rom. 12:1; 2 Cor. 7:1; 1 Thess. 4:3; Heb. 12:14; and so forth). . . . Scripture always holds on to both facets: God's all-encompassing activity and our responsibility.[61]

At the heart of sanctification is "'continued repentance,' which, according to the Heidelberg Catechism, consists in the dying-away of the old self and the coming-to-life of the new self."[62]

---

[59] *RD*, 4:186.
[60] *RD*, 4:248.
[61] *RD*, 4:253.
[62] *RD*, 4:253.

Not only must we acknowledge our own responsibility as disciples of Jesus Christ to strive for holiness; we need also to be reminded that we do not do this on our own. We cannot do it without the empowering work of the Holy Spirit, and—here we are able to conclude our discussion of Spirit and *means*—we have also been given the gift of the body of Christ as the place and space within which our dying to self and rising to Christ should take place. The church is, among other things, a social institution, a reflection of our nature as social creatures or, in Aristotle's language, "political animals." We are born into community and cannot escape it. And because the most powerful bond between people "is the bond that unites people in religion," Bavinck reminds us that "there exists in religion a powerful social element."[63] For that reason, corporate, social cultic activity serves an important role in helping people flourish within the human community.

But the church of Jesus Christ is much more; it is a *divine* institution gathered and equipped by the Holy Spirit at Pentecost and commanded by the ascending Lord to "go therefore and make disciples of all nations, baptizing them in the name of the Father and of the Son and of the Holy Spirit, teaching them to observe all that I have commanded you" (Matt. 28:18–20). Preach to, evangelize, baptize, and disciple "the whole world"—that is the calling of the church and the calling of the Christian. When we add to this our Lord's command to eat the bread of his broken body and drink the cup of the new covenant in his blood, we are not left in doubt about what we need to do to flourish in our discipleship and grow in our sanctification. Much more can be said, of course, and we will examine the life of holiness in greater detail in the next chapter as we consider the imitation of Christ; for now, let us be satisfied with the reminder that we can hardly do better than to use the *means* provided for us by our Lord himself. Those who are united with Christ go to church, participate in the sacraments, and bear witness to their faith with their words and deeds. And when they do, they flourish as human beings; they will be blessed and be a blessing.

---

[63] *RD*, 4:276.

PART 2

THE SHAPE OF CHRISTIAN DISCIPLESHIP

CHAPTER 5

FOLLOWING JESUS

The preceding chapters have laid a foundation for the building of Christian discipleship, and the next two chapters will describe the overall *shape* of the building in whose various rooms our life vocations take place. The final four chapters will then examine the content of those rooms as they are shaped by a Christian worldview in which the imitation of Christ plays a central role. As we explore Bavinck's key ethical themes, we must never forget that they are framed by creation, law, and union with Christ.

Bavinck wrote two significant essays on the imitation of Christ, one in 1885–1886,[1] and the other in 1918.[2] In addition, in his unpublished manuscript "Reformed Ethics,"[3] Bavinck explicitly identifies the imitation of Christ as "the heart of spiritual life."[4] After a general historical overview of the imitation theme, we will consider Bavinck's understanding of the Sermon on the Mount, focusing on key hermeneutic questions: Is the imitation theme valid for all times and applicable in all circumstances? Do changing contexts call for different attitudes toward the world and our Christian discipleship in the world?

---

[1] "Imit. I." In references to this work, the first page number refers to the Dutch original, and the bracketed number cites the page of the translation in *Analysis*, appendix A, 372–401.
[2] "Imit. II." In references to this work, the first page number refers to the Dutch original, and the bracketed number cites the page of the translation in *Analysis*, appendix B, 402–40.
[3] For the story about the discovery of this manuscript and details about its content, see Dirk Van Keulen, "Herman Bavinck's *Reformed Ethics*: Some Remarks about Unpublished Manuscripts in the Libraries of Amsterdam and Kampen," *The Bavinck Review* 1 (2010): 25–56.
[4] Ibid., 38.

History of a Popular Ethical Theme

The imitation of Christ as an ethical ideal has had its ups and downs in the history of the church, but it never disappears altogether, as the recent popular practice of wearing WWJD (What would Jesus do?) wristbands shows. This specific formulation can be attributed to Charles Sheldon's 1897 best seller, *In His Steps*. *"What Would Jesus Do?"* was the book's subtitle. However, the imitation-of-Christ theme has a much longer pedigree. Thomas à Kempis's fifteenth-century *De imitatione Christi* remains one of the most widely read devotional books of all time. The original German title of Dietrich Bonhoeffer's influential *The Cost of Discipleship*, first published in 1937, is simply *Nachfolge*, literally "following after," or "imitation." The popularity of the theme should not surprise us in light of the numerous New Testament calls to be a follower or disciple of Jesus, especially our Lord's own call to "deny [your]self and take up [your] cross and follow me" (Matt. 16:24). Because the theme has been appealed to at different times and in different circumstances, we find great variety in its understanding and application. We will begin our consideration of Bavinck's understanding as he himself did, with a historical survey in which he highlights aspects of the imitation of Christ of which he approves and those of which he does not.

Bavinck's first effort to unpack the imitation theme—in his 1885/1886 essay—was primarily a historical overview of imitation spirituality from the postapostolic period to the modern era. This overview was necessary, he notes, because, given the difficulty and severity of the demand, which is "quite contrary to the natural inclinations of the human heart and also difficult to understand and follow in a spiritually healthy manner," this ideal has "a history filled with error and misconception." The earliest Christians "simply lived as [their] Lord had. For the most part the church members were members of the lower classes of society rather than the wise, the wealthy, the powerful or the noble of this world. Only by means of a distinct lifestyle could the church be a letter of Christ to the world."[5] Bavinck points to the second century *Epistle to Diognetus* as a summary of the new outlook and lifestyle of Christians and includes a large quotation from the letter in his own essay. While Christians follow the language and ordinary customs of the people among whom they live, their manner of life is distinct in a "wonderful and confessedly striking" way. They are sojourners and pilgrims rather than settlers: "As citizens they share in all

---

[5] "Imit. I," 101 [372].

things with others, and yet endure all things as if foreigners. Every foreign land is to them as their native country, and every land of their birth as a land of strangers." Christians are "in the world" but not "of the world"; they do not despise earthly goods and loyalties, but they do relativize them in the light of an eternal hope and destiny. This posture gives rise to conduct that is truly singular and sounds like it could have been written for the twenty-first century as well as the second: "They marry as do all others; they beget children; but they do not destroy their offspring. They have a common table, but not a common bed."[6]

Bavinck has nothing but praise for the life of self-denial and cross bearing that characterized the earliest Christians, even speaking of it as a "pure" form of imitation piety. However, because the Christian faith made absolute claims and "refused to be ranked with or absorbed by other religions," but claimed "to be the only true religion [and] desired a place of supremacy above all religions," it "soon came into unavoidable conflict with the power of the Roman State." This struck a deadly blow against the pretensions and tolerance of the Roman state, conflict ensued, and persecution of Christians began. Bavinck points out that contrary to all worldly standards of power, Christians actually had the superior might. "In fact," he adds, "the church endured the persecutions of the world better than its subsequent embrace." "Poverty-stricken though they were according to worldly standards, they were all conscious of being bearers, albeit in earthen vessels, of an inestimably valuable treasure." Even under conditions of poverty and suffering persecution, Christians considered themselves rich and superior. "Possessing the truth of divine forgiveness and reconciliation, fearing neither worldly power nor its knowledge, scorning death—why should they fear persecution?" They possessed a "powerful self-consciousness, the deep conviction that one is fighting for the very glory of God." This leads Bavinck to marvel that "this posture seems so strange to us today that we cannot sufficiently be amazed by it and envy it." Even the martyrdom they faced counted as victory rather than defeat: "The Christians were killed but their dying was life, their defeat was triumph, their death days were regarded and remembered as birth-days."[7]

However, it is here in the field of martyrdom that Bavinck discerns a serious problem. It is understandable, he notes, that martyrdom increasingly

---

[6] *Epistle to Diognetus*, quoted in "Imit. I," 102–3 [373–74].
[7] "Imit. I," 103 [374–76].

became glorified for its own sake, because even to this day "the accounts of their heroic suffering and faithfulness" serve as a "source of amazement" and inspiration to all. The martyr who "stood firm and even sang, prayed, gave thanks and rejoiced amidst the crackle of flames" honored both Christ and his church. In this way "martyrdom gradually became regarded as a matter of glory and fame," which, Bavinck notes, is a "heathen notion." There arose among many Christians "a deep longing for the fame which martyrdom brings with God and with man." In this view, martyrdom becomes the "supreme ideal of the true Christian" and "the martyr becomes the truest and best imitator of Jesus Christ." Bavinck judges that this is where "Christianity became pathological."[8]

The next phase in the development of the imitation ideal took place after the so-called "Constantinian turn" in the West, the recognition and legitimation of the Christian faith and church by the imperial power of the state. This effectively ended the systemic persecution of Christians by state powers, but introduced a new problem for the church. Jesus had told his disciples that the world would hate them (John 15:18; 16:33) and that they would be persecuted and reviled (Matt. 5:11–12). Furthermore, following Jesus meant self-denial and cross bearing. What happens to the church when the powers of this world no longer persecute you but acknowledge and affirm you? You are no longer reviled; you now sit with the powerful.

We know the outcome all too well: as Bavinck noted, "The church endured the persecutions of the world better than its subsequent embrace." This embrace was deadly. Not only was the church recognized by the state; it also "became dependent upon the state and lost its freedom. As the church became dependent on temporal power, she no longer sought and exercised her real strength in her spiritual, moral power." Put in the language of the New Testament, the church became "worldly." "When the church pressed forward into the world, the world also entered the church."[9] In these circumstances, a new type of imitation spirituality arose that challenged the church's accommodation to the state and worldly powers: monasticism.

Monasticism arose as a protest against a worldly church and shared with other, more extreme, forms of protest "the desire to safeguard the purity of the church." Whereas movements such as Montanism and Donatism were sectarian and motivated by a desire to "keep church and state sepa-

---

[8] "Imit. I," 105 [376, 377].
[9] "Imit. I," 104 [375]; 107 [378].

rate," monasticism came from "within the church and was even supported and sustained by it." Bavinck provides a helpful sociological analysis here. In the earliest period of the Christian church, during the days of marginalization and persecution, "Christians had been excluded from numerous areas of life. They could not participate in the games or in many businesses." This posture was fully in line with Jesus's teaching "against the dangers of riches" and his declaration of "salvation as being for the poor. In order to follow Jesus, his disciples were expected to deny even parents, brothers, sisters as well as possessions." When we consider the world to which the church was accommodating itself, "a world of self-indulgence and gluttony," says Bavinck, "it is no surprise that many withdrew from the world in loneliness in order to live only for God and for heaven."[10]

But Bavinck also detects some troubling influences on monasticism, namely, "Stoic, neo-Platonic, and gnostic philosophy which sharply set spirit and flesh against one another."[11] Motives for entering the monastic life were therefore mixed. Bavinck asks, "Why did so many members of the noblest and highest levels of society desire the lonely life of hermit or monk?" Many of them, he suggests, were undoubtedly "motivated by a genuine desire to die to this world and live totally and completely for God and for eternal, imperishable things." But others held just as strongly that the rigorous ascetic life was the best way to tame "the passions and desires which continually arose in ordinary life." In this way,

> the hermits and monks became the successors of the martyrs, those voluntary and powerful witnesses in whom the Christian ideal was most purely and fully expressed and preserved. . . . Monasticism became the true imitation of Christ, who had also not been married, had wandered through the land and had even periodically isolated himself in the desert.[12]

Bavinck's chief objection to monasticism is its ambition "to achieve a higher level of perfection than was possible in ordinary life, [resulting in] a pernicious distinction of two kinds of morality, of higher and lower obligations, of counsels and commandments." Practically, this promoted "pride and trust in good works among those striving for perfection, and a complacent indifference to the ideals of holiness in the practical daily

---

[10] "Imit. I," 108–9 [378–79].
[11] "Imit. I," 109 [379].
[12] "Imit. I," 110–11 [379–80].

lives of ordinary people." Bavinck is quick to point out that Protestantism has not entirely rid itself of such double morality, and that "many clear and distinct vestiges of monasticism remain in the way many Protestants regard this earthly, natural life and human calling in society." As evidence of this, he singles out "renunciation of certain foods and beverages" as well as principled refusals to become involved in key political or business enterprises, along with hostility to art and science. But there is something as bad or possibly even worse: "An even greater number regard the natural realm as totally independent of Christian faith and fail to see this natural life as a calling to be undertaken in faith, as a task given by God and therefore to be freely and joyfully done for him."[13]

Historical Deviations and Union with Christ

I will treat more briefly the remaining types of imitation spirituality Bavinck covers in his historical overview. As the Christian church grew in the Middle Ages with the conversion of the Germanic peoples, the "hierarchical nature of the church, which corresponded well with the feudal order of medieval society," became "firmly established." A sharp division arose between the clergy and the laity, and this period was characterized by immaturity in the laity and "incompetence and an unspiritual life-style" among the clergy. This explains the protest movements that arose during the second half of the Middle Ages, movements that "desired reformation of the existing order." Among these protest movements, including the Cathari and other radical groups, Bavinck singles out the Waldensians for singular praise, noting that they "are especially honored by Protestants and regarded as true and pure Christians." Notwithstanding some serious problems among them, including excess spiritualism (often accompanied by gross immorality), Bavinck appreciates these movements for their call to reform and renew the church by "returning to the model of the early church." We must not, he says, "lose sight of what was correct in this development. While Catholicism stressed orthodoxy and liturgy, these groups simplified doctrine and placed the emphasis on holy living."[14]

A special variant of monasticism—in fact, a "new era" according to Bavinck—began under the influence of Francis (1182–1226) and Dominic (1170–1221). Independent monasteries became attached to *orders* and ac-

---

[13] "Imit. I," 112–13 [381–82].
[14] "Imit. I," 202–5 [383–84].

quired "increased temporal power" that overshadowed their spiritual role. Bavinck speaks of "mendicant armies," who were "subject to the Pope" and exalted "the ideals of poverty, chastity, and obedience." "The dominant ideal of these mendicant orders was, of course, the imitation of Christ." What is striking about them, however, is that though they disparaged possessions and were dependent "on others for the basic needs of life," they did not separate from but were active participants in society. The monastic ideal of separation from human society was "discarded in order to emphasize even more strongly another ideal, namely that of poverty." This poverty became a visible sign *within* society and not detached from it. Bavinck provides a pithy summary of this move: "The monk is no longer an anchorite but becomes a mendicant [beggar]."[15]

Mendicant imitation piety paid attention to the entire life of Jesus, but especially his suffering. "The true imitation of Christ was understood to consist of reflection upon and repetition of his suffering." Aided by the numerous thirteenth- and fourteenth-century "'lives of Jesus,' all portraying in brilliant colors a life to be meditated upon and internalized as well as read," monks sought "daily and even hourly, to relive the very life of Jesus. The imitation of Christ became the dominant means by which the truly pious attempted to wean their souls from the sensible realities of this world and to become Christ-like in contemplation and meditation." Thomas à Kempis's *The Imitation of Christ* represents one of the high points of the mystical turn to the cross and suffering of Jesus. Bavinck insists that "this mysticism bore tremendous fruit for some," and he singles out Bernard of Clairvaux (1090–1153), Bonaventure (1221–1274), and Johannes Tauler (1300–1361), along with Thomas. Bavinck especially praises Thomas's "strong ethical and practical emphasis, in addition to this inward mystical note." He objects to the excessive literalism of those who seek to copy Christ's specific suffering and criticizes the "subjective nature" of phenomena such as the stigmata of St. Francis, which he attributes to the "power of the imagination . . . continually nurtured by visible representations."[16]

In addition to the three types of imitation we have already covered, Bavinck also briefly considers what he calls a "rationalist" conception, in which the historical Jesus is taken as a mere human whose purpose was to be an example of the ideal moral human being. Bavinck protests that "he

---

[15] "Imit. I," 208–9 [387].
[16] "Imit. I," 209–13 [388–90].

who sees Jesus only as an example is overwhelmed and becomes discouraged. To see Jesus is to experience judgment on our own conscience and our powerlessness to truly imitate him. Indeed, if he is only an example then he comes to judge us and not to save us."[17]

Though the specific shape of his objection differs slightly, the loss of focus on Jesus as the Mediator and Redeemer is also at the heart of Bavinck's concern about medieval mysticism. "Jesus Christ as mediator is pushed to the background in medieval mysticism. Rather than the one who makes atonement for sin and removes human guilt, he becomes instead the example of mystical union with God." Using some biblical allegory, Bavinck compares these mystics to "the Jewish women on the road to Golgotha; they merely sympathize with Jesus rather than being struck with a consciousness of sin and seeking their reconciliation with God in him."[18]

To summarize: Bavinck introduces the imitation theme by considering four distinct types of imitation spirituality: the martyr, the monk, the mystic, and the modern rationalist. Yet, reading between the lines we might identify what Bavinck calls the "pure" imitation spirituality of the early church as a fifth type. "In its earliest period, the newly formed Christian church simply lived as its Lord had." Although he notes that the purity of this imitation was soon lost, Bavinck nevertheless must have regarded the ideal as lasting well into the second century, since he considers the description of the Christian lifestyle in the fifth chapter of the *Epistle to Diognetus* as an accurate portrayal of this earliest and still pure understanding of the imitation of Christ.[19] Bavinck's brief appreciative comments about the medieval Waldensians also suggest that he considers some of the protest movements of the Middle Ages as continuing the "pure" imitation spirituality of the early church.

We learn a number of things about Bavinck's own understanding of proper imitation piety from his survey. Negatively, he questions all forms of imitation piety that fail to do justice to the unique mediatorial role of Jesus Christ. One becomes guilty of this either by excessive imitation—attempting literally to duplicate even the redemptive suffering of Christ—or by reducing Jesus to a mere example and model for humans to emulate. Positively, Bavinck affirms the "purest" form of the ideal, which he describes simply in his explanation of the "earliest" Christians: "Denying itself and freely

---

[17] "Imit. I," 325 [394].
[18] "Imit. I," 324 [393–94].
[19] "Imit. I," 101–3 [372–74].

taking up its cross, the early church followed the example left behind by its Lord and Master." Bavinck points out, however, that even while Jesus was on earth, externally "following him" was never enough. "It is likely that Jesus was accompanied on his travels by a multitude of disciples. This external fellowship however revealed a deeper relationship of genuine love to Jesus." As our Lord himself pointed out, there were costs involved in following him, and his disciples had better be prepared. "No one who puts his hand to the plow and looks back is fit for the kingdom of God" (Luke 9:62). "The required itinerant life, filled as it was with unrest and rejection, could only be undertaken by those who truly loved Jesus and were willing to forsake everything for him."[20]

Even for those who were literally and physically following Jesus during his sojourn on earth, Bavinck points to the deeper, intimate fellowship that characterized this following. Already in the Gospels themselves the imitation is extended and goes deeper than the literal and physical. "At this point the imitation of Christ was utilized in a metaphorical sense and acquired an ethical, spiritual significance. Consequently, the demand to follow Jesus is then indiscriminately placed before all who hear him (Mk. 8:34; Lk. 9:23)." The conclusion, therefore, for Bavinck is that "this mystical union, this spiritual, living, communion with Christ is the primary element of the imitation of Christ." On this point, one of Bavinck's sharpest critiques is applied to what he sees as the literalism and externalism of monasticism:

> The monk incorrectly understands the imitation of Christ to consist of a simple repetition and copying of the personal life of Jesus. As a result, it is all too possible for someone outwardly to be Christ-like yet inwardly very unChrist-like, to appear to be one with him while actually very far from him. The essence of the imitation of Christ is lost in a number of external and obvious deeds which repeat those of Jesus.[21]

The inward union with Christ is primary, but things must not be left on the purely "spiritual" plane. "This primary spiritual fellowship with Jesus Christ must also find concrete expression in the realm of the ethical." Even as he notes this, Bavinck continues to emphasize the primacy of spiritual union with Christ. "This second dimension of the imitation of Christ is of

---

[20] "Imit. I," 103 [374]; 328 [397].
[21] "Imit. I," 328 [397]; 322 [391–92].

course rooted in, and an expression of, the mystical union with Christ." The ethical imitation of Christ includes aspects of Jesus's life on earth that continue to serve his followers as an example. "We have the privilege," Bavinck notes, "of following in his footsteps and walking in the same way in which he walked (1 John 2:6)."[22] To explore that further we need to consider Bavinck's treatment of the Sermon on the Mount and move our attention to the second imitation essay.

Bavinck's Understanding of the Sermon on the Mount

In the first imitation essay, when discussing his favorite medieval group, the Waldensians, Bavinck observes that all the medieval sectarian groups "were agreed upon this one thing that the words and commands of Jesus had the supreme value and authority, especially the Sermon on the Mount. The Sermon on the Mount was the new evangelical law, and the mark of the true church was its adherence to that law." While it is true that "the obligations of a literal understanding of the Sermon on the Mount were for all men," other of our Lord's commands, "such as those in Matthew 10 and elsewhere were only applied to ministers of the Word."[23] Bavinck does not venture further beyond this general point in his 1885/1886 essay. In particular, he does not consider the hermeneutic problem of the Sermon on the Mount as a part of New Testament ethics more broadly. Even if we reject all double moralities—those that apply the sermon's teaching only as "counsels of perfection" to those in religious orders and insist that the sermon is for all Christians—we are still left with questions about whether the instruction to "turn the other cheek" is appropriate for soldiers and policemen. "Imitation I" gave the impression that one might come to a "pure" imitation spirituality if one only purged it of certain aberrations and excesses.

All this changes in "Imitation II"; there the very ideal itself appears in crisis. The full title of the essay and the date of its publication are significant. "The Imitation of Christ and Life in the Modern World" was released in 1918, at the conclusion of the Great War. It was the war that shattered the moral sensibilities of Europe and exposed, says Bavinck, the deeper underlying problem of how the gospel relates to culture: "The conflict which many experience between Christianity and war is but one aspect of the tre-

---

[22] "Imit. I," 330–31 [399].
[23] "Imit. I," 206–7 [385].

mendous tension that exists between the gospel of Jesus Christ and human culture in its various aspects of state, vocation, industry, business, science, art, etc." After a quick survey of the material covered in greater depth in "Imitation I," Bavinck takes a closer look at the modern era and the various efforts to "rescue" Jesus and his teaching from their misappropriation by the Christian church. Some (John Stuart Mill, Leo Tolstoy) were convinced that Christians could only be true to their Master's teaching by literally living according to his example. Liberal Protestantism of the late nineteenth century, represented by Albrecht Ritschl (1822–1899) and Adolf von Harnack (1861–1930), "regarded the developments in church and dogma as serious deviations from the original, pure Christianity. Thus the cry arose to return to the simple gospel that is concerned with God and the individual soul and regards Jesus as only a prophet and teacher." Others, however, upon seeing "the great gulf between the original gospel and contemporary Christianity, . . . concluded that Christianity had outlived its usefulness. Any reconciliation between the demands of the New Testament and the responsibilities of modern culture was judged to be impossible." The world of science, art, industry, and politics and statecraft cannot be reconciled with the Gospel's demands "that we love neither the world nor what is in it, that we build up no treasures on earth, that we cut off our hand if it offends us, that we do not resist evil, that we be longsuffering, etc."[24]

Bavinck finds none of these postures satisfactory and also rejects the move to grant "the validity of Christian morality for private life while denying its adequacy for life in state and society." He acknowledges that the imitation of Christ presents us with major challenges in the modern era: "Is there even room in the cultural life of the present for such an imitation? Can it still be taken seriously by people in the state, industry, business, marketplace, stock-exchange, office or factory, in science and art, in war, even at the front?"[25] But he does not yield; the crisis of the imitation ideal in the modern world is part of a more general crisis concerning the continuing relevance of the New Testament ethic. We will look at Bavinck's answer by considering his interpretation of the Sermon on the Mount in the context of New Testament ethics more broadly.

Imitation of Jesus, which includes accepting a life of suffering, should not, says Bavinck, be taken in a literalistic way. Imitation is fundamentally

[24] "Imit. II," 118–19 [407–8].
[25] "Imit. II," 119–20 [408–9].

a matter of obedience to the law of God. "The true imitation of Christ does not consist of an external following or a mere listening to his words, or even in saying 'Lord, Lord,' but in doing the will of the Heavenly Father as he himself perfectly fulfilled it. True imitation is thus a matter of being conformed to the image of Christ."[26] We saw in chapter 2 that Bavinck's emphasis on the primacy of creation led him to reject all notions that the gospel creates a new world, a new culture, a new social order. He now applies this to the Sermon on the Mount, which he refuses to consider a "new law" or the order for a totally "new creation," but sees as a *clarification* of the imitation of Christ through concrete images and examples. Those who are united to Christ in faith desire to follow him as obedient children of their heavenly Father just he was an obedient Son. Jesus not only fully acknowledges the authority of Old Testament law; he also never sets "himself beyond or above its authority; his attitude is characterized by 'It is written' (Mt. 4:4, 7, 10; 11:10; 21:13)." Bavinck emphasizes that it is in "the Sermon on the Mount that Jesus emphatically declares that he has not come to annul the law and the prophets but to fulfill them. In other words, Jesus declares that he has come to concretize and heighten the demands of the law and prophets."[27]

What then are we to do with the specific commands themselves, particularly those that strike us as going beyond Old Testament law? According to Bavinck, Jesus takes issue not with "the words of the law itself, but with its incorrect interpretation and application. Jesus never contradicts what is written in the Old Testament law but always that which his disciples had heard of old from the Scribes, that which had been told to the fathers." But Bavinck also introduces a new and significant qualification to the ongoing importance of the imitation theme: circumstance. The original Sermon on the Mount, he notes,

> was directed especially to the disciples. It was not intended for the nation of Israel as a whole or even for its prominent leaders, but for the relatively small band of disciples who were not members of the upper echelon of society but of the lower classes which possessed very little eminence and influence.

Furthermore, it was directed to disciples who would be reviled and persecuted for the sake of Christ. "Jesus himself had told them that in the world

---

[26] "Imit. II," 123 [412].
[27] "Imit. II," 123–24 [412, 414].

they would experience tribulation (John 16:33), and not to expect justice from the judges and rulers since such great men exercise an authority that is based on oppression and power (Mt. 20:25)."[28]

The Sermon on the Mount, Bavinck argues, exalts "precisely those virtues which his disciples would require about everything else in such circumstances." Jesus does not give his disciples a cultural or social mandate in the Sermon on the Mount; in fact, "it would have been quite inappropriate." In the circumstances in which the earliest disciples found themselves, "they would not be able to influence the world by means of any exercise of might but were called to let their light shine through their good works by which men would be moved to glorify their Father in Heaven (Mt. 5:16; John 15:8)." It is in "loving service that his disciples are called to follow him (Mt. 20:26–8)." Their righteousness must exceed that of the Scribes and Pharisees. "They must first of all seek the kingdom of God and its righteousness, strive to be perfect as their Father in Heaven, be as ready to forgive as he forgives (5:21–26), be chaste within and outside of marriage in heart as well as in deed (5:27–32), submit to and love their enemies (5:39–44) etc." This reading of the Sermon on the Mount, Bavinck contends, is reinforced by the rest of the New Testament. In a world where they were regarded as "misanthropes, as enemies of the societal and civil order" because "they refused to participate in the official public cults and gathered together in their own meeting places," Christians "viewed themselves as strangers and pilgrims, having their citizenship in heaven, and longed for the return of Christ (Phil. 3:20, 21; Hebr. 13:14; James 1:1; 1 Peter 1:1; 2:11 etc.)."[29]

Bavinck points out that there was little else the earliest Christians could do. "If one wanted to be a child of God and an heir to eternal life it was necessary to flee the world and its pleasures (James 4:4; 1 John 2:15; 5:19)." If the early church had tried to transform its world through cultural engagement, it "would have quickly drowned in the world's maelstrom." Survival required retreat. "During its earliest period it was necessary for the church simply to preserve its independent identity and establish its own position in the world." This is the reason why the New Testament extols what Bavinck calls the "passive virtues" of

> truth, righteousness, holiness (Eph. 4:24); purity, modesty, temperance (Eph. 5:3–5); prayer, vigil, and fasting (Acts 14:23; Rom. 12:12; 1 Cor. 7:5;

---

[28] "Imit. II," 125 [415–16]; 125–26 [416]; 126 [416–17].
[29] "Imit. II," 126 [417]; 128 [419].

1 Peter 4:7, 8); faith, love, longsuffering (1 Tim. 6:4); brotherly love, generosity, hospitality (Rom. 12:[13]); compassion, lowliness, meekness, patience (Col. 3:12); all those virtues which Paul acclaims as fruits of the Spirit and contrasts with the works of the flesh (Gal. 5:19–22).[30]

The ethic of the New Testament is specific to the circumstances of its day; it "was written from the vantage point of an oppressed and persecuted body of believers" who "lived with the expectation that Jesus was returning shortly, that the present generation would be the last (1 Thess. 4:15; 1 Cor. 15:51)." Though the early church did not set out intentionally to transform the Roman world—its culture, social order, and politics—an amazing and surprising thing happened. "By exercising these virtues the Christian church, in the first and second centuries, powerfully influenced the world, overcoming it by the cross, even as God, by the cross, had triumphed over the principalities and powers (Col. 2:15)." But with this transformation, the Christian posture toward the world also had to change. "The exercise of negative and passive virtues was no longer sufficient to sustain it in its new task of reforming and renewing the world in accord with Christian principles."[31] Put in starkest operational terms, "How should a Christian emperor conduct himself?"

Bavinck does not abandon the Sermon on the Mount in his answer but provides it with a broader theological context. He points to the incarnation as "a sign of the gracious love of God the Father through the Son." Christ came not to destroy the world "but to preserve it by destroying the works of the devil in it (John 3:17; 9:39; 12:47; 1 John 3:8)." Furthermore, God's love is not opposed to justice "but, as it were, takes justice up into itself" in the cross, which "is at the same time a revelation of the highest love and of strict justice, simultaneously a fulfillment of the law and gospel (Rom. 3:25–26)." The cross is not the end: "The death of Christ is followed by his resurrection, his humiliation, by his exaltation." Believers who "temporarily forfeit their rights on earth and patiently suffer injustice" do not reject justice but entrust their cause to God who will vindicate them. When Christ ascended, his "bodily presence" and "daily communion" with disciples ceased, and he sent another Comforter in his place, who would create a new communion with their Lord and make them his temple.

---

[30] "Imit. II," 128–29 [420].
[31] "Imit. II," 130–31 [422–24].

The imitation of Christ thus acquired a much deeper meaning and a much richer significance. The focus was no longer on the example given by his earthly life but on the complete Christ, the pre- and post-existent Christ, the crucified and glorified Christ, the one anointed to be priest and king as well as prophet and teacher.[32]

Union with Christ is therefore the heart of the imitation of Christ. By directing our attention to the whole Christ, the Creator as well as incarnate Redeemer, and the one who now rules from heaven, Bavinck has taken the theme of the imitation of Christ and framed it by creation, law, and eschatology. The Sermon on the Mount is not a new law, and the life of Jesus is not simply a model for us to copy. His description of the call to imitate Jesus is somewhat startling as well as liberating: "The example of Christ becomes for the apostles a noteworthy illustration of the most important virtues which the law requires of us, especially love (Rom. 12:9; Gal. 5:14)."[33] With the phrase "a noteworthy illustration" Bavinck relativizes the specifics of the sermon while maintaining its foundation in the law, framed by love. Bavinck does not, it is important to emphasize here, allow us to spiritualize the concreteness of the sermon. While he cautions against excessive literalism, he also insists that "it is not true . . . that Jesus is only concerned here with the disposition of the heart and considers concrete deeds as of lesser significance." In opposition to mere external legalism, Jesus is concerned about the heart, but there is no hint in the sermon that Jesus is concerned *only* about one's heart. Instead, "from the beginning to the end he deals with concrete deeds and places them as examples before his disciples." While the references to plucking out one's eye, cutting off one's hand, resisting evil, and turning the cheek (Matt. 5:29–42) "are not to be taken literally, all these examples are nonetheless to be understood practically and concretely." "In all of this, Jesus means exactly what he says and says exactly what he means. He demands that his disciples not only be *disposed* to follow his instruction but that they actually *do* as he says."[34]

Summary and Conclusion

Our following Jesus in lawful obedience is grounded and shaped by our union with the whole Christ. Bavinck admittedly relativizes the Sermon

---

[32] "Imit. II," 132–33 [424–25].
[33] "Imit. II," 133 [426].
[34] "Imit. II," 127 [418].

on the Mount by emphasizing its historical context as an address to a persecuted and oppressed minority living in a hostile environment. This is why the "so-called passive virtues occupy the prominent place in the ethics of the New Testament; . . . believers are constantly enjoined to fulfill their obligations and virtually never called to insist upon their rights." In the engagement with the cultural, social, and political powers of the day, the early church had only spiritual weapons at its disposal. There is in fact no other way. The church's "particular responsibility with respect to nature and culture" is to oppose sin, and it has only one means at its disposal.

> In this ongoing struggle which the gospel of Jesus Christ is called to continue to wage against sin, the church is permitted to use only those spiritual weapons consonant with its own nature. The weapons of coercion, power, riches, might, flattery, and hypocrisy are forbidden to her. The only legitimate weapons are the Word and faith, truth and righteousness. These weapons alone are powerful for God.

And these weapons are more than adequate for the task. Historically, "the church, by purely ethical and spiritual means, overcame the world."[35]

Bavinck's application to his own day, and to ours, is subtle. Most importantly, the imitation of Christ as an ethical ideal rooted in union with Christ remains valid for all times and places. "In principle there is no other way [the church] can wage the war against sin." Bavinck even acknowledges that "there exist great similarities between the age that gave birth to Christianity and ours." In addition, the gospel of the cross is a "scandal for the Jews and foolishness for the Greeks" in every age. At the same time, he argues, "It is difficult to prove the contention that our position vis-à-vis our culture must be identical to that of the early church." Since the Sermon on the Mount and the example of Christ are together a "noteworthy illustration" of the law, neither can provide us with a complete ethic for Christian discipleship. God's law remains the boundary and base for discerning God's will; life in creation, culture, and society is to be lived in union with Christ and in obedience to God's laws. This cultural engagement "in all its diversity has a life of its own and is subject to its own laws. It is not the calling of Christianity to annihilate this life of culture and to resist its inner laws, but rather fully to honor and respect that life with its own rules. Grace does

---

[35] "Imit. II," 129 [420]; 136 [430]; 134 [427].

not suppress nature but restores it." God's ordinances for our life in culture and society

> can only be uncovered by man through experience and investigation. Whoever desires to understand nature must study nature; whoever wants to be a farmer must actually engage in farming; whoever wants to be a salesman must get busy in commerce, etc. It is not the study of Scripture but careful investigation of what God teaches us in his creation and providence that equips us properly for these tasks.[36]

What this amounts to is a strong affirmation of Christian liberty and a call to spiritual discernment. We *are* pilgrims and sojourners in this life; we cannot be entirely at home as long as the battle against sin remains. In all circumstances we are called to follow Christ. "Naturally the application will vary depending upon circumstances. Although all are subject to one and the same moral law, the duties under that law vary considerably. . . . Thus while the virtues to which the imitation of Christ calls us are the same, circumstances may modify the application." The degree to which we are estranged from our own culture and marginalized in our society will depend on the degree to which both are hostile to the Christian faith. Bavinck judged that the culture and society of his own day, "whatever moral objections one may have about" it, could still not "be simply designated as pagan." He did, however, add this somber warning:

> How it will develop further remains to be seen, we simply do not know. There are developments that fill our hearts with sorrow and fear. If some of the principles being proposed for a future moral order are accepted by society and pass into legislation we shall experience difficult times ahead. But that day has not yet arrived.[37]

It is not for me to say whether those "difficult times" are here; it does appear to me that they are nearer than they were then. In any case, what Bavinck said nearly one hundred years ago remains true: "In general it must be said that our society, unlike that faced by the early church, does not make the imitation of Christ impossible. The Christian church today enjoys a freedom for which it must be truly grateful."[38] This liberty is also

---

[36] "Imit. II," 137 [430]; 137 [431]; 137 [431]; 135 [429]; 136 [430].
[37] "Imit. II," 143 [438]; 138 [433].
[38] "Imit. II," 139 [433].

a challenge, especially as we look back and recall the martyrs who lacked it and yet stood firm in their devotion to our Lord. Surrounded by the cloud of such witnesses as these, how could we do less? With liberty comes responsibility, the responsibility of mature Christian discipleship. We must pray for discernment, recognizing that discerning the Holy Spirit's guidance is a communal project and not an individual one. Discipleship is a function of *body* life; we are members together of the body of Christ.

CHAPTER 6

A CHRISTIAN WORLDVIEW

It was Abraham Kuyper, in his 1898 Stone Lectures at Princeton Seminary, who introduced the notion of worldview (*Weltanschauung*, world-and-life view), or as Kuyper called it, "life system," and made it the defining characteristic of Dutch neo-Calvinism. This emphasis on worldview was rooted in Kuyper's conviction that Calvinism was a global or universal faith with implications far beyond the church, matters of salvation, and the life of piety. His cosmic, Trinitarian definition of Calvinism is intentionally set in contrast with Lutheran Christianity. According to Kuyper, the "dominating principle" of Calvinism "was not, soteriologically, justification by faith, but, in the widest sense cosmologically, the *Sovereignty of the Triune God over the whole Cosmos*, in all its spheres and kingdoms, visible and invisible."[1]

Worldview was Kuyper's chief weapon in the battle—stated in Augustinian categories—of the city of God against the earthly city. Kuyper had in mind especially the battle against the spirit of modernity he saw embodied in the atheistic cry of the French Revolution *Ni Dieu, Ni Maître*! (No God, No Master).[2] It was imperative for Christians to draw clear battle lines over against this dominant "life system," and Kuyper saw himself and the ecclesiastical and sociopolitical movement he inspired as engaged in a cosmic conflict of principles.

---

[1] Abraham Kuyper, *Lectures on Calvinism* (Grand Rapids: Eerdmans, 1931), 79; emphasis added.
[2] Ibid., 10, 87, 109.

> If the battle is to be fought with honor and with a hope of victory, *then*
> *principle* must be arrayed against *principle*; then it must be felt that in
> Modernism the vast energy of an all-embracing *life-system* assails us,
> then also it must be understood that we have to take our stand in a life-
> system of equally comprehensive and far-reaching power.[3]

Kuyper found in Calvinism the life system that most evidently manifested the Christian principle needed to do battle against modernism.

> In Calvinism my heart has found rest. From Calvinism have I drawn the
> inspiration firmly and resolutely to take my stand in the thick of this
> great conflict of principles. . . . Calvinism, as the only decisive, lawful and
> consistent defense for Protestant nations against encroaching, and over-
> whelming Modernism.[4]

According to Kuyper, the very future of Western civilization was at stake
in this struggle.

Though usually absent the militaristic imagery and the civiliza-
tional hubris evident in the preceding, the use of worldview as a comprehensive interpretive key is common to neo-Calvinism in the century
after Kuyper himself. This is true of Bavinck, whose 1904 university
rector's address begins with observations about two conflicting late
nineteenth-century worldviews—emancipation and repristination—in
their common rejection of classic Christian orthodoxy.[5] Worldview,
in other words, is an *antithetical* notion; it posits one set of ideas over
against another comprehensive complex. This conflict is fundamentally religious in nature; the deepest questions of life's meaning are
at stake. According to Bavinck, these always boil down to three basic
issues captured by the Greek division of philosophy into dialectics
(thought), physics (nature/being), and ethics (doing). Over the centuries, the names may change to, "for example, logic (noetics), the natural and spiritual sciences, but every division in the end comes back to
this old trilogy." Bavinck concludes: "The problems that confront the
human spirit always come back to these: What is the relation between
thinking and *being*? Between *being* and *becoming*? Between *becoming* and

---

[3] Ibid., 11–12.
[4] Ibid.
[5] *Wereldb.*, 8–10.

acting? Who am I? What is the world? What is my place and task within this world?"[6]

The Place of Worldview

Before we proceed further to explore Bavinck's understanding and application of a Christian worldview, we need to put the whole notion into perspective. The academy is of course the natural arena for the "worldview app." An antithesis between the biblical understanding of reality and modern secular views has been in place since the eighteenth-century Enlightenment. Whereas Christians seek to understand their faith, devotees of autonomous reason repudiate faith altogether, leading to the many misnamed faith-versus-science clashes of the modern era. That is why Kuyperian neo-Calvinism, with its demonstrated commitment to the life of the mind as a key ingredient of Christian discipleship, has had such an appeal to North American evangelical Christians in the last few decades.

When Mark Noll's much-discussed 1994 indictment *The Scandal of the Evangelical Mind* pointed to the anti-intellectualism in evangelical churches and the absence of institutional commitment to serious Christian scholarship, he did allow for exceptions in the Dutch Reformed community, including Calvin College, the flagship educational institution of the Christian Reformed Church. He summarizes, "As they grew closer to evangelical networks, the Dutch Reformed offered their American counterparts a heritage of serious academic work and experienced philosophical reasoning."[7]

In a similar vein, an essay by James C. Turner explores the "puzzling" American evangelical revival in the 1980s and 1990s: "How did a religious movement that has historically produced preachers rather than professors . . . manage to generate within a couple of decades a distinguished cohort of scholars? How could so sturdy an intellectual life arise on such feeble intellectual traditions?" Noting that "evangelicals, in fact, did not build, could not have built—on their own foundations," he introduces Calvin College into his story and traces its history and location within the Christian Reformed Church (CRC), which he describes as "a fairly small denomination . . . though weak in numbers . . . sturdy in mind." Furthermore, Turner points out that the CRC and Calvin College are themselves

---

[6] *Wereldb.*, 14.
[7] Mark Noll, *The Scandal of the Evangelical Mind* (Grand Rapids: Eerdmans, 1994), 216.

heirs to the distinctive Dutch Reformed tradition known as neo-Calvinism, the tradition of Abraham Kuyper and Herman Bavinck.[8]

As someone who has been profoundly shaped by this tradition myself, I truly value the way in which neo-Calvinism has contributed to the nurture of a Christian mind in North America, and I trust that the previous chapters have provided sufficient evidence of it. Every culture is a cauldron of conflicting ideas and values striving for hegemony. Ideas are important, and a mind shaped by the Bible is needed if one is to resist the idolatries of bad ideas that are so destructive to individuals and communities. A disciple of Christ needs to understand the ideas of the age and be able to counter them with biblical truth if he or she is to live a spiritually healthy and whole life. Though we need not endorse all aspects of Kuyperian neo-Calvinism, North American evangelical Christians who value the life of the mind do owe a debt of gratitude to those Dutch Reformed Christian immigrants who took Abraham Kuyper, Herman Bavinck, and neo-Calvinism along with them to North America.

It is, therefore, as an appreciative "insider" that I now raise some cautions about the neo-Calvinist project, cautions in the spirit of Herman Bavinck himself. At the most basic level, the development of a Christian worldview is an integral part of a larger project of cultivating a Christian mind, making everything captive to Christ (2 Cor. 10:5). A Christian mind is not identical to a Christian worldview; a Christian worldview is not the whole of a Christian mind or even the most important part of it. When the apostle Paul commended "the mind of Christ" to the church at Philippi (Philippians 2), he was not talking about becoming a Christian philosopher but was calling the church to have the heart and attitude of a servant. Our attitudes, dispositions, habits, desires, and feelings—key ingredients of our *character*—include but cannot be reduced to our intellect.

The placement of this chapter on worlview in the overall structure of this book is quite intentional. The discussion of worldview is not found in part 1, "Foundations for Christian Living," and it is the second chapter in part 2, "The Shape of Christian Discipleship," after the chapter "Following Jesus." I am distancing myself from the tendency of some neo-Calvinists to lead with worldview when discussing Christian discipleship.[9] While it is

---

[8] James C. Turner, "Something to Be Reckoned With: The Evangelical Mind Awakens," *Commonweal* 126 (January 19, 1999): 11–13.

[9] For an affirmation of this point, applied to Christian higher education, see James K. A. Smith, *Desiring the Kingdom: Worship, Worldview, and Cultural Formation* (Grand Rapids: Baker, 2009); Smith's balanced

a significant error for Christians to be indifferent to the life of the mind or intellect, it is no less a mistake to think that we serve Christ *primarily* with our intellects. Ideas and the life of the mind *are* important; they are just not of *first* importance. When they become important beyond their appropriate place, they fuel an elitist intellectualism and become the building blocks of ideologies.

Worldview analysis becomes an ideology when it is used as an interpretive grid that excludes insights from other viewpoints because of religious disagreement. For example, a Christian philosopher would then refuse to acknowledge "truth" in a pagan (Greek) or modern secular thinker, strictly on the basis of a crucially different starting point. At that point worldview practitioners lose the ability to correct themselves and be corrected by others; they already know the "right" answers. Both of these shadowy tendencies—intellectualism and ideology—can be found in the history of Kuyperian neo-Calvinism, and therefore our appreciation of worldview interpretation must be tempered by an acknowledgment of its proper place in Christian discipleship. Worldview *follows* faith and union with Christ; it does not create faith and is no substitute for it.

Bavinck underscores this point when he looks closely at concrete religion, religion as it is actually practiced by people and not just derived from reading texts. Religion is like language; we are born with a native capacity for speech, but whether we grow up speaking English or Korean depends on the community into which we are born. Religions, too, are not products of our mind; we receive them as "gifts" from our environment. Religion, says Bavinck, "never occurs in a pure form and without content." The parallel here is with all the latent, potential abilities in each newborn: "However rich a talent for science and art may be hidden in a baby, it is nevertheless born in a state of helplessness. It depends on the 'grace' of its environment." The particular communities into which we are born not only determine the language we speak and the social customs we live by; they are also determinative for our religious beliefs and convictions.

> We receive food and drink, shelter and clothing, ideas and concepts,
> perceptions and wants from the circle in which we are born and reared.
> Religion also is instilled in us by our parents and caretakers. As with
> language, so it is with religion. The faculty of speech is something we

treatment of the neo-Calvinist preoccupation with worldview is constructive and resonates well with much of what I will develop in this chapter.

possess at birth, but the language in which we will later express our thoughts is given us by our environment.

At this point, Bavinck reiterates his contention that religious commitments should not be confused with philosophical ideas. Proving that he is no ideologue but willing to learn even from those with whom he fiercely disagrees, he cites the nineteenth-century idealist philosopher Arthur Schopenhauer:

> Schopenhauer correctly remarks, therefore, that religions have a great advantage over philosophical systems since they are instilled in children from their earliest youth on. Religion develops from childhood on in conjunction with the most intimate and tender parts of life and is in part for that reason ineradicable.

Bavinck concludes by pointing to the intractability of religious convictions in most people: "The [general] rule is that people die in the religion in which they were born. . . . conversions are rare. A change of religion is the exception, not the rule. Most people even live and die without ever being shaken in their religious beliefs by serious doubt."[10]

Bavinck's last point is important for our purposes. Healthy believers who "find more or less satisfaction in their faith," he argues, just don't obsess about whether or not their faith has adequate intellectual grounding. Finding solace and meaning in their religion, they simply practice it. "A hungry man does not first examine the way the bread that is put before him has been prepared." Bavinck provides a useful dictum for the church, one that is directly relevant to the topic we are considering here: "We live first, then we philosophize, since there is a great difference between life and reflection."[11] Though "the idea of God . . . is undoubtedly logically antecedent to religion," human affirmation that God exists is not the fruit of cognitive processes; it is the gift of revelation to religious beings. The "God concept never arose from a line of reasoning but was well established prior to all reasoning and proof in virtue of God's revelation and the corresponding religious nature of human beings."[12] Furthermore, excessive concern about the intellectual, philosophical warranting of one's faith is not a sign of a healthy faith. "It is evidence, not of the richness, but rather of the poverty of their religious life when people devote most of their attention to

---

[10] RD, 1:502.
[11] RD, 1:502.
[12] RD, 1:523.

such formal questions." It is when people's "faith has lost its vitality and confidence" that "they explore the grounds on which it rests."[13]

I emphasize this point not to undermine the value of Christian philosophizing and worldview thinking but to place it in proper perspective. Worldview is not a substitute for faith, and, as Bavinck said with respect to philosophical epistemology, it "cannot compensate for the loss of faith." Furthermore, faith does not require prior intellectual justification; for most believers faith is its own proof. "A person who is hungry and eats experiences automatically the nourishing power of the food consumed and has no need to study its chemical components." Much of the clamor for intellectual justification of faith overlooks the fact that faith is "so deeply hidden in the life of the soul and so closely interwoven with the finest and most tender fibers of the human heart that it almost completely eludes our own perception and even more that of others." The question How and why do I believe? is among the most difficult of all. "It is a riddle to us, inasmuch as we cannot plumb the depths of our own heart or penetrate with our eyes the darkness that lies behind our consciousness. And to others it is an even greater mystery." The ultimate ground for one's faith finally is not a matter of persuasive argumentation and satisfactory apologetics; in the end, "faith maintains itself and says, 'I cannot do otherwise, so help me, God.'"[14]

Just to be clear, Bavinck is not only concerned about the virus of rationalism in Christian understandings of discipleship. Accounts of coming to faith and then to religious certainty, he says, can appeal to the heart, to feeling, and to conscience, as well as to the intellect and reason. They all have something destructive in common. Because they locate the source of religion in ourselves, Bavinck regards such appeals as evidence of "a lack of psychological and epistemological sophistication." Religion does not arise from our minds, our wills, or our conscience. Religion is not like anything else—culture, science, art, or morality—that can be understood as arising solely from human effort. Religion, Bavinck contends, can only find its source in revelation. "Religion presupposes and demands the existence, self-revelation, and knowability of God."[15] Our search for the source of religion does not begin with our minds, our wills, or our conscience; it begins with God's address to us, with revelation.

---

[13] *RD*, 1:502.
[14] *RD*, 1:503–4.
[15] *RD*, 1:504–5.

Worldview Sins

Intellectual elitism, exalting the life of the mind beyond its proper place in Christian discipleship, is the first and perhaps most obvious sin associated with worldview analysis. Closely related to it is the sin of abusing worldview analysis by turning it into an ideology, applying it in ways that exclude legitimate insights from those with other, even conflicting, worldviews. Recall our earlier point that for Abraham Kuyper worldview was an antithetical notion; it served as a rallying cry to mobilize Christians in opposition to the revolutionary worldview of modernity. Kuyper, recall, described this as a battle of ultimate principles arrayed against each other, of life systems in mortal conflict. Over against the "all-embracing life-system of Modernism," he insisted, "we have to take our stand in a life-system of equally comprehensive and far-reaching power."[16]

The emphasis on principles—*Reformed* principles—became the rallying cry for Kuyper and his followers and served to distinguish friend from foe even within the Dutch Reformed camp itself. Shortly after Kuyper founded the Free University of Amsterdam in 1880, a controversy about a key article in its bylaws that called for all instruction in the school to be in accord with "Reformed principles" led to the dismissal of a prominent member of the law faculty. Article 2 of the university's controlling body, the Society for Higher Education on a Reformed Basis, read as follows: "The Society supports all education taking place in its schools which completely and exclusively rests on the foundation of Reformed principles and acknowledges as basis for the education in theology, the three forms of unity as fixed in 1618–19 by the National Synod of Dort."[17] The difficulty with this basis was that, apart from the three forms of unity (Heidelberg Catechism, Belgic Confession, Canons of Dort), the content of these "Reformed principles" was uncertain, and the principles themselves became the subject of bitter debate.

The Dutch jurist Jonkheer Alexander Frederik de Lohman (1837–1924) was appointed to the law faculty of the Free University in 1884. On June 17, 1895, at a public meeting of the Society for Higher Education on a Reformed Basis, questions were raised about Professor Lohman's instruction and his fidelity to the provisions of article 2. A commission of inquiry,

---

[16] Kuyper, *Lectures on Calvinism*, 11–12.

[17] J. C. Rullmann, *De Vrije Universiteit: Haar onstaan en haar bestaan* (Amsterdam: De Standaard, 1930), 180.

headed by Bavinck, was appointed to investigate the Reformed character of Lohman's teaching. It turned out that Kuyper and his followers understood "the expression '*Reformed principles*' in article 2 of the statutes [to] refer to *the principles of Calvinism*";[18] they also believed that they had arisen *historically* in the Reformed Churches and could be found in the confessions, liturgical formulations, and church orders, as well as in the writings of Reformed theologians, especially their polemics against Romanists, Anabaptists, Libertines, Socinians, Lutherans, and others. The scientific and artistic efforts (especially in poetry) of Calvinists through the centuries provided an additional source. Lohman, however, understood "Reformed principles" simply to mean fidelity to Scripture in the light of the Reformed confessions. The commission of inquiry, under Bavinck's guidance, came down uncompromisingly on the side of Kuyper. In Lohman's teaching, the commission judged, the Reformed principles indicated in article 2 of the statutes do not properly come into their own. In a letter to Kuyper, Bavinck states his own position clearly: "Prof. Lohman's conception and article 2 cannot be reconciled."[19]

Bavinck thus stood unequivocally at Kuyper's side in defense of "Reformed principles." While this stance undoubtedly reflects his own commitments and priorities at the time, we must take into account the situation in the union *Gereformeerde Kerken in Nederland* (GKN) during the 1890s. The decade saw a prolonged struggle about theological education in which the GKN was pulled in two different directions. The members of the Secession Christian Reformed Church not only took pride in their theological school at Kampen but, in addition, regarded a commitment to a church-related seminary as the proper place for training future ministers as a matter of principle. For Kuyper, however, it was no less a principle that such training should take place at a theology faculty in a Christian university in dialogue with other sciences and faculties. Bavinck's definite commitment to an academically responsible theological education undoubtedly influenced his conclusions and led to his siding with Kuyper.

In our biographical sketch in chapter 1, I called attention to Bavinck's indefatigable labors in the decade of the 1890s to bring together these two opposing visions for theological education. Over against those in his own church who prized their theological school at Kampen, Bavinck insisted

---

[18] Ibid., 186.
[19] *Tijdg.*, 103.

that theology as the study of God must be related to other areas of human knowledge and that a university is thus a fitting place for a theological faculty. But, facing Kuyper's intransigence in meeting the concerns of the Secession community, Bavinck began increasingly to emphasize the role of the church in theology and theological education. It is worth repeating our citation from an 1899 brochure by Bavinck: "In 1896 it had to do with the right and freedom of the discipline of theological science. Now in 1899 it appears to me that it has to do with the right and freedom of the churches."[20]

Without going into more historical detail than is necessary, we can say with some confidence that over time, the more intimately Bavinck became involved with Kuyper and the organizations Kuyper founded and ruled with a strong hand, the more critical he became, and this criticism also applied to the much-beloved "Reformed principles." We will look at two important signals of Bavinck's increasing distance from Kuyper: the internal critique of Kuyper's leadership of the Anti-Revolutionary Party, and Bavinck's direct criticism of the manner in which Kuyper used "Reformed principles" as a tool to run roughshod over his opponents. Kuyper became leader of the Anti-Revolutionary Party in 1871, almost single-handedly fashioned it into a political power, and was its undisputed leader. When he became prime minister in 1901, he reluctantly relinquished the reins as chairman of the ARP but managed to have his own personal choice, Bavinck, appointed in his place. Kuyper resumed the chair in 1909, at which time Bavinck also resigned from the executive of the ARP, apparently because of his dissatisfaction with Kuyper's leadership.[21]

The growing opposition to Kuyper within the ARP came to a head in 1915 when Bavinck and four others published a grievance against Kuyper's leadership.[22] We need not dwell on this episode, save to note it here because it helps explain Bavinck's more direct critique of Kuyper's famous "principles" only a few years later. One brief citation from this grievance, however, is significant because it indicates Bavinck's use of the imitation-of-Christ theme as a *critical principle against aspects of Kuyper's practice.* Calling for a unity and freedom in the party, Bavinck insists that all honest differences need to be dealt with openly rather than suppressed, and he calls for all members of the party to

---

[20] *Het recht der kerken en de vrijheid der wetenschap* (ET: "The right of the churches and the freedom of science/scholarship"), cited in Gleason, 256.
[21] See *Tijdg.,* 209–32.
[22] H. Bavinck et al., *Leider en leiding in de Anti-Revolutionaire Partij* (Amsterdam: Ten Have, 1915).

practically begin to live the apostolic injunction: Brothers, be like-minded, having the same love, being one in spirit and purpose. Do nothing out of selfish ambition or vain conceit, but in humility consider others better than yourselves. Each of you should look not only to your own interests, but also to the interests of others. Your attitude should be the same as that of Christ Jesus [Phil. 2:1–5].[23]

Even in the rough and tumble of politics and party conflict, Bavinck wanted to showcase "the mind of Christ" as summarized in Philippians 2.

That brings us to Bavinck's explicit critique of "Reformed principles." One of the problems with Kuyper's practice was his equivocal use of the term *principles*. On the level of basic biblical teaching about God's sovereignty, the distinction between Creator and creature, the sinfulness of humanity, religious liberty, and so forth, Bavinck was unwavering in his commitment. But Kuyper had a habit of also including specific policies and strategies deduced from core principles—such as opposition to women's suffrage—as matters of nonnegotiable principle. This had the effect of turning Kuyper's political program into an inflexible ideology, and Bavinck pleaded for a more fluid application of the more fundamental principles. When Bavinck published his book on the role of women in contemporary society in 1918,[24] his mildly progressive stance on matters such as women's suffrage gave rise to significant and vocal criticism, and he was accused of abandoning good Reformed (ARP) principles. When he finally publicly defended himself—at a gathering of ARP deputies in 1918—he also openly criticized Kuyper. He reminded the delegates that it was not he who had changed the party's position on any number of issues such as state pensions, general suffrage, and even women's suffrage. And then, directly facing Kuyper, he observed, "Long ago, the 'honored' leader of our party did."[25] He followed this with an observation about principles and concrete application: "Both are necessary: Principle and its on-going, ever-changing application, idealism and realism, ideal and practice. But in all these developments we must remain bound to established, ethical principles (norms)."[26] Bavinck was committed to "established, ethical principles (norms)," but much more than Kuyper and his followers seemed to allow, he was equally committed to the "on-going, ever-changing application" of those principles.

---

[23] Ibid., 56.
[24] *De vrouw in de hedendaagsche maatschappij.*
[25] Bavinck, "Politieke rede 1918" (unpublished manuscript, n.d.), 11, Archive Bavinck, HDC.
[26] Ibid.

It was the failure of many in the Reformed community during the second decade of the twentieth century to distinguish principle from application and to demonstrate their willingness to change application in a changed time that Bavinck regarded as problematic for the church. Intransigence on the application of principles led to a devaluing of principles altogether.

In 1920 the GKN was experiencing turbulent times, including a challenge to its understanding of scriptural authority. In a set of notes for a brochure Bavinck was preparing for these difficult days, he again raised questions about the way Kuyper and his followers in the GKN appealed to principles. The confusion about these principles, he contended, was a major contributor to the upheaval in the church: "Of the so-called principles not a single one remains pure and unsullied, not a single one remains standing before the onslaught of reality. This led to a feeling of malaise; of disbelief in principles."[27] The Reformed world was facing new challenges, and the old theological wineskins no longer sufficed to hold the new wine of modern questions. Facing new and difficult questions, some took refuge in solutions that "no longer held water." "Other [questions] were avoided altogether." Simple appeals to longstanding principles no longer persuaded: "The long-held belief that one could solve every problem with an appeal to 'principles,' by working theoretically and deductively, was shattered by reality. Reality imposed itself and set up a barrier against all abstract principles. Facts were more powerful than principles." "Reality imposed and set up a barrier . . . facts [proved to be] more powerful than principles." What Bavinck describes here is the public unmasking of an ideology; Kuyperian ideology was being "mugged by reality."

There is also an important *theological* issue involved in this difference between Bavinck and Kuyper. If we recall the discussion in chapter 4 about Kuyper's understanding of regeneration, we may take it one step farther. Regeneration or rebirth refers to that mysterious internal work of God the Holy Spirit that turns a rebellious human heart toward God. In Kuyper's speculative hands, the possibility that the Holy Spirit had planted a "seed" of regeneration in an infant's heart became one of the key grounds—a *presumed* regeneration—for the practice of infant baptism. But Kuyper did more with the doctrine of regeneration. It is classic Christian—notably Augustinian—teaching that being "born again" takes one from the earthly

---

[27] G. Harinck et al., *'Als Bavinck nu maar eens kleur bekende'* (Amsterdam: VU Uitgeverij, 1994), 48–50. The quoted material in this and the next paragraph is from these pages.

city (the "world," in New Testament terms) into the city of God; one is now a member of the body of Christ, the new people of God. In that sense, regeneration is an *antithetical* term; at the ultimate spiritual level, the world's population is divided in two: the citizens of this world and the pilgrim people of God.

Kuyper extended this *spiritual* antithesis into the concrete spheres of life, especially to the world of influential ideas. Regeneration is the foundation of Kuyper's antithetical use of principles, his passion to enter into battle with "principle set against principle" and "life-system against life-system."[28] For Kuyper, the consequence of regeneration—"which changes man in his very being, and that indeed by a change or transformation which is effected by a supernatural cause"—is a radical division in humanity itself: "This 'regeneration' breaks humanity in two, and repeals the unity of the human consciousness."[29] Consequently, we "have to acknowledge *two kinds of human consciousness*; that of the regenerate and the unregenerate; and these two cannot be identical."[30] The implication Kuyper draws from this is that "two kinds of people" will develop "two kinds of science."[31] The conflict in the scientific enterprise is not between faith (or religion) and science, but between "*two scientific systems . . . each having its own faith.*"[32] Different religious perceptions of reality result in different scientific conceptions. And, by extension, they result in different cultural, social, and political visions, strategies, and policies. It is not hard to see how this religiously rooted vision could lead to ideological blindness and dogmatism.

Bavinck does not repudiate worldview analysis rooted in religious vision and commitment. In his book-length treatment outlining the contours of a Christian worldview, he also sets that worldview over against the religious errors of pantheism, materialism, monism, vitalism, atomism, individualism, socialism, Darwinism, and historicism.[33] Yet Bavinck's own approach to the question of worldview is strikingly different. In particular, Bavinck repudiates Kuyper's famous dictum that divides Christian scholars from non-Christians: "Two kinds of people—two kinds of science." In an unpublished series of lectures given to students at Kampen in 1896–1897

---

[28] Kuyper, *Lectures on Calvinism*, 11–12.
[29] Abraham Kuyper, *Principles of Sacred Theology*, trans. J. Hendrik De Vries (Grand Rapids: Eerdmans, 1954), 152.
[30] Kuyper, *Lectures on Calvinism*, 133.
[31] Kuyper, *Principles of Sacred Theology*, 155–82.
[32] Kuyper, *Lectures on Calvinism*, 133.
[33] *Wereldb.*, 27, 39, 41, 43, 74, 79, 84, 91.

and available only in the form of a *dictaat* or student notes,[34] Bavinck expresses deep criticism of this application of the doctrine of regeneration. To conflate the scientific distinction between truth and falsehood with the personal one of regenerate and unregenerate people is to commit a logical fallacy technically known as *metabasis eis allo genos* (crossing over into a different genus). To mix a metaphor, it is to substitute an orange for an apple in an argument. In this instance, according to Bavinck, to identify the scientific work of the regenerate with truth and that of the unregenerate with the lie is categorically false. Not only is there much that is true in the scientific work of unregenerate people, but Christian faith in itself gives no one a corner on scientific truth. According to Bavinck, Kuyper is operating with a speculative and highly abstract conception of science and fails to adequately distinguish between faith in a saving sense and faith in a scientific sense. Science should be empirical, not speculative. As Bavinck puts it, "[Kuyper] does not attempt to derive his idea of science from the data as they appear in human life and are gathered together under the umbrella of science, but he attempts to establish it apart from empirical data, from the 'idea' of science."[35]

Worldview as a Gift of Revelation

How then does Bavinck himself approach the matter of worldview without lapsing into intellectualism or ideology? He does it by beginning with human experience in general, rather than with the doctrine of regeneration. Our worldview is not in the first place a product of our mental processes, our intellect, or our reason; rather, it arises out of experienced response to revelation. For Bavinck, revelation is that communicative act of God—Father, Son, and Holy Spirit—whereby he *manifests* himself, *discloses* himself, and *displays* who he is. With this definition in mind, we can understand how Bavinck, beginning with creation itself, roots all reality in revelation; God who became incarnate in Christ, who speaks to us in Scripture, is none other than the one who created all things by his *Word* (John 1; Colossians 1). "The world itself rests on revelation; revelation is the presupposition, the foundation, the secret of all that exists in all its forms. . . . The foundations of creation and redemption are the same. The Logos who became

---

[34] Bavinck biographer Bremmer, who had a copy of this "dictaat" available to him, gives an extensive analysis of Bavinck's critique of Kuyper's *Encyclopaedie* in *Dogmaticus*, 37–45.
[35] *Dogmaticus*, 39.

flesh is the same by whom all things were made."[36] From this, Bavinck concludes that all worldviews are attempts by human beings to navigate their
way between three realities present to us: ourselves and other humans,
the world, and God. With all their variations and permutations, there are
therefore only three basic worldviews possible:

> And as every world-view moves between the three poles of God, the world,
> and man, and seeks to determine their reciprocal relations, it follows that
> in principle only three types of world-view are distinguishable—the the-
> istic (religious, theological), the naturalist (either in its pantheistic or
> materialistic form), and the humanistic.[37]

All this still sounds rather intellectual, so let us look at Bavinck's own starting point in human self-consciousness as the gateway to understanding
revelation.

Human self-consciousness can be explained in simple terms. A newborn infant does not differentiate between herself and the surrounding
environment, including the environment that will come to be known as
"Mom." This coming to awareness is one of the most mysterious and wonderful things in all God's creation, and observing it carefully is one of our
greatest possible joys. Hold an infant before a mirror and at first she will
regard the image as another baby rather than herself. When prompted and
asked, "Who is that?" she might say, "be-be." And then, over time and after
repeated visits to the mirror, something mysterious and amazing happens:
she learns to recognize herself and say her name, "Anna." That is when
we speak of *self*-consciousness; the awareness that I am a "self," that I am
"me." It is the reflective ability to think of ourselves in the third person.
Bavinck develops his whole understanding of revelation by starting with
this ordinary but wonderful and observable path of human development.

Bavinck's 1908 Stone Lectures at Princeton Seminary are titled "The
Philosophy of Revelation" rather than "The Theology of Revelation" because he wants to explore the reality of revelation in general and not
just the particular revelation in the Bible. When we think of revelation
as a universal phenomenon, what do we have in mind? Can we explain
phenomenologically how revelation "happens"? What is it that we "receive" in revelation? Bavinck explains it by reminding us of the way in

---

[36] *PofR*, 27.
[37] *PofR*, 33.

which we become aware of ourselves, other people, and the external world. In particular, he calls us to reflect on how we knowingly differentiate ourselves from other human beings. His answer points us to something deeply experiential and intuitive; it may even initially startle us: "It is all *revelation.*" "In consciousness our own being, and the being of the world, are disclosed to us antecedently to our thought or volition; that is, they are *revealed* to us in the strictest sense of the word."[38] The normal human developmental process of becoming aware of ourselves as distinct persons and the awareness that there is a real world external to us are *revelations.* Bavinck also includes human awareness of God as part of this awareness: "In self-consciousness God makes known to us man, the world, and himself."[39] All this is entirely gratuitous, a gift; we cannot create this awareness by our own effort: "[The gift of self-consciousness] is received on our part spontaneously, in unshaken confidence, with immediate assurance."[40]

That last point about confidence and "immediate assurance" is very important to Bavinck's understanding of worldview. Without delving into a full discussion of what French philosopher René Descartes (1596–1650) may have meant with his famous *cogito ergo sum* (I think, therefore I am), Bavinck's approach turns this on its head. We *are* and are quite sure that we *are* before we begin to question our existence. *Being* always precedes thinking. To believe that we could prove our own existence by thinking about it seems bizarre; to believe that we create the world around us by our thought (as in some forms of idealism) seems even more bizarre. Most bizarre of all would be the idea, initiated in the modern era by philosopher Ludwig Feuerbach (1804–1872), that we create God, that he is only the outward projection of our inner life. It is, so the Scriptures teach us, the height of folly (Ps. 14:1). Imagine what it must be like to consider yourself the total master of your own destiny, a god unto yourself. Upon reflection, can anything be more unsettling and frightening?

By contrast, Bavinck claims that a sense of dependence is at the heart of human self-consciousness: "We feel ourselves dependent on everything around us; we are not alone [and] we feel ourselves, together with all creatures, wholly dependent on some absolute power which is the one infinite being." It is crucial to regard this not as a matter of philosophical reason-

---

[38] *PofR,* 75.
[39] *PofR,* 79.
[40] *PofR,* 62.

ing or as an abstraction, "but a fact which in point of certainty is equal to the best established fact of natural science." Bavinck adds, "It is something genuinely empirical, universally human, immediate, the very core of self-consciousness, and involves the existence of both the world and God."[41] With this emphasis on dependence, we now have in place the essential basic building blocks for a biblical, Christian worldview. Christians know themselves and their fellow humans to be image bearers of God, dependent on him as creatures, and living in a world that is a cosmos, an orderly reality providentially upheld by our heavenly Father.

And here we also have the antidote to all ideology, including Christian ideologies. Practically speaking, a biblical worldview calls us to trust our basic commonsense perception of the world. In the same way that we can be confident that we exist, so too can we be confident that our mind has a reliable grasp of the physical world outside us. We can be as sure about the world around us as we are of our own existence: "For the representation [of the world in our mind] is connected with reality by the same tie that binds self-consciousness to the self."[42] With trust comes a spirit of openness, of curiosity, and a willingness to change one's mind. With it also comes humility and modesty; we recognize that while God is all-knowing and faithful, we are finite and fallible.

The spirit I have just described was Bavinck's by family inheritance and personal temperament, but it was also a matter of *principle* for him. At Leiden he had learned "to attempt to understand the opponent,"[43] and in the foreword to the first edition of his *Reformed Dogmatics*[44] he spells it out as a methodological principle. Noting that his work is definitely a *Reformed* work of theology, he indicates his desire to honor the past and yet avoid simple repristination; he also tells us that he intends to leave his own stamp on it.

> The author who has a preference for the older generation whose freshness and originality exceeds that of later ones thus reserves the right of a dogmatic theologian to distinguish kernel from husk in the history of Reformed theology. To cherish the ancient simply because it is ancient is neither Reformed nor Christian.

---

[41] *PofR*, 66–67.
[42] *PofR*, 68.
[43] Hepp, 84.
[44] "Herman Bavinck, 'Foreword' to the First Edition (Volume I) of the *Gereformeerde Dogmatiek*," trans. John Bolt, *Calvin Theological Journal* 45 (2010): 9–10; the quotes that follow are from this foreword.

His desire is to be contemporary, to address issues of his own day. God who led great leaders of the past in reforming and teaching the church continues to do the same today. "For that reason this work of dogmatic theology is eager to carry the imprint of its own time. It would be an unending task to loosen one's ties to the present; but it would also not be pleasing to God who speaks to us as seriously and loudly as to previous generations."

A contemporary theology, one that takes seriously the challenges and demands of modernity, requires a certain amount of polemics. But Bavinck's description gives the strong impression that he views with distaste much of the way such theological debate is carried out: "Some blows will definitely be struck at numerous theological movements that crucify each other; in the midst of all of them I have sought and taken my own place." His conclusion underscores what we have already noted about Bavinck's fairness and openness to learn from others: "Where duty obligates that a different path be taken, I shall provide reasons. But even then I strive to appreciate what is good where it is found. Frequently this study will set forth newly discovered relationships that initially may seem not to exist." As someone who has spent most of his scholarly life working closely with Bavinck's *Reformed Dogmatics*, I gladly testify that he achieved his goal magnificently.

Contours of a Christian Worldview

We have now considered the place of worldview in Bavinck's understanding of the Christian life and seen how his conviction that worldview *follows* faith is characterized by a sense of *trusting dependence* on God's faithfulness. The important human capacity for self-consciousness—our awareness of self, the world, and God—is pure *gift*; it is *revealed* to us. And with that we have the answers to the three worldview questions introduced at the beginning of this chapter: What is the relation between *thinking* and *being*? Between *being* and *becoming*? Between *becoming* and *acting*? Put more simply: Who am I? What is the world? What is my place and task within this world?[45]

To answer the first: Thought follows being and self-consciousness, and all thought must be measured by its fidelity to reality, by the way things really are. And because the Logos who created and ordered all things is

---

[45] *Wereldb.*, 14.

also the Word who addresses us in revelation, our capacity to receive revelation—including the ability to use our small *l* logos or mind to discern the order of the world—gives us confidence that our perceptions are real and true. From this, we honor who we are, who God is, and our place in his world by being open to his revelation, to learning more about the world, to self-correction, and to humility and modesty in our claims. This is the part of Bavinck's Christian view of the world that is often overlooked, and sadly neglected, by those who turn to the Dutch neo-Calvinist tradition for help on worldview matters.

As we now turn to the key elements of Bavinck's Christian worldview, we must acknowledge the problem that sin introduces into the picture. Bavinck acknowledges that our self-knowledge and our knowledge of the world are distorted by sin. When it comes to knowing God, sin compounds the problem. In much the same way that we can come to know others only if they *reveal* themselves to us, so too we can know God only if he reveals himself to us. "A man must reveal himself, manifest himself by appearance, word, and act, so that we may somewhat learn to know him." Similarly,

> no knowledge of God is possible except that which proceeds from and by God (Matt. 11:27; 1 Cor. 2:10ff.). Earlier theology had an axiom for it: "What we need to understand about God must be taught by God himself, for this cannot be known except by the author himself." The fact that the creature knows anything of God at all is solely due to God. He is knowable only because and insofar as he himself wants to be known.[46]

The human analogy breaks down, however, because our self-revelation is always problematic: "We often reveal ourselves in totally arbitrary ways and in spite of ourselves; we often manifest ourselves in character traits and peculiarities that are unknown to us. Sometimes our self-manifestation belies who we are—it is false, untrue, misleading." And then, here is the difference: "But none of this is true of God." Because "the source of our knowledge of God is solely God himself," we can know that our knowledge of God is genuine and true.[47] God's self-revelation is true, has integrity, and is disclosed with power.

The subjective response to God's revelation involves the work of the Holy Spirit. Bavinck makes an important distinction "between the external

---

[46] *RD*, 1:212.
[47] *RD*, 1:212.

and internal principle of knowing, the external and internal word, revelation and illumination, the working of God's Word and the working of his Spirit."[48] True knowledge of God, in other words, requires *regeneration*, a work of the Holy Spirit transforming a person's consciousness and will.[49] Regeneration is the *sine qua non* for any assurance that we truly know God. However, unlike Kuyper, Bavinck does not use regeneration as a criterion or condition for our knowledge of the world, for scientific inquiry. Even when he begins his antithetical description of worldviews contrary to the Christian faith, it is as *religious* postures that he distinguishes them from the Christian worldview. As he begins his book *Christian Worldview* and outlines the various streams of thought he will be engaging, it is their antithetical stance to the Christian religion that draws his attention. The idols of emancipation, restoration, patriotism, socialism, classicism, and so forth are destructive forces arrayed against the Christian message of reconciliation. Bavinck judges that there is a "deep, sharp contrast between the Christian faith and the modern person" that demands choice. "Decisive choice is an obligation. As much as we would love peace, the conflict has been placed upon us."[50]

Bavinck does not shirk away from the conflict that so occupied Kuyper, and he picks out many of the same targets; but unlike Kuyper (and Cornelius Van Til), he does very little with the cognitive disruptions due to the fall into sin. He clearly acknowledges them, as we have already noted in his comments about our self-revelation to others. Having spent some time on this earlier in this chapter, I will add only a few additional nuances here.

Bavinck explicitly unlinked sin and regeneration from science. "In many aspects of science, regeneration has no influence. Whether one is re-born or not, one can do science."[51] In fact, Bavinck adds, even Kuyper acknowledges this. In the very section of his *Principles of Sacred Theology* where his topic is "two kinds of people, two kinds of science," Kuyper says the following (with his emphasis): "The formal process of thought has *not* been attacked by sin, and for this reason palingenesis [regeneration] works no change in this mental task."[52] Instead of locating the religious divide

---

[48] *RD*, 1:213.
[49] Technically and strictly speaking, illumination is not identical with regeneration. Since they have in common a direct work of the Holy Spirit, and Kuyper's use of "regeneration" that we discussed earlier is probably more accurately described as illumination, I have also conflated the terms here.
[50] *Wereldb.*, 12–13.
[51] *Dogmaticus*, 40.
[52] Kuyper, *Principles of Sacred Theology*, 159.

among conflicting modern worldviews in the original fall into sin, Bavinck places it *historically* in the rise of humanism. Ever attuned to the political and ecclesiastical currents swirling about, Bavinck asks, somewhat mischievously, "In the final analysis, is this whole principle enlisted to place the Free University over against the others?"[53]

The irony of all this is that the content of Bavinck's and Kuyper's worldview is virtually identical. I will provide a brief synopsis of it here, but the next four chapters will explore this worldview in marriage and family, in work and vocation, in culture and education, and in civil society.

Bavinck's worldview can be neatly summarized by two adjectives: *Trinitarian* and *organic*.[54] It is a theological worldview and rooted in the Christian doctrine that God is triune, one in essence and three in persons. The Trinity provides the necessary perspective for viewing all reality. Bavinck regularly defines the Christian faith in Trinitarian terms such as these: "The essence of the Christian religion consists in the reality that the creation of the Father, ruined by sin, is restored in the death of the Son of God, and re-created by the grace of the Holy Spirit into a kingdom of God."[55] According to Bavinck, we must learn to think in Trinitarian terms: "The Christian mind remains unsatisfied until all of existence is referred back to the triune God, and until the confession of God's Trinity functions at the center of our thought and life."[56] In fact, because creation as a whole reflects the very Trinitarian being of God, Bavinck grants that "there is much truth to the belief that creation everywhere displays to us vestiges of the Trinity. And because these vestiges are most clearly evident in 'humanity,' so that 'human beings' may even be called 'the image of the Trinity,' 'humanity' is driven from within to search out those vestiges."[57]

Practically and operationally, this conviction leads Bavinck to insist that the world's unity in diversity can only be understood from the perspective of God's tri-unity, and here we encounter Bavinck's emphasis on the *organic*. Bavinck follows Kuyper in his concern about all monistic forms of thought, notably nineteenth-century pantheism, which he judges to be the age's dominant heresy.[58] In contrast with pantheism, Bavinck insists that Christian

---

[53] *Dogmaticus*, 40.
[54] I am indebted to James Eglinton, *Trinity and Organism: Towards a New Reading of Herman Bavinck's Organic Motif* (Edinburgh: T&T Clark, 2012), for his thorough discussion of these two closely linked themes.
[55] *RD*, 1:112.
[56] *RD*, 2:330.
[57] *RD*, 2:333.
[58] H. Bavinck, "Hedendaagsche wereldbeschouwing" ("Contemporary Worldviews"), *De vrije kerk* 9 (1883): 435.

theology "recognizes a life and consciousness in God, distinct from the world," and God and his attributes are not to be identified with the laws of the universe. There is no point of unity for all things within the universe itself; its existence, its continuation, its duration and consummation are in God's hands. He alone is the one source from whom all things come and to whom all things return. Pantheism blurs the boundaries between God and creation, a primal blurring that leads to additional destruction of creation boundaries and distinctions.[59] A refusal to recognize the diversity created by God is rooted, in Bavinck's judgment, in the Renaissance-Enlightenment ideal of radical human autonomy and sovereignty. Man, as the Creator of his own destiny, is free and not subject to the law of God. God and his law must be incorporated within man's rational ordering of cosmic reality. God is not the transcendent ruler of the cosmos; he is radically immanent within it.

The Christian world finds its unity in the triune God, in the conviction that reality, which is an incarnation of God's thought, is created by the same Logos who created the laws of thought in us and holds them *organically* together. Here Bavinck intentionally distances himself from the *mechanistic* (deist) thinking of his own teachers at Leiden, namely J. H. Scholten and L. W. E. Rauwenhoff. A closed-system universe with fixed laws of cause and effect, set in motion by a deistic God who then lets it run its own course, simply cannot be reconciled with a biblical worldview. Mechanistic materialism fails to account for the world's unity in diversity no less than does pantheism.

> Pantheism attempts to explain the world dynamically; materialism attempts to do so mechanically. But both strive to see the whole as governed by a single principle. In pantheism the world may be a living organism (*zōon*), of which God is the soul; in materialism it is a mechanism that is brought about by the union and separation of atoms.

Both are intellectually bankrupt because "both fail to appreciate the richness and diversity of the world . . . and dissolve all distinctions in a bath of deadly uniformity. Both deny the existence of a conscious purpose and cannot point to a cause or a destiny for the existence of the world and its history."[60] Bavinck's description of the contrasting biblical worldview is worth quoting at length:

---

[59] Ibid., 445.
[60] *RD*, 2:435.

Scripture's worldview is radically different. From the beginning heaven and earth have been distinct. Everything was created with a nature of its own and rests in ordinances established by God. Sun, moon, and stars have their own unique task; plants, animals, and humans are distinct in nature. There is the most profuse diversity and yet, in that diversity, there is also a superlative kind of unity. The foundation of both diversity and unity is in God. It is he who created all things in accordance with his unsearchable wisdom, who continually upholds them in their distinctive natures, who guides and governs them in keeping with their own increated energies and laws, and who, as the supreme good and ultimate goal of all things, is pursued and desired by all things in their measure and manner. Here is a unity that does not destroy but rather maintains diversity, and a diversity that does not come at the expense of unity, but rather unfolds it in its riches. In virtue of this unity the world can, metaphorically, be called an organism, in which all the parts are connected with each other and influence each other reciprocally. Heaven and earth, man and animal, soul and body, truth and life, art and science, religion and morality, state and church, family and society, and so on, though they are all distinct, are not separated. There is a wide range of connections between them; an organic, or if you will, an ethical bond holds them all together.[61]

Bavinck's worldview is rooted in the very Trinitarian being of God; God's own three-in-oneness is reflected in the world he created. Since "the Christian mind remains unsatisfied until all of existence is referred back to the triune God,"[62] the Christian disciple must think in Trinitarian, organic terms. As James Eglinton puts it, "Organic thinking begins by seeing the universe as the general revelation of God's Trinity."[63] We will not explore this further in this chapter but leave it to four chapters in the third part of this volume, where we will consider how Bavinck applies this worldview to marriage and family, work and vocation, culture and education, and civil society.

---

[61] *RD*, 2:435–36.
[62] *RD*, 2:330.
[63] Eglinton, *Trinity and Organism*, 67–68.

PART 3

THE PRACTICE OF CHRISTIAN DISCIPLESHIP

CHAPTER 7

MARRIAGE AND FAMILY

The previous chapter, on the role of worldview in Bavinck's understanding of the Christian life, emphasized the Trinitarian shape of his vision. We must learn to think about everything in Trinitarian terms: "The Christian mind remains unsatisfied until all of existence is referred back to the triune God, and until the confession of God's Trinity functions at the center of our thought and life."[1] In addition, Bavinck points to the creation itself as displaying "vestiges of the Trinity," with human beings as the most clearly evident display of those vestiges. Bavinck is even willing to say that human beings may be called "the image of the Trinity."[2]

It is especially in marriage and family that we recognize the most profound analogy of the unity in diversity found archetypally in the tri-unity of God. Bavinck's book *The Christian Family* begins with an unexpected note of playfulness, a note that is sustained throughout the volume. Through striking imagery and prose, the book frequently celebrates the love between a man and a woman and between parents and their children. The very first sentence reads, "The history of the human race begins with a wedding."[3] "God did not create the earth so that it would remain empty," Bavinck goes on to say, "but he formed it so that people would inhabit the earth (Isa. 45:18)." The creation of humanity is then described in Trinitarian terms:

---

[1] *RD*, 2:330.
[2] *RD*, 2:333.
[3] *Family*, 1.

So he created this humanity after a special [intra-Trinitarian] consultation; he created humanity according to his own image and likeness; he created humanity immediately as distinct sexes, as man and as woman. And when he had created them, he blessed them and gave them the whole earth as their territory.[4]

The Family in Bavinck's Social Vision

The foundational role of the family is an essential ingredient in Bavinck's social vision. In the narrative of Genesis 1 and 2 there "lies embedded everything we need to know about the origin, the essence, and the destiny of humanity. They contain a wisdom that far surpasses the understanding of the erudite."[5] Lest there be any doubt about the matter, Bavinck makes a point of stating that men and women alike are the full image bearers of God. "The woman, just like the man, is a special creation of God, bearing his image and likeness."[6] But it is a mistake to think of the man and the woman only in solitary, individual terms as image bearers of God because "both together are said to have been created in God's image (Gen. 1:27)." And to be sure that we don't miss the point, Bavinck adds this: "Not merely one of them, but both, and not the one separate from the other, but man and woman together, in mutual relation, each created in his or her own manner and each in a special dimension created in God's image and together displaying God's likeness." That is the reason, according to Bavinck, that "the Lord compares himself not only to a Father who takes pity on his children (Ps. 103:13), but also to a mother who cannot forget her nursing child (Isa. 49:15). He chastens like a father (Heb. 12:6), but he also comforts like a mother (Isa. 66:13), and replenishes for the loss of both (Ps. 27)."[7]

If Bavinck were writing his book today, he would need to include a chapter on the challenges presented to our biblical understanding of men, women, sexuality, and marriage by our culture's preoccupation with homosexuality. The topic does not get Bavinck's attention in *The Christian Family*, but what he says about male and female sexual identity is directly relevant to it. Sex comes from God; he is the one who designed it. "God is the Creator of the human being, and simultaneously also the Inaugurator of sex and of sexual difference." Bavinck directly confronts the inclina-

---

[4] *Family*, 1–2.
[5] *Family*, 1–2.
[6] *Family*, 3.
[7] *Family*, 3.

tion of some pious people to construe sexual desire itself as in some sense linked to a sinful human sensuality. "This difference [between the sexes] did not result from sin; it existed from the very beginning, it has its basis in creation, it is a revelation of God's will and sovereignty, and therefore wise and holy and good." This calls for contentment with one's sexual identity as male or female. "Therefore, no one may misconstrue or despise this sexual difference, either within one's own identity or in that of another person. It has been willed by God and is grounded in nature." To summarize:

> God is the sovereign Designer of sex; man and woman have God to thank not only for their human nature, but also for their different sexes and natures. Both are good, even as they both come forth from God's hand. Together in mutual fellowship they bear the divine image. God himself is the Creator of duality-in-unity.[8]

Admittedly this does not address the manifold complications that arise from people's actual experience as sinful sexual beings: homosexual or bisexual desire, transgender emotional conflicts, and so forth. We who are more aware of this complexity today than Bavinck was a century ago must be sensitive and compassionate in our response to all whose experiences of sexual identity are broken. We also need to remind ourselves that we are all broken to some degree or other, including sexually. It also needs to be said that the Christian church has a great deal to learn on this subject, not to mention plenty of which to repent. Nonetheless, Bavinck's treatment remains helpful in putting the *created norm* for human sexuality front and center. That too is an act of pastoral love. As in all cases of human brokenness and moral failing, those who are broken and have failed need the norm even more than those who "are well [and] have no need of a physician" (Matt. 9:12). Failure to put the norm before sinners dishonors them as responsible moral agents. To refuse to recite the eighth commandment to a thief and call him to stop stealing is not an act of compassion; it is to resign him to an inevitable fate of remaining a criminal. Quite apart from giving him carte blanche to be a lawbreaker, such "compassion" is soul destroying; it does not call for repentance and asks for no moral sacrifice. It is cruel.

Bavinck's real interest in the duality-in-unity of the man and the woman is less personal and individual than it is social. The fullness of

[8] *Family*, 5.

the image of God is found in community. "For only in the human race is the image of God unfolded, and only in its dominion over the whole earth does the human race achieve its vocation and purpose." This engagement with the creation, this subduing and serving, is a task performed together. "Both—man and woman—stand thus with their distinct gifts in a united sacred service, both fulfill a shared precious calling, and labor at a single divine work." But now we come to the heart of the matter for Bavinck: this shared calling must be performed in obedience to God's commands and in respect for each other's unique gifts and tasks. "But they are able to respond to this their exalted vocation only when together they continue to obey the divine command, before everything else, to continue respecting the image of God in themselves and in each other, and as a consequence, keep living in the most intimate mutual fellowship." Bavinck then makes a point with prepositions: "God created the woman *from* the man and *for* the man (1 Cor. 11:8–9), but also *unto* the man, even as he created the man *unto* the woman. God made two out of one, so that he could then make the two into one, one soul and one flesh." Marriage between a man and a woman is a unique and holy union, a "kind of fellowship [that] is possible only between two." The very nature of marriage is that it must be monogamous, "an essential bond between one man and one woman, and therefore also a lifelong covenant, indissoluble by human authority." Bavinck concludes, "No other love resembles God's love so closely, or reaches such height."[9]

Again, though Bavinck does not explicitly address the issue of homosexuality, his description of human heterosexual union within the bounds of marriage is directly relevant. This is even more apparent when we consider what he goes on to say about the entrance of children into the picture and the creation of families. God's blessing rests upon marriage. "He is the Creator of man and of woman, the Inaugurator of marriage, and the Sanctifier of marriage." But marriage is not simply about the sexual intimacy and fulfillment of two people; it also has procreation in view. As the "cultural blessing and mandate" of Genesis 1 makes clear, God blesses humanity in its activity of "being fruitful and multiplying." Children, too, are a sign of God's blessing and an image of the triune diversity-in-unity.

> Each child born is the fruit of fellowship, and as such is also the fruit of
> divine blessing. The two-in-oneness of husband and wife expands with a

---

[9] *Family*, 7.

child into a three-in-oneness. Father, mother, and child are one soul and one flesh, expanding and unfolding the one image of God, united within threefold diversity, and diverse within harmonic unity.[10]

It is here, in cooperating with God to create new life, a new human soul, that we achieve the high point of what it means for humans to image God the Creator. And it is here that homosexual love fails the creational structure of marriage. There is no unity-in-duality, only a unity of sameness; there is no possible two-in-oneness expanding into three-in-oneness. The divine command of Scripture against homosexual activity should be sufficient for us; nonetheless, a Christian worldview rooted in the tri-unity of God also provides us with a clear metaphysical grounding for the command.

Heterosexual, monogamous marriage producing a family is the tri-unity of relationships that is foundational to all life in society, according to Bavinck. "The authority of the father, the love of the mother, and the obedience of the child form in their unity the threefold cord that binds together and sustains all relationships within human society." In Bavinck's view, there is also a feedback loop benefitting the individual because this threefold pattern is the norm for a harmonious life in each person and in society. Every individual, to be complete, requires masculine, feminine, and childlike qualities. "Within the psychological life of every integrated personality this triple cord forms the motif and melody. No man is complete without some feminine qualities, no woman is complete without some masculine qualities, and to both man and woman, the child is held up as an example (Matt. 18:3)." Bavinck then describes these three characteristics in terms of "authority, love, and obedience," which he says "are the pillars of all society." "These three characteristics and gifts are always needed in every society and in every civilization, in the church and in the state."[11]

Roles, Rights, and Reformation

From the preceding we see clear hints of sex-ascribed roles for men and women in marriage and in society, roles that are linked to their respective and distinct natures. Indeed, Bavinck does ascribe to women a primary calling in the home, and he points to human history, as well as the narratives and laws of the Old Testament, as evidence for a patriarchal structure

---

[10] *Family,* 7–8.
[11] *Family,* 8.

of human society. Before we dismiss this as a typical Victorian-era bias, we need to consider the several ways in which Bavinck nuances his views. Speaking of patriarchal Israel, he warns against making unwarranted assumptions from our modern context. "One would be mistaken," he says, "to conclude from this extensive power of the head of the family that his wife and children lived in a state of slavery."[12] It is true that there were no laws "describing the rights of wives and children," but that does not mean "that in reality they were devoid of all rights, and were handed over to the master's kindness or lack thereof." Instead, such "rights" "were established in large part not in the law but in the mores." When one looks at the narratives of the Old Testament, one notices from such stories as Rebekah and, later, Rachel at the well (Gen. 24:15–16; 29:10), along with Jethro's daughters at the well (Ex. 2:16), that women were given considerable freedom and independence outside the home, even in dealing with strangers. "Wives like Sarah, Rebekah, Rachel, Hannah, Abigail etc., hardly give the impression of being slaves; they are free women who are honored and loved by their husbands."[13]

In connection with this, Bavinck also notes that the multiplication of laws that attempt to enshrine "rights" for women is a symptom of social and moral decline, not advance.

> Rather than concluding from the limited number or complete absence of laws that people live in a situation without rights, in many cases we can with more warrant argue just the reverse and say: the more laws we need, the more it becomes evident that rational and moral understanding, that natural love and natural bonds, are losing their influence and power.

The preoccupation with "rights" that *must* be established by law is "due largely to self-interest undermining the moral character of society."[14]

There is more to be said about scriptural teaching concerning marriage. "The sacredness of marriage comes to fullest expression in that it serves as an image of the covenant of fidelity between God and his people."[15] While the pagan nations around Israel also brought marriage into their relationship with the deity, they had no concept of God's holiness and

---

[12] *Family*, 32.
[13] *Family*, 32–33.
[14] *Family*, 32–33.
[15] *Family*, 35.

simply "transferred to the deity the distinction of sexes, along with various immoral relationships and acts." By contrast, the covenant Lord enters into a relationship with Israel "as with no other nation on earth." Having betrothed himself to her as a Bridegroom and Husband "out of pure grace (Is. 61:10; 62:5; Jer. 2:32; Ezek. 16; Hosea 1–3)," he is now "jealous of his honor, and regards all apostasy of his people as harlotry and adultery, as sexual immorality and infidelity (Lev. 20:6; Num. 14:33; Ps. 73:27; Isa. 1:21; Jer. 3:1; Ezek. 16:32; etc.)."[16] Apart from our Lord himself, the true Israelite, "the Israelitess par excellence, who does not run ahead and act on her own, but who receives in childlike faith what God bestows upon her" is Mary, the mother of Jesus. "Whereas Eve detached herself from the word of God and went her own way, Mary accepted the word of God without murmuring or arguing; by God himself she was prepared and formed to be the receptor of his most sublime revelation."[17]

Thus, "the holy family is the example of the Christian home." By the example of his words and deeds, Jesus honored marriage and family. "Jesus dealt with women with complete openness and freedom; women were among his most beloved disciples; they follow him in Galilee and Judea, minister to him from their possessions, and are witnesses of his crucifixion and burial, his resurrection and subsequent appearances."[18] Jesus honored marriage by his presence at the wedding in Cana (John 2) and restored the original, creation meaning of marriage in his comments about adultery and lust (Matt. 5:27–28) and divorce (Matt. 19:4–6). He also restored the force of the fifth commandment in his comments about the way the rabbis of his day evaded their duties with their declarations of "Corban" (Matt. 15:4–6; Mark 7:10–12).[19] His several healings of sick children (Matt. 17:14–20; John 4:46–54), even twice raising them from the dead (Luke 7:11–15; 8:41–56), demonstrate "a profound understanding of the tender relationship that exists between parents and children."[20] In short, "Christ honored the woman and lifted her once again after her fall," and "at the same time he honors and restores marriage."[21]

Bavinck thus sees a restoration of marriage and family as a fruit of the completed work of Christ. "Christianity," he insists, "has been a rich

---

16 *Family*, 36.
17 *Family*, 38.
18 *Family*, 40.
19 *Family*, 42–43.
20 *Family*, 43.
21 *Family*, 41.

blessing for family living."[22] "Christianity sanctified marriage, liberated it from various evils, and once again established it on the foundation of the divine commandment."[23] However, as Bavinck looks at the state of marriage and family in his own day, he judges both to be under serious attack. "There has never been a time when the family faced so severe a crisis as the time in which we are now living. Many are not satisfied with remodeling; they want to tear things down to the foundation."[24] Christians have an opportunity and a responsibility to contribute to healthy, flourishing marriages and families by calling for inner, spiritual renewal.

> If family life is indeed being threatened from all sides today, then there is nothing better for each person to be doing than immediately to begin reforming in one's own circle and begin to rebuff with the facts themselves the sharp criticisms that are being registered nowadays against marriage and family.[25]

Such inner reformation differs from modern attempts to deny or change human nature; it acknowledges and promotes principles that are in tune with nature and thus do not "conflict with the facts and demands of reality." The gospel is not at war with nature; on the contrary, the gospel only "battles against sin across the entire spectrum of reality." "Everywhere and always it seeks the reformation of natural life, but only in such a way and by such means that nature is liberated from unrighteousness."[26]

True Distinctions versus Stereotypes

With respect to marriage and family, the first principle that flows from Scripture is the distinction between man and woman. While it is true that the particular way in which these differences are socially expressed varies over time and from place to place, the distinction itself "has existed from the very beginning, provided by nature itself and consequently called into existence by God, who placed it before our eyes as an undeniable fact."[27] This does not mean that it is always easy to describe "crisply and clearly the distinction between man and woman." Extremes arise in history: women

---

[22] Family, 47.
[23] Family, 50.
[24] Family, 61.
[25] Family, 63.
[26] Family, 64.
[27] Family, 64.

haters and women worshipers; "the woman is an angel or a devil, a queen or a vixen, a dove or a serpent, a rose or a thorn."[28] Nonetheless, Bavinck insists that there are important, perennial differences: physically, emotionally, and mentally. In all this, "each of the two is complete as a person" and "each of the two has a fully human nature and is a uniquely independent person." As a result, with respect to individual persons, it is very difficult to answer questions about sex-ascribed aptitudes, much less see them in absolute terms.[29]

This confirms what I spoke of earlier as "hints of sex-ascribed roles for men and women in marriage and in society, roles that are linked to their respective and distinct natures." In terms of a contemporary debate among North American evangelicals between "complementarians" and "egalitarians,"[30] Bavinck is clearly on the side of the former. It would be a mistake, however, for either side in this debate to brush aside Bavinck's views except as a confirmation of already-held biases or as an illustration of a typical nineteenth-century Victorian male whose ideas are best left behind. The views I have described in this chapter are nuanced to avoid all extreme forms of sex-determined identity and role ascriptivism. Bavinck's insistence that a fully integrated person possesses qualities usually attributed to each sex is a clear antidote to the extremes of will-to-power, macho masculinity and eroticized or subservient, passive femininity. Nor can it be said that Bavinck was simply reflecting the reactionary sex stereotypes of his own day and insufficiently sensitive to emancipatory currents that were changing the roles of women. Bavinck intentionally acquainted himself with the changes taking place with respect to women's roles in society, even attending the 1913 exhibition "The Woman, 1813–1913," held in Amsterdam from May through October.[31] Furthermore, he acknowledged the inevitability of many of these changes with these remarkable words:

---

[28] *Family*, 67.

[29] *Family*, 66–67.

[30] The "complementarian" position, represented by the Council on Biblical Manhood and Womanhood and articulated in the Danvers Statement (http://cbmw.org/core-beliefs/, accessed October 10, 2013), holds the view that men and women have equal dignity and worth as image bearers of God but are called to different roles, notably by restricting women from some governing and ruling roles. On the other side, the website for Christians for Biblical Equality states, "CBE affirms and promotes the biblical truth that all believers—without regard to gender, ethnicity, or class—must exercise their God-given gifts with equal authority and equal responsibility in church, home and world" (http://www.cbeinternational.org/content/about-cbe, accessed January 9, 2015).

[31] Hepp, 314. An overview of Bavinck's views on the public role of women can be found in Niels M. Van Driel, "The Status of Women in Contemporary Society: Principles and Practice in Herman Bavinck's Socio-Political Thought," in *Five Studies in the Thought of Herman Bavinck, A Creator of Modern Dutch Theology*, ed. John Bolt (Lewiston, NY: Edwin Mellen, 2011), 153–95; Van Driel spends most of his essay with Bavinck's work, *De vrouw in de hedendaagsche maatschappij* (Kampen: Kok, 1918).

"The soul of the woman has awoken and no power in this world will bring it back to its former state of unconsciousness."[32] And finally, his writing and speaking on the subject in the 1918 publication *Women in Contemporary Society*[33] and his address "The Vocation of Married Women," delivered to the Second Christian Social Congress in Amsterdam on March 10–13, 1919,[34] generated controversy and opposition in the circles of the Union Church (*Gereformeerde Kerken in Nederland*) for their progressive stance.

On two issues—women's suffrage and vocations for married women outside the home—Bavinck's views challenged his church community and the political leadership of the Dutch Calvinist political party, the Anti-Revolutionary Party. Though Bavinck was an ARP member of the Dutch Senate during the years—especially in the 1910s—when women's suffrage was a controversial issue in the Dutch Parliament, his openness to women's suffrage meet with considerable resistance. He objected to treating the issue as a matter of abstract "principles" and insisted that the developments in society that strengthened women's positions could and should also be seen in a positive light. And although not an advocate of women's suffrage and even acknowledging that some of the objections to it had partial validity, he "regarded women's suffrage as a natural consequence of legitimate historical developments."[35]

In his address to the Second Christian Social Congress,[36] Bavinck suggested that most married women who worked outside the home did so from economic necessity; combining home and outside work was very difficult. His judgment was that outside work was "inadvisable" but not forbidden by Scripture.[37] From 1910 to 1940, there were no fewer than ten attempts to pass legislation in the Dutch Parliament to forbid women from working outside the home. This was the climate and context within which Bavinck's "moderate" voice spoke. In our day, when the issue of women's suffrage is settled, other issues about sexuality, marriage, and role ascriptivism continue to be part of a simmering cauldron of social uncertainty and debate.[38]

---

[32] Bavinck, *De vrouw*, 78; cited by Van Driel, "The Status of Women," 156–57.
[33] See note 31 above.
[34] H. Bavinck, "De beroepsarbeid der gehuwde vrouw," in *Tweede christelijke sociaal congres gehouden te Amsterdam op 10, 11, 12 en 13 Maart* 1919 (Rotterdam: Libertas, 1919), 5–25.
[35] Van Driel, "The Status of Women," 179.
[36] In addition to the literature cited in notes 31–34, see H. J. van de Streek, "Haar eigenlijke taak in het huis," *Vereniging van Christen-Historici* 1, no. 1 (1990).
[37] Ibid.
[38] To take just one example, consider the intense conversations generated by books like Alison Wolf, *The XX Factor: How the Rise of Working Women Has Created a Far Less Equal World* (New York: Crown, 2013); Hanna Rosin, *The End of Men: And the Rise of Women* (New York: Riverhead, 2012); and articles like

Obviously, there is a great deal about the roles of women as wives, mothers, and professionals that remains unclear; not everything is settled. The issues that Bavinck and his contemporaries wrestled with around the turn of the twentieth century have not disappeared; we can still learn from his thoughtful attention to them.

A Beautiful Symmetry

We noted at the outset of this chapter the opening line from Bavinck's book on the Christian family: "The history of the human race begins with a wedding."[39] Marriage, however, even when not blessed with children, remains a good: "For husband and wife marriage is meaningful and is for them a means for fulfilling their earthly and spiritual calling." But Bavinck is quick to add, "Just as marriage is to be recommended in general, so too a marriage blessed with children is what may generally be described as a customary, normal marriage." Bavinck refers to this "trinity" of father, mother, and child in aesthetic terms as "beautiful symmetry."[40] It is fitting, therefore, to conclude this chapter with Bavinck's own eloquent testimony to the rich joys of family life:

> For children are the glory of marriage, the treasure of parents, the wealth of family life. They develop within their parents an entire cluster of virtues, such as paternal love and maternal affection, devotion and self-denial, care for the future, involvement in society, the art of nurturing. With their parents, children place restraints upon ambitions, soften the differences, bring their souls ever closer together, provide them with a common interest that lies outside of them, and opens their eyes and hearts to their surroundings and for their posterity. As with living mirrors they show their parents their own virtues and faults, force them to reform themselves, mitigating their criticisms, and teaching them how hard it is to govern a person. The family exerts a reforming power upon the parents. Who would recognize in the sensible, dutiful father the carefree youth of yesterday, and who would ever have imagined that the lighthearted girl would later be changed by her child into a mother who renders the greatest sacrifices with joyful acquiescence. The family transforms ambition into service, miserliness into munificence, the weak into the strong,

---

Anne-Marie Slaughter, "Why Women Still Can't Have It All," *The Atlantic*, July/August 2012, http://www.theatlantic.com/magazine/archive/2012/07/why-women-still-cant-have-it-all/309020/.
[39] *Family*, 1.
[40] *Family*, 96.

cowards into heroes, coarse fathers into mild lambs, tenderhearted mothers into ferocious lionesses.[41]

It is in families that we nurture our true humanity. "A person's becoming human occurs within the home; here the foundation is laid for the forming of the future man and woman, of the future father and mother, of the future member of society, of the future citizen, of the future subject in the kingdom of God."[42]

---

[41] *Family*, 96–97.
[42] *Family*, 108.

CHAPTER 8

WORK AND VOCATION

Next to marriage and producing a child in the love union of husband and wife, the closest we humans come to being "cocreators" with God is in our work. There we embody the royal dignity we enjoy as God's image bearers. In the end, of course, we are created for Sabbath, for eternal fellowship with God, but before we who are sinners are ready for such fellowship, we need to be reconciled with God. At the same time, Bavinck insists, being reconciled with God and assured of eternal life is not the whole picture.

> The Calvinist, therefore, is not satisfied when he is personally reconciled with God and assured of His salvation. His *work* begins then in dead earnest, and he becomes a *co-worker* with God. For the Word of God is not only the fountain of the truth of salvation, but also the norm of the whole life; not only glad tidings of salvation for the soul, but also for the body and for the entire world. The Reformed believer continues therefore, "*ad extra*," that reformation which began with himself and in his own heart.[1]

Our work begins once we are personally reconciled with God and assured of our salvation. Stated differently, eternal destiny has a priority over earthly vocation, but the two must never be separated or seen as competitors. The shape of the latter is determined by the former. From another perspective, however, Bavinck does give a creation-based priority to our work in the world: "The spiritual does not come first; the natural does. The first man was earthly, from the earth (1 Cor. 15:45–47), and was given a vocation

---

[1] "Moral Infl.," 52; emphasis added.

also for this world."[2] These two orders of priority are not a contradiction. The former is a *teleological* order referring to our final human destiny, the destiny that shapes our discipleship; the second is a *structural* or *anthropological* order pointing to human creaturely, embodied existence as the arena in which we exercise our discipleship. "Thanks to his body, man is connected to the earth, dependent on it for his existence, and in many respects shares its life." Bavinck then divides our connection to the earth into two responsibilities: "With a view to earth, humans are given a double task, *to fill the earth* and *rule* over it (Gen. 1:[26]; 2:15)."[3] We considered the first of these tasks in the preceding chapter; this chapter is devoted to the second.

Why Work? What Work?

The language of "co-workers," along with "ruling," reminds us that we are God's *covenant* partners who have been given great dignity, responsibility, and liberty. As we noted in chapter 2, God values our moral responsibility and liberty so much that he even gave us the freedom to rebel against him. It is this high and noble view of human beings in their bounded freedom that gives earthly vocations their eternal significance. While the apostle Paul had in mind the gospel ministry when he told the Corinthians to be "always abounding in the work of the Lord, knowing that in the Lord your labor is not in vain" (1 Cor. 15:58), his words are applicable to all faithful work. We work for eternity because the purpose of our work is to glorify God.

> It is this dual vocation that sets the responsibility of work before humans. God, who himself is always at work (John 5:17) and calls us to be like him in this, did not create us for idleness and blissful inactivity. He gave us six days, therefore, for all sorts of labor involving our heads and our hands as we subdue the earth; our work is also a divine institution.[4]

Why do we work? Largely, because of necessity. As the apostle Paul put it—in a warning, to be sure—"If anyone is not willing to work, let him not eat" (2 Thess. 3:10). We can think of this necessity in primarily negative ways as an unfortunate consequence of our fall into sin and God's curse on the man's work in Genesis 3:17–19:

---

[2] "Gen. Prin.," 438.
[3] "Gen. Prin.," 438.
[4] "Gen. Prin.," 438–39.

Cursed is the ground because of you;
  in pain you shall eat of it all the days of your life;
thorns and thistles it shall bring forth for you;
  and you shall eat the plants of the field.
By the sweat of your face
  you shall eat bread,
till you return to the ground,
  for out of it you were taken;
for you are dust,
  and to dust you shall return.

There can be no denying the enormous pain involved in work, from the extremes of body-destroying physical toil and child labor, on the one hand, to unemployment and disability, on the other. There is nothing romantic about the reality of work in our world.

At the same time, however, this is not the only thing to be said about work. Bavinck acknowledges that

> work, then, is certainly made more difficult and onerous as a result of sin—many languages use the same word for "work" and "difficulty" or "trouble"—but work existed before the fall; it was included in being created in God's image and consisted in subjecting in terms of what nowadays is referred to as culture.[5]

We miss a proper understanding of work, he adds, when we "do not continually keep in view the relationship between work and being created in the image of God. Work is rooted in human beings as rational beings and is a likeness of the work that God accomplishes through creation and providence." Here Bavinck takes issue with an evolutionary understanding of humanity, which considers the development of religion and morality, culture and civilization, simply "as the fruit of labor [that] are acquired in the struggle to live." It is of course true "that struggle and need often compel human beings to exert all of their powers; . . . [and] being in need makes one resourceful." What is missing in this explanation, however, is the awareness that human beings "cannot create what does not exist, and people cannot invent new gifts and powers. Work does not *make* a person a rational, moral, and religious being, but presupposes that one *is* such a

---

[5] *Family*, 117–18.

being; in work, a person's humanity comes to light."[6] Our work does not make us; we make our work and through our work we make our world.

Because humans are psychosomatic wholes, work is not just a physical or material activity; "all work displays a spiritual and a material side." Bavinck appeals to biblical anthropology as a ground for this: "The human being consists of body and soul both in one person, and shows this in all his work." This insight is important for our understanding of work because it helps us to avoid what Bavinck calls the "regrettable" and prevalent notion that the word *work* "usually refers only to working with one's hands." In this view, held by many, especially among the "laboring" classes, farmers, plumbers, auto mechanics, and sanitation workers do *real work* while preachers, professors, lawyers, stockbrokers, and writers do not. Bavinck thinks this is all wrong: while it is true "that in one kind of work the spiritual side comes to the fore [and] in another kind of work the physical side predominates," this is a matter of degree rather than absolute difference. "Even in the most spiritual work, a person exerts the body more or less, the philosopher thinks, but only with his brains; the day laborer works with his hands, but also needs his soul, his mental acumen." And Scripture permits no class division along such lines, such as restricting "real work" to physical labor: "Scripture puts it differently, speaking, in connection with the servant of the Lord, of the labor of his soul (Isa. 53:11), talking of working in wisdom, knowledge, and skill (Eccles. 2:21), and often identifying the activity of the apostles with the term *work*." Work is a universal human activity, grounded in our created human nature. "There is no single distinct class of workers, but all people are workers, created in God's image, ordained for service. All work bears and ought to bear a human, that is, a rational and moral character."[7] We have here the highest possible view of human vocation.

This is the appropriate place then to briefly resume the discussion begun in chapter 2 about radical discipleship. I raised questions about "heroic" visions of Christian service being elevated above "ordinary" vocations in "marriage, family, business, vocation, agriculture, industry, commerce, science, art, politics, and society." My intention was not to devalue extraordinary devotion to Christ or to lower the bar for Christian discipleship but to insist upon the legitimacy and holiness of all honest human vocations, each in its own distinct way. Furthermore, we also saw that these "ordi-

---

[6] *Family*, 118.
[7] *Family*, 118–19.

nary" vocations, rooted as they are in our created nature as image bearers of God "ruling" over his world, actually precede the specific call of gospel ministry and kingdom service. The creation order, we noted, is prior to God's work of redemption: "God's act of creation and his creational, natural gifts to humanity all precede the redemption begun with the call of Abraham." *All* Christians who follow Christ in stewarding God's "good and perfect gift[s]" (James 1:17), in whatever vocation, are acting as responsible Christian disciples. As I said then, "We live our Christian lives in the vocations to which God calls us, whatever they may be."

A Christian's Work and "Good Works"

Does this mean that our work is relatively neutral, that we simply work according to the standards of natural law or creation ordinances? Or course not! Does our new identity in Christ then have nothing to say to us about our work? Of course it does! *Who we are* in Christ must definitely affect *what we do* in the world. Our work is at the heart of our sanctification; it is as new creatures in Christ, empowered by the Holy Spirit that we are called to our vocations and work out our holiness in them. But it is precisely here that our considerations of Christian discipleship become tricky. The moment we introduce the language of "work" (and "works") into our discussion of what it means to be a Christian, we are thrown back into the polemics of the Reformation and Counter-Reformation, not to mention the age-old "Paul versus James" discussion. Since we have already traveled along this path in chapter 4, I will not repeat what was said there but focus our attention singly on the issue of work and "works."

In the polemics with Roman Catholic ecclesial teaching and theology, the Reformers were always pressed to distance themselves from "cheap grace," from an understanding of justification by faith alone that led to indifferent and lazy Christians. To capture that age-old debate in a snapshot, let's consider an imaginary dialogue between a representative of Rome and a Reformation Protestant:

> PROTESTANT: We are saved by grace alone, received by faith; there are no "works" needed on our part. Christ has done all the work.
> ROMAN CATHOLIC: If I understand this right, you are saying that you don't have to do *anything* at all. Really? You don't need to cooperate with the Holy Spirit to do good works?

PROTESTANT: Right, not for our justification we don't.

ROMAN CATHOLIC: I can accept this only in part. I too "am persuaded that in the cross and blood of Christ all my faults are unknown, this is indeed necessary, and forms the first access we have to God, but it is not enough. For we must also bring a mind full of piety toward Almighty God, and desirous of performing whatever is agreeable to Him; in this especially, the power of the Holy Spirit resides."[8]

PROTESTANT: So, you are saying that without our works we cannot be justified before God?

ROMAN CATHOLIC: "If anyone says that the sinner is justified by faith alone, meaning that nothing else is required to cooperate in order to obtain the grace of justification, and that it is not in any way necessary that he be prepared and disposed by the action of his own will, let him be anathema."[9]

The challenge to the Reformation doctrine of justification is set before us with a striking contrast in Trent's "Decree on Justification," canon 20: "If anyone says that a man who is justified and however perfect is not bound to observe the commandments of God and the Church, but only to believe, as if the Gospel were a bare and absolute promise of eternal life without the condition of observing the commandments, let him be anathema."

This canon may be less of a challenge to the Reformed tradition than it is to the Lutheran because Reformed people place a high value on law as a rule of gratitude for those who have been saved by grace. Reformed Christians do believe that they ought to obey God's law out of thankfulness for their deliverance from sin, and classic Reformed liturgies include a reading of the Ten Commandments in worship. But significant questions remain for Reformed people as well. Can we be *saved* without doing *anything*? Would this not be "faith without works" and therefore "dead faith"? What about the epistle of James? Is it satisfactory to think of justification as something *only* forensic or legal, a changed status before God's judgment seat? If this is indeed the case, how do we avoid encouraging spiritual sloth? So, then, in a volume where Christian living is understood as "following Jesus in *lawful obedience*," and in a chapter where we are considering our work as part of that lawful obedience, we need to be clear on the relation between grace, faith, works, and our work.

---

[8] Taken from the March 1539 letter of Roman Catholic cardinal Jacopo Sadoleto to the Genevans, in *A Reformation Debate: Sadoleto's Letter to the Genevans and Calvin's Reply*, ed. John C. Olin (New York: Harper Torchbooks, 1966), 35.

[9] Council of Trent, "Decree on Justification," canon 9, http://www.ewtn.com/library/councils/trent6 .htm.

The Heidelberg Catechism recognizes the problem in two different Lord's Days. Lord's Day 24 addresses the question of "good works." Our good works cannot save us because they can never measure up to the requirements of God's law (Q&A 62), and therefore they merit us absolutely nothing (Q&A 63). Then comes the pastorally important question:

> Q. 64. But doesn't this teaching make people indifferent and wicked?

The answer points to a believer's union with Christ as the antidote:

> A. No. It is impossible for those grafted into Christ through true faith not to produce fruits of gratitude.

As though aware of the persistence of either Roman Catholic objections or Reformed practice (or perhaps both), the authors begin the third section of the catechism ("Gratitude") with this question:

> Q. 86. Since we have been delivered from our misery by grace through Christ without any merit of our own, why then should we do good works?

The answer points us to a life of growth in holiness or sanctification:

> A. Because Christ, having redeemed us by his blood, is also restoring us by his Spirit into his image, so that with our whole lives we may show that we are thankful to God for his benefits, so that he may be praised through us, so that we may be assured of our faith by its fruits, and so that by our godly living our neighbors may be won over to Christ.

When the catechism goes on to consider the content of that "godly living," it directs us once again to the law of God:

> Q. 91. What are good works?

> A. Only those which are done out of true faith, conform to God's law, and are done for God's glory; and not those based on our own opinion or human tradition.

In that same vein, the 1891 Christian Social Congress in Amsterdam, responding to Bavinck's report "General Biblical Principles and the Relevance of Concrete Moral Law for the Social Question Today," passed the following as its first resolution: "Holy Scripture teaches that human society must not be ordered according to our own preferences but is bound to those laws that God himself has firmly established in Creation and His Word."[10] The twofold command of love is at the heart of the law: "God's law—written on human hearts—was given as a rule and guide for our entire existence in its internal and external dimensions, covering our daily walk and our commerce. This law is summarized in the duty to love God and the neighbor."[11] In summary, if we regard our work as an integral part of our sanctification in holiness and the new life in Christ that must be guided by God's law, then love of God and love of neighbor are together the key to our understanding and practice of work.

In the preceding paragraphs we traveled the reverse road of our approach in chapter 4, where we began with our union with Christ and moved back to our created nature as human beings. Our concern then was to insist that our union with Christ did not elevate us above our humanity but restored and healed it: "In Christ, the Second Adam, the true man, we become fully human by participating in his humanity. Union with Christ in the power of the Spirit renews us in the true righteousness and holiness for which we were created. We are Christian to be truly human." This restoration is both a new status before God (justification) and a process of inward renewal that is traditionally spoken of as sanctification. We who are declared "not guilty" are also inwardly renewed by the Holy Spirit and united with Christ.[12] Our union with Christ is most definitely *not our work*; sanctification *is* our work, albeit one that cannot be done without the empowering work of the Holy Spirit within us. So, in the same way that we underscored the true humanity that is ours in Christ, the *true man*, we now move in the reverse direction: forward from our new identity to consider our work as *Christians*. Maintaining this order—from redeemed identity to our work in the world—is crucial if we are to avoid the several "work sins" to which we are inclined.

The Reformation and the "Sins" of Work

The preceding broad overview of Reformation teaching may seem obvious to many readers, but from the perspective sketched above I do need to em-

---

[10] "Gen. Prin.," 445.

[11] "Gen. Prin.," 438–39.

[12] Once again, I refer the reader to J. Todd Billings, *Union with Christ: Reframing Theology and Ministry for the Church* (Grand Rapids: Baker, 2011), for a vision of the Christian life that does not set justification as a forensic category over against the pneumatological category of union with Christ but fully embraces both. See the discussion above in chap. 4, pp. 90–95.

phasize two important implications for our perspective on work. The first is that we are not saved by our works, and the second is that our work does not save us. As redundant as that may sound, it is a shorthand warning of two perennial temptations related to work. To say that "we are not saved by our works" is to draw a contrast between two fundamentally different approaches to salvation, the deliverance from the basic mess in which all humans find ourselves. We are saved by grace, not by our own deeds or works. The second phrase, "our work does not save us," directs us to our attitude toward work; as much as we value work, we must not think of it more highly than it deserves.

The first temptation, the Reformation notwithstanding, arises in all our continuing efforts to save ourselves even when we outwardly profess *sola gratia*. Without accusing all who preach the necessity of heroic, radical discipleship of the sin of trying to save themselves, we do need to note how strong the temptation remains in this emphasis, especially when we apply the language of incarnation, of "being Jesus to people," to our own acts of discipleship.[13] The second temptation is the inclination, historically linked especially to Calvinism, of placing so much emphasis on our work, our duty to labor "for the glory of God," that our work becomes an idol that enslaves us. The influential German sociologist Max Weber (1864–1920), best known for his book *The Protestant Ethic and the Spirit of Capitalism*, believed this idolatry to be the condition of modern man and described it as "an iron cage" (*stahlhartes Gehäuse*; literally, "steel-hard shell/case").[14]

When our work exerts that much influence over us, it becomes a kind of heroic discipleship into which we pour all our energy and toil in an effort to do well. While we believe the gospel message and profess that we can be saved only by God's grace in Christ, we still rely far more than we ought to on the work of our hands to meet our needs, ameliorate our hurts, provide for our present and future security, and give us a sense of well-being. We retain a penchant to use our work in redemptive ways. If the first temptation is to think of our heroic discipleship as a salvific activity, as "building God's kingdom on earth," the second temptation is to look for something redemptive in and through our work, to think of what we do as somehow redeeming the sphere of work, at least for ourselves.

---

[13] For a brutally honest, self-critical treatment of the spiritual pitfalls of heroic discipleship, see Peter Greer, with Anna Haggard, *The Spiritual Danger of Doing Good* (Bloomington, MN: Bethany House, 2013).
[14] Max Weber, *The Protestant Ethic and the Spirit of Capitalism*, trans. Talcott Parsons, new introduction by Randall Collins (Los Angeles: Roxbury, 1998), 181.

To help us sort this out, we will briefly consider the significance of the Protestant Reformation on our understanding and practice of work, guided by Bavinck's September 22, 1892, lecture to the Fifth General Council of the Alliance of the Reformed Churches Holding the Presbyterian System, meeting in Toronto, Ontario: "The Influence of the Protestant Reformation on the Moral and Religious Condition of Communities and Nations."[15]

First, a caution is in order. As we reflect on the changes in attitudes toward work brought about by the Reformation, we must be careful not to exaggerate its influence. The Reformation was not the first movement in Western history to emphasize the dignity of work; the idea can be found in the New Testament itself. When the apostle Paul instructs Christian slaves to be obedient to their masters, he tells them: "Whatever you do, work heartily, as for the Lord and not for men, knowing that from the Lord you will receive the inheritance as your reward. You are serving the Lord Christ" (Col. 3:23–24).

Social historians have noted that the early Christians especially viewed menial work quite differently than did their Greco-Roman fellow citizens. At the same time, this too needs to be put into perspective, as Ernst Troeltsch observed in his classic *Social Teachings of the Christian Churches*: "The saying that 'Christianity has dignified labour' ought not to be exaggerated. The appreciation of labour was only natural since so many of the early Christians belonged to the lower classes."[16] As we draw contrasts between the Reformation and medieval Catholicism, we must also remember that the monastic ideal, notably the Rule of Saint Benedict, insisted on the importance of work. Chapter 48 of the Rule begins: "Idleness is the enemy of the soul; and therefore the brethren ought to be employed in manual labor at certain times, at others, in devout reading."[17] Hence the Latin motto *Ora et labora* (pray and labor), which has generally been associated with the Benedictine order.

So, then, what did the Reformation achieve, especially with respect to work? According to Bavinck, the Reformation was a "religio-ethical movement . . . [that] sought peace of soul with God, liberty to serve Him according to His word, [and] satisfaction for deep spiritual yearnings." Over against the "sacramental system and outward morality" of Rome, the

---

[15] I.e., "Moral Infl."
[16] Ernst Troeltsch, *The Social Teaching of the Christian Churches*, trans. Olive Wyon, 2 vols. (Louisville: Westminster John Knox, 1992), 1:119.
[17] Accessed October 29, 2013, http://www.ccel.org/ccel/benedict/rule2/files/rule2.html#ch48.

Reformation believed that "the entire ethical life originates in religion, in faith, and is itself nothing but a serving of the Lord. The antithesis of consecrated and unconsecrated collapses and makes way for that of holy and unholy. The natural is recognized in its value, and is sanctified by faith in Christ."[18]

It is helpful here to compare and contrast Bavinck's description of the Reformation viewpoint with that of Rome's great medieval teacher Thomas Aquinas.[19] Thomas divides human life into two parts, the *active* life and the *contemplative* life, or the *practical* and the *speculative* life. The first in each pairing is represented in Holy Scripture by Leah and Martha, and the second by Rachel and Mary.[20] In addition, Thomas says that all contemplation, in the final analysis, is a matter of seeking God and not just any truth whatsoever.[21] The contemplative life is superior to the active life in several ways. In the first place, only the contemplative life endures into eternity: "The active life ends with this world."[22] Second, the superiority of the contemplative life was taught by our Lord when he said to Martha that her sister Mary "had chosen the better part."[23] The contemplative life also results in greater merits than the active life,[24] even though the active life precedes the contemplative "in the order of generation." What finally seals the deal for Thomas is the direction of each: "The contemplative life is directed to the love of God, not of any degree but to that which is perfect; whereas the active life is necessary for any degree of the love of neighbor."[25] The perfection of the Christian life for Thomas consists chiefly and "radically" in Christian charity, which itself is further divided between love of God and love of neighbor.[26]

Thomas's remaining questions on the two different lives[27] are careful, thoughtful, and nuanced, challenging many simplistic Protestant commentators who far too easily dismiss his views as elevating the contemplative life of the "religious" and the three counsels of perfection (poverty, chastity, obedience) so high that there is no room for the "ordinary" active

---

[18] "Moral Infl.," 48, 49.
[19] The summary that follows is taken from Thomas's *Summa theologica*, IIaIIae, qq. 179–89, in Thomas Aquinas, *Summa Theologica*, 5 vols., trans. Fathers of the English Dominican Province (Allen, TX: Christian Classics, 1981), 4:1923–2010.
[20] Q. 179.
[21] Q. 180, art. 4.
[22] Q. 181, art. 4.
[23] Q. 182, art. 1.
[24] Q. 182, art. 2.
[25] Q. 182, art. 4.
[26] Q. 184, arts. 1, 4.
[27] Qq. 185–89.

life of loving one's neighbor. Such claims distort the subtlety of Thomas's thought and violate the ninth commandment against bearing false witness. It is fair, nonetheless, to say that Thomas does provide the theological grounds for thinking about the Christian life in hierarchical terms that are linked to merit. *Some* ways of living in *some* areas—notably in the "religious" life of orders and monasteries—are morally superior to others and more meritorious. The Reformation's doctrine of justification deleted the category of merit from all thinking about the Christian life and dramatically leveled the notion of Christian vocation. *All* Christians in *all* vocations were equal in their standing before God—both before and after the pardon of justification—and were *free* to serve, honor, and glorify their Maker and Redeemer, wherever they were placed.

As we resume our quick summary of Bavinck's 1892 Toronto address, we observe that Bavinck's argument is mostly historical. He points to the actual changes that took place in Europe, notably in Switzerland, the Low Countries, and the British Isles, and finally in America. This, it is worth noting, is also the precipitating factor in Max Weber's famous study on Protestantism and capitalism. Here is his opening sentence:

> A glance at the occupational statistics of any country of mixed religious composition brings to light with remarkable frequency a situation which has several times provoked discussion in the Catholic press and literature, and in Catholic congresses in Germany, namely, the fact that business leaders and owners of capital, as well as the higher grades of skilled labour, and even more the higher technically and commercially trained personnel of modern enterprises, are overwhelmingly Protestant.[28]

The influence on the "religious condition of nations" came about, says Bavinck, because the Reformation "made religion a personal matter, and encouraged liberty of conscience." More so than Lutherans, Reformed people grasped the "great and rich thought . . . that Christ is not only king of the soul, but of the body as well; not only of the church, but of the entire plane of all human life." "The Swiss Reformation was radical and total." Calvinism was not satisfied with justification by faith, "but had no peace until it had found the eternal in and behind the temporal." The temporal was seen to be the "bearer of the eternal"—*caducum eterna tuetur.*

---

[28] Weber, *Protestant Ethic*, 35.

The Calvinist found no rest for his thinking, no more than for his heart, until he rested in God, the eternal and unchangeable. He penetrated into the holiest of holies of the temple, to the final ground of things, and did not cease his search after the "αἰτία" ["cause," "reason"], the "διότι" ["wherefore"] of things, till he had found the answer in the eternal and sovereign pleasure, in the " εὐδοκία τοῦ θεοῦ" ["good pleasure of God"].

A Calvinist "looks over the whole world" from a "high spiritual, theological standpoint"; "he sees everything *sub specie aeternítatis,*—broad and wide and far. In his system all depends, not on any creature but only, on God Almighty." In sum:

> In the religious life, as it reveals itself in Reformed circles, as well as in doctrine, *the Sovereignty of God stands foremost.* Not the love of the Father, as in many modern circles; not the person of Christ, as among the Moravians; not the inner testimony of the Holy Spirit, as among the Anabaptists and Friends; but the Sovereignty of God, in the entire work of salvation, and over the whole expanse of the religious life, *is here the starting-point and the ruling idea.*[29]

This belief in the sovereignty of God, fed by "strict preaching of God's justice and law, awakens a deep feeling of guilt and unworthiness in man, and . . . prostrates him deeply in the dust before God's sovereign majesty." At the same time, "it elevates him to a singular height of blessedness, and . . . it causes him to rest in the free, eternal, and unchangeable good pleasure of the Father." The result is sturdy Christians, "men of marble, with a character of steel, with a will of iron, with an insuperable power, with an extraordinary energy." Bavinck points to the importance of predestination in one's understanding: "Elected by God, he recognizes in himself and in all creatures nothing but instruments in the Divine hand. He distinguishes sharply between the Creator and the creature, and, in his religion, he will know nothing but God and His Word." Convicted by the sovereignty of God and passionate about liberty of conscience, sturdy and fierce men such as this defied bishops, rebelled against tyrants, and created impressively successful commercial societies such as the Golden Age of Dutch history in the seventeenth century.[30]

---

[29] "Moral Infl.," 49–51.
[30] "Moral Infl.," 51.

Calvinism's Legacy and Challenge

To consider work the activity of free people who have been set apart by God in grace and called to glorify him in their daily vocations elevates both the person and the work to royal status and dignity. In our work we become partners with God, co-laborers in creative development of the plenitude of resources God has placed within creation. Taking the Word of God "as the norm of the whole life; not only glad tidings of salvation for the soul, but also for the body and for the entire world," the Reformed person moves beyond "that reformation which began with himself and in his own heart" and seeks God's glorifying work in all areas of life. "The family and the school, the Church and Church government, the State and society, art and science, all are fields which he has to work and to develop for the glory of God." Bavinck acknowledges a shadowy side to Calvinism's "seriousness": "Puritanism has thus sometimes nourished a hardness of sentiment, a coldness of heart, and a severity of judgment, which cannot impress favourably. The free, the genial, the spontaneous, in the moral life, have often been oppressed and killed by it." Yet, whatever asceticism one might discover in Calvinism's history, Bavinck insists that this was not rooted in a hostile attitude to natural life: "But the Calvinistic rigorism was born from the desire to consecrate the whole life to God"; it was an attempt not to "bridle the natural man" but rather "to sanctify him." And, furthermore, any honest self-examination will lead us to acknowledge that ascetic restraint is an understandable, even if excessive, response to sin's reality within each of us.

> And if [Calvinism] has thus been guilty of exaggeration, and if it has often disowned and killed the natural, everyone who recognizes the power and extensive dominion of sin will feel the difficulty here to walk in the right way, and equally to avoid conformity to and flight from the world, the worship and the despisal of the same.[31]

Furthermore, Calvinism's "innerworldly asceticism" (Weber's term) has produced valuable "bourgeois" virtues for our life together.

> The strict morality of Calvinism has, moreover, nourished a series of beautiful virtues: domesticity, order, neatness, temperance, chastity, obedience, earnestness, industry, sense of duty, etc. These may not be-

---

[31] "Moral Infl.," 52–54.

long to the brilliant and heroic virtues; they are specially civic virtues, and are of inestimable value to a people. Thereby the Calvinistic nations have laid by, in store, a capital of moral possessions, on which the present generations are still living.[32]

Calvinism, according to Bavinck, is a religious-ethical vision of the world and the human person that "tolerates neither hierarchy in the Church, nor tyranny in the State" and serves as a "principle of liberty" for people in "Switzerland, the Netherlands, England, and America." "All the nations, among whom Calvinism became a power, distinguish themselves by extraordinary activity, clearness of thought, religious spirit, love of liberty, and by a treasure of civic virtues, which are not found, to that extent, among Catholic nations."[33]

As we saw earlier, observing this difference inspired Max Weber to do his research for *The Protestant Ethic and the Spirit of Capitalism*. Toward the end of the twentieth century, as many in Latin America responded to the economic plight of the southern Americas with various forms of liberation theology, theologian Michael Novak pointed out that religion was an obvious key difference between the success of North America and the stagnant economies of South America. "Both continents were discovered by Europeans at about the same time. Both continents were colonized by the greatest naval powers in the world at that time, Spain and Britain." Populations of both grew "side by side" and "for more than a century, South America seemed far richer than North America, yielding silver and lead to ornament the churches and public buildings of Spain, while North America produced corn, tobacco, furs, and cotton."[34] However, while North America developed a new political economy built on liberty, private property, and a rich voluntary associational life, Latin America "retained the aristocratic traditions of Europe," including a "plantation system and agrarian ethos" much like the Southern US states prior to the Civil War.

The economic system of South America was mercantilist or, in Max Weber's phrase, *patrimonial*; state controls and family heritage governed it; there were hardly any free markets or industry; there was not much of a

---

[32] "Moral Infl.," 54.
[33] "Moral Infl.," 54–55.
[34] Michael Novak, ed., *Liberation South, Liberation North* (Washington, DC: American Enterprise Institute, 1981), 1.

middle class, little tradition of widespread home ownership, and only a little small, independent farming.[35]

And religious difference lay at the root of this disparity.

In religion, Latin America was not merely very largely Catholic, but Latin, with greater affinity to the Catholicism of Spain, Portugal, and Italy than to the Catholicism of France, Germany, Great Britain, Ireland, and Eastern Europe. By contrast, North America had a more Protestant ethos, shared more or less by most of the Catholics (about one-quarter of the population) that now dwell in it.[36]

I have included this brief note from a contemporary Roman Catholic writer to show that Bavinck's understanding of the Protestant Reformation's profound influence on nations and communities with respect to work has stood the test of time very well. Yet, these observations must be understood properly and used carefully. In the first place, it would be a mistake to point to a particular doctrine, such as justification, and attribute all the good of the modern world, including liberty and prosperity, to a single teaching. Historical causality is never that simple. Nor does it mean that Christians need to traverse the complex theological paths of Reformation debates about justification before they can do their work faithfully. This is what is important about the Reformation teaching on justification: *because of the atoning work of Christ on our behalf and in our place, and the justifying work of God the Holy Spirit in believing hearts, we are set free from works righteousness so that we can work.* Justification by grace, through faith, means that our work must never be given redemptive significance; our work does not redeem us and we do not redeem our work. And it is important to *know* that—to be convinced in one's soul that one is free to work.

With that in mind we can now look at the reality of sin in the development of our modern democratic, free market societies. The narrative we just completed underscored the important role of Protestant, and especially Calvinist, Christianity in creating this new order. This portrayal simply describes the influence, focusing on the result, without going into detail about how the greater freedom and prosperity of key nations like

---

[35] Ibid., 2.
[36] Ibid., 3.

the Netherlands, England, and the United States historically came about. In particular, it overlooks the darker side of this history, such as the dislocation and suffering that accompanied the move to industrialization and urbanization. Thus, the narrative I provided must not be seen as a single uninterrupted progressive realization of greater freedom and prosperity. "Progress" came with significant costs. The Industrial Revolution—driven by technological innovation in iron and steel production and a shift from cottage industry to factory production—led to mass movements of working people from rural areas into the urban centers of Europe during the nineteenth century. The result was a growing number of urbanized poor who struggled to meet the basic necessities of life and lived in appalling conditions. This is why "the social question" was on the front burner of European Christian consciousness during the second half of the nineteenth century, producing such important works as Pope Leo XIII's 1891 encyclical *Rerum Novarum* (on the plight of the worker), and Abraham Kuyper's opening address to the Amsterdam First Christian Social Congress, "The Social Question and the Christian Religion."[37] And it was for this Social Congress that Bavinck prepared his report "General Biblical Principles and the Relevance of Concrete Mosaic Law for the Social Question Today," which we will now consider.

Bavinck's essay strikes us immediately with its indirectness. Unlike many of the social critics of his day, such as Karl Marx (1818–1883), and Christian socialists, such as the Anglicans F. D. Maurice (1805–1887) and Charles Kingsley (1819–1875), as well as American social-gospel theologian Walter Rauschenbusch (1861–1918), he does not start with a description of the lamentable conditions he has seen and ask, What must we do about them? Nor does he begin by summarizing the "spirit of revolutionary change, which has long been disturbing the world," as Pope Leo XIII did in his encyclical on capital and labor, *Rerum Novarum*. Instead, Bavinck begins with a *normative* description of human calling before the face of God and with reflections on our dual—earthly and heavenly—destiny and calling. God gave us six days to work and a seventh day, which he blessed and hallowed "so that humans could rest from their labors and make heaven

---

[37] Leo's encyclical has been published in many different formats. A handy one-volume collection of Roman Catholic social teaching is Michael Walsh and Brian Davies, eds., *Proclaiming Justice and Peace: Papal Documents from Rerum Novarum to Centesimus Annus*, rev. ed. (Mystic, CT: Twenty-Third Publications, 1991). Abraham Kuyper, *De sociale vraagstuk en de Christelijke religie* (Amsterdam: Wormser, 1891); ET: *The Problem of Poverty*, ed. James W. Skillen (Washington, DC: Center for Public Justice; Grand Rapids: Baker, 1991).

rather than earth the final goal of their work. Together with all creatures humans are called to find their rest in fellowship with God."[38]

This is followed by a discussion of sin and the way sin destroys our relation not only to God but also to other human beings and to creation. God's command concerning our work does not change: "We are still given the responsibility to fill the earth and subdue it." But everything *has* changed in ourselves and in the conditions under which we do our work: "The character of our labor now is changed: women bear children in pain and sorrow, and men eat bread by the sweat of their brow because nature is no longer cooperative but antagonistic." Even the creation has become a hostile power arrayed against us: "Human dominion over creation has given way to [a] situation where nature is indifferent even hostile, where 'thorns and thistles,' the animals of the field, and the forces of nature are our enemies." The result is very familiar and lamentable: "Our labor has become a struggle merely to survive. Paradise is closed behind us and we are sent out into the raw, wasted world without any weapons." Consequently, we feel God's judgment on us: "Rebellion against God's law never goes unpunished; sin is itself misery and is followed by an ocean of disasters." Bavinck is no naïve romantic but brutally honest about the ravages of sin.

> Shattered souls and broken bodies are the wrecks of justice; inner dis-
> turbance, a sense of guilt, an agonized conscience, and fear of punish-
> ment gnaw at the hidden life of every human being. Illness and troubles,
> tragedies and evils, mourning and death, all take away the joys of our
> earthly life. Dust celebrates its triumph in the grave; destruction sings
> its victory song.[39]

Bavinck does not shy away from the brokenness of work in our world; but he also refuses to regard as mere victims the people who suffer because of the curse on work. By calling attention to human responsibility, sin, guilt, and God's judgment, he upholds human royal dignity. We are rebels and lawbreakers and bring upon ourselves the miseries and disasters that beset us, either individually or corporately.

At the same time, God providentially upholds his creation and even restrains the "devastating path of sin's work over time." "In his role as

---

[38] "Gen. Prin.," 438.
[39] "Gen. Prin.," 439–40.

Creator and Sustainer God redirects sin, opposes it and reins it in so that sin does not annihilate creation and frustrate his decree." Remarkably, Bavinck begins his list of ways that God does this by referring "in the first place, [to] the punishments and judgments that he [God] links to sin." As we human beings experience the consequences of our own sin, as well as the corporate sins of others, we experience both the judgment and the mercy of God.

> Restless souls, the trials of life, the struggle for existence, the toils of our daily labor, all of these are, at the same time, revelations of divine wrath and instruments of his common grace, by which he throws obstacles in the path of sin's progress and opposes the most horrific outbursts of sin.

In addition, God allows "a few weak remnants of his image and likeness to remain [after the fall]. He grants them reason and conscience; preserves in them some knowledge of his existence and character, a seed of religion; a moral sense of good and evil; and a consciousness of our eternal destiny." God also "awakens in the human heart a natural love between men and women, parents and children [and] nurtures a variety of social virtues among people: a pull toward social relationships and a longing for affection and friendship."[40]

But since none of this is enough, God also called a people unto himself, made a covenant with them, established them in their own land, and gave them laws by which to live, laws that if kept would lead to social peace and human flourishing. This community, called to obedience, is also challenged to be merciful. In cases where people fell into poverty and need, Israel was given clear instructions about the ministry of mercy, including rights of poor people to glean in the fields, debt forgiveness in Sabbath and jubilee years, and the expectation that those with disabilities and the elderly were well treated. Bavinck adds:

> God's law even provided for the life and well-being of animals, including their rest (Ex. 20:10; Deut. 25:4; 22:6; 23:9, etc.). This entire ministry of mercy is repeatedly predicated on Israel's oppression and sojourning in Egypt (Ex. 22:20; 23:9; etc.). Israel's moral law is written from the vantage point of the oppressed.[41]

---

[40] "Gen. Prin.," 440.
[41] "Gen. Prin.," 442.

In addition to affirming their royal dignity and responsibility, Bavinck also insists that God's people are called to *priestly* compassion.

Recall that the congress is wrestling with a biblical answer to the pressing "social question" of the day. Bavinck is not satisfied with only paying attention to the external symptoms of the social upheaval and unrest of his day but wants to penetrate deep into the very heart of the problem: human sin. Before we can deal with the symptoms, we must cure the disease itself. The first step is clear:

> Thus, the first order of the day is restoring our proper relationship with God. The cross of Christ, therefore, is the heart and mid-point of the Christian religion. Jesus did not come, first of all, to renew families and reform society but to save sinners and to redeem the world from the coming wrath of God. This salvation of our souls must be our ultimate concern for which we are willing to sacrifice everything: father and mother, house and field, even our own lives, in order to inherit the kingdom of heaven (Matt. 6:33; 16:26).

When we are brought into a proper relationship with God in Christ, then "all other human relationships are given a new ordering and led back to their original state."[42] Our relationships and the differences that characterize them are relativized by our union in Christ. "Distinctions in our social life remain but they lose their sharp edge." Here's how Bavinck applies that directly to our work:

> The New Testament is overflowing with warnings against riches (Matt. 6:19; 19:23; 1 Tim. 6:17–19, etc.), but poverty is no virtue and the natural is not unclean in itself (Mark 7:15ff.; Acts 14:17; Rom. 14:14; 1 Tim. 4:4). Work is commended and tied to food and wages (Matt. 10:10; 1 Tim. 5:18; Eph. 4:28; 2 Thess. 3:10).[43]

In the face of massive dislocation and pauperization, Bavinck does not come up with a grand scheme for reordering society or redistributing wealth. His effort is more basic: to point to the spiritual renewal and moral uplift that all people need in order to flourish. He is not suggesting that individual repentance and renewal will by itself result in social and economic uplift; only the moral renewal of a community, a collective people,

---

[42] "Gen. Prin.," 443.
[43] "Gen. Prin.," 444.

a nation can accomplish that, and such moral renewal needs to be accompanied by just laws and social policies. We will take a closer, more detailed look at Bavinck's understanding of society and social relationships in chapter 10, but for the purposes of this chapter, notice the important principle adopted by the 1891 congress with respect to human calling. Individual responsibility is maintained here, but there is also a clear recognition that human flourishing in work and vocation also requires conditions of *liberty* and *opportunity* that can come about only through corporate decision and action.

> [Resolution] #5: According to Scripture the important general principle for a solution to the social question is that there be justice (*gerechtigheid*). This means that each person be assigned to the place where, in accord with their nature, they are able to live according to God's ordinances with respect to God and other creatures.[44]

Bavinck's insistence that we start with the fact of human sin and the need we all have to be reconciled to God is not the end of the matter; he calls for practical, concrete steps to create the conditions under which people can flourish. Scripture, he says, directs us not only to be concerned about people's eternal destiny "but also to make it possible for them to fulfill their earthly calling." Christians should therefore seek to "uphold the institution of the Sabbath" and work for polices that

- prevent poverty and misery, especially pauperization,
- oppose the accumulation of capital and landed property; [and]
- ensure, as much as possible, a "living wage" for every person.

Bavinck is clear about the realistic character of his vision; Christian hope is not utopian. Resolution 8 says, "There remains, in addition to this, a very large role for the ministry of mercy since, thanks to the working of sin and error, all kinds of miseries will always be with us, and in this earthly dwelling can never be removed by justice [alone]."[45]

In sum: Without any work on our part, we are set free to work and to do good works, knowing that "our labor in the Lord is not in vain." If we are to flourish in our work, we must be free from all "works righteousness"; we

---

44 "Gen. Prin.," 445.
45 "Gen. Prin.," 446.

cannot save ourselves by our work, and if we use our work as an attempt to satisfy our anxieties about our own security and welfare, our work will kill us, spiritually as well as physically. We cannot justify our existence by our work, and shouldn't try to, because we don't need to; we are already justified in Christ. Strictly speaking, there is nothing *redemptive* in our work.

Once we have stopped justifying ourselves through our work, however, we are liberated to honor God in our work as an integral part of our Christian discipleship and sanctification. Honest labor remains a noble and high calling in which we are able to use God's gifts in creation, in society, and in ourselves to praise him. That's what it is all about. Therefore, *Labora ad maiorem Dei gloriam* (Work for the greater glory of God).

CHAPTER 9

CULTURE AND EDUCATION

Our work produces culture. Since the word *culture* comes from the same root as *cultivate* (and that root means "to till [the soil]"), the link between the most basic and essential kind of human work and culture seems apparent. Working is integral to our humanity, and culture is thus produced whenever and wherever humans work, starting with the most basic product: agri*culture.* In our reflections on culture we must not begin with or restrict ourselves to those rarified ("cultivated"?) understandings that point to good taste and refined sensibilities in the arts, humanities, and the like, as in this dictionary definition: "enlightenment and excellence of taste acquired by intellectual and aesthetic training." A subsequent definition in the same dictionary captures it much better: "the integrated pattern of human knowledge, belief, and behavior that depends upon the capacity for learning and transmitting knowledge to succeeding generations."[1] Culture is therefore more than skills and technical know-how; culture is the product of accumulated communal wisdom about the world that can be passed on to develop cultured people and build a civilization. For that reason education is intrinsically connected with the notion of culture; cultures are multigenerational phenomena, and people have developed effective ways to educate new generations so that civilization can continue.

Religion, Nature, Work, and Culture

From a social point of view, culture begins in the family, the crucible of all civilizing. Thinking *theologically* about culture, however, one has to begin

---

[1] *Merriam-Webster's Collegiate Dictionary*, 11th ed. (Springfield, MA: Merriam-Webster, 2008), senses 4a and 5a.

with religion, with the reality that human beings live in the presence of God. Says Bavinck:

> Religion is not limited to one single human faculty but embraces the human being as a whole. The relation to God is total and central. We must love God with all our mind, all our soul, and all our strength. Precisely because God is God he claims us totally, in soul and body, with all our capacities and in all our relations.

Anthropologically speaking, "head, heart, and hand are all equally— though each in its own way—claimed by religion; it takes the whole person, soul and body, into its service."[2] While it is true that nothing falls outside the scope of religion, it is important to distinguish religion "from all the forces of culture" and acknowledge its independence. Here Bavinck rests his case on a faculty psychology of the human person. "While religion embraces the whole person, science, morality, and art are respectively rooted in the intellect, the will, and the emotions." Bavinck resists all attempts to explain the origin of religion by scientific historical means. To the best of our knowledge, he notes, religion and culture go together: "Wherever we witness human beings in action, they are already in possession of religion. Strictly speaking, cultureless peoples do not exist, and 'primitive man,' the human without religion, morality, reason, or language, is a fiction."[3]

Bavinck considers human persons as richly blessed because of the numerous relationships that arise from our nature as embodied spirits. This makes us the crown of God's creation: "Creation culminates in humanity where the spiritual and material worlds are joined together."[4] Humans are "spiritual" creatures because, unlike the animals,

> man . . . did not . . . come forth from the earth, but had the breath of life breathed into him by God (Gen. 2:7); because he received his life-principle from God (Eccles. 12:7); because he has a spirit of his own, distinct from the Spirit of God (Gen. 41:8; 45:27; Ex. 35:21; Deut. 2:30; Judg. 15:19; Ezek. 3:14; Zech. 12:1; Matt. 26:41; Mark 2:8; Luke 1:47; 23:46; John 11:33; Acts 7:59; 17:16; Rom. 8:16; 1 Cor. 2:11; 5:3–5; 1 Thess. 5:23; Heb. 4:12; 12:23; etc.); and because as such he is akin to

---

[2] *RD*, 1:268.
[3] *RD*, 1:269.
[4] *RD*, 2:511.

the angels, can also think spiritual or heavenly things, and if necessary also exist without a body.[5]

Bavinck explicitly compares humans with angels, detailing no fewer than five reasons why we humans should consider ourselves "superior" to angels. Notwithstanding its length, Bavinck's fourth reason is worth citing in full because its details are highly relevant to our consideration of culture:

> Fourth, angels may be the mightier spirits, but humans are the richer of the two. In intellect and power angels far surpass humans. But in virtue of the marvelously rich relationships in which humans stand to God, the world, and humanity, they are psychologically deeper and mentally richer. The relations that sexuality and family life, life in the family and state and society, life devoted to labor and art and science, bring with them make every human a microcosm, which in multifacetedness, in depth, and in richness far surpasses the personality of angels. Consequently also, the richest and most glorious attributes of God are knowable and enjoyable only by humans. Angels experience God's power, wisdom, goodness, holiness, and majesty; but the depths of God's compassions only disclose themselves to humans. The full image of God, therefore, is only unfolded in creaturely fashion in humans—better still, in *humanity*.[6]

Human beings work and create culture because they are spiritual beings, embodied *souls*. We are material creatures but our spirits enable us to rise above the limits imposed by our materiality. The human capacity for rising above basic bodily appetites and creating structures of meaning, including social institutions, provides safety and order for our physical existence. As embodied spiritual beings we cannot escape our physical world altogether, but we are also not bound to it as something unalterable and limited. We cannot control the weather, but we can build homes with central heating and air conditioning; we cannot eliminate illness and disease completely, but we have eradicated smallpox worldwide and polio in all but a few countries, and are significantly prolonging the lives of people with HIV/AIDS. Our capacity to do all these things is spiritual and defines us as cultural creatures. We have nothing like this at all in mind when we speak, let us say, of "bee cultures" or "ant colonies." Bavinck says, in summary:

---

[5] *RD*, 2:556.
[6] *RD*, 2:462.

But man is "soul," because from the very beginning the spiritual component in him (unlike that of the angels) is adapted to and organized for
a body and is bound, also for his intellectual and spiritual life, to the
sensory and external faculties; because he can rise to the higher faculties only from a substratum of the lower ones; and hence, because he is
a sentient and material being and as such is related to the animals. Man
is a rational animal, a thinking reed, a being existing between angels
and animals, related to but distinct from both. He unites and reconciles
within himself both heaven and earth, things both invisible and visible.

It is precisely in this way that we see ourselves as the image and likeness
of God.[7]

Work and culture are related to each other as nature is to history; culture is the product of *purposive* work that creates history. Human beings till
the soil for crops, husband fruit trees, and domesticate animals, all to meet
the basic need for food. But they also cut down trees for lumber and shelter
and mine coal from the earth for fuel and heat. They do this in community
with other humans and create distinct patterns of agriculture, eating and
drinking, architecture and social life, all of which are accompanied by cer-
emonies and rituals to produce *civilizations*. God created the world with
all its resource potential and providentially upholds it, but he also gave
humans the responsibility to work in cooperation with his purposes and
in response to his continuous omnipresence. All culture is a response to
God's (general) revelation; clarity about the proper place of human beings
in the ways of God with the world came through the special revelation to
Israel and in Jesus Christ. In Bavinck's words:

> Christianity was conceived of as a cooperation of the will of reasonable
> creatures with Divine providence which wants to lead people to an es-
> tablished goal, namely, the kingdom of God. . . . With Christianity God
> himself enters history and leads people to the realization of his goal. In
> Christianity God becomes the God of history. For the ancient peoples God
> always remained a force of nature . . . but in Christianity God is the God
> of history who fulfills his council in the world.[8]

With the coming of the gospel of Jesus Christ into the Greco-Roman world
the very conception of God was changed; he was seen no longer as merely

---

[7] *RD*, 2:556.
[8] *ESSR*, 97.

"supreme reason" and "substance," but as a "person" who is "almighty, holy, gracious Will." The course of the world was understood no longer as a simple "development of nature," but as a "wonderful drama" because human cooperation with God's own purposes takes place alongside willful resistance to them.[9]

Remarkably, the preceding excerpts were from a presentation first delivered not to an audience of sympathetic Reformed Christians but to the Upper Chamber (Senate) of the Dutch Parliament on December 29, 1911. The occasion was a debate about the government's budget for its colonial management in the Dutch East Indies, particularly the schools.[10] A previous speaker argued that the colony needed modernization and that the superstitions of Christianity often impeded such progress. Education, particularly in the natural sciences, needed to be placed "under the protection of the Enlightenment, and proceed from the thesis that phenomena can be explained from natural causes." The speaker concluded:

> Therefore, the *Enlightenment* must be brought to the Dutch East Indies, lest a knowledge of natural science enter it too slowly, and we must be very careful that the natives do not receive a poor understanding of Christianity, and turn it into a weapon for animism and in that way thwart the enlightenment.[11]

In response, Bavinck contended that culture and education cannot be divorced from their religious roots. Furthermore, after the decline of Greece and the fall of Rome, "the scholarship of classical antiquity" was preserved and even "augmented and expanded in many respects" first by Arab schools and then by Christian academies.[12] Bavinck disputes the modernist dismissal of the medieval period as "dark ages," calling this "a judgment [that] rests on ignorance and is very one-sided." He points to three factors that show how irresponsible such a contemptuous dismissal is:

(1) Medieval Christianity brought about the Christianization and civilization of the new peoples;
(2) it gave life to the oldest and most famous universities;
(3) it tackled the most basic issues with tremendous intellectual power and raised the humanities to an exceptional height never achieved before.[13]

---

[9] *ESSR*, 97.
[10] *ESSR*, 81n.
[11] *ESSR*, 89; Bavinck's speech was a response to fellow senator C. Th. van Deventer; cf., *ESSR*, 81n1.
[12] *ESSR*, 94.
[13] *ESSR*, 94–95.

Bavinck acknowledges that the medieval achievement "suffered from many deficiencies," such as awarding "too much authority to antiquity," neglecting "observation" of nature, and believing "it could find all wisdom in books." These deficiencies, he says, are even acknowledged by Roman Catholics, and Protestants should not be reluctant to follow suit. Nonetheless, these deficiencies were a historical accident, not a matter of principle, because scholasticism was committed to observation as the path to knowledge and rejected the notion of innate ideas.[14] As he considers the great intellectual changes that took place "when the knowledge of nature and the philosophy of nature of the Greeks and Arabs invaded Western Europe," Bavinck points to the "unmistakable influence" of Christianity in the process, owing to its exalted view of nature.

> The Holy Scriptures—through psalmists and prophets, Jesus and the apostles—presented a view of nature so rich and beautiful that it not only produced an unsurpassed poetry of nature in Israel but also brought into being in the Christian church a lofty, and yet basically very sound, philosophy of nature as is found nowhere else, through men such as Gregory of Nyssa, Athanasius, Saint Augustine, and Thomas Aquinas.[15]

The biblical worldview transformed human attitudes toward nature and profoundly shaped the culture that arose from human interaction with nature.

> While paganism always hovers between reckless abuse of the world and a childish fear of its mysterious forces, the Hebrew with sovereign self-assurance encounters nature without being afraid of it, and yet with an awareness of being highly responsible, because as a man of God he has the calling to subdue and manage it.[16]

Nature, History, and Culture

Following Bavinck's lead in his *Philosophy of Revelation*,[17] we may tie several thoughts together and provide some key definitions. "Culture," he says, "in the broadest sense thus includes all the labor which human power exerts on nature." In speaking of nature, however, we need to distinguish

---

[14] *ESSR*, 95.
[15] *ESSR*, 96.
[16] *ESSR*, 96.
[17] In the chapter "Revelation and Culture," in *PofR*, 242–69.

"the whole visible world of phenomena which is outside man" from "man himself; not his body alone, but his soul also." The gifts given to human beings are also gifts from God; "they are a gift of nature, and these gifts are a means for cultivating the external world, as well as an object which must be cultivated." Consequently, we must speak of

> two great circles of culture. To the first belong all those activities of man for the production and distribution of material goods, such as agriculture, cattle rearing, industry and trade. And the second circle includes all that labor whereby man realizes objectively his ideals of the true, the good, the beautiful, by means of literature and science, justice and statecraft, works of beauty and art, and at the same time works out his own development and civilization.[18]

In the previous section I introduced the category of *history*, adding the notion of purposiveness to *nature* as the working material of human culture. We also took note of Bavinck's witness to a biblical worldview in a remarkable speech to the Upper Chamber of Parliament about Dutch colonial policy in the East Indies. Because the Bible reveals God to be a person and his law a personal will, and because this personal God is the Creator and Sustainer of all, and human beings are created in his image, we are called to "cooperate" with God in a "wonderful drama." Bavinck's historical review of developments from the Middle Ages on pointed to the significant role that Christianity played in the creation of the modern world, notably its science. However, in his speech to the Senate Bavinck did not limit himself to showing how a biblical view of nature was essential for the development of modern science and thus how it changed history; the very understanding of *history* itself was transformed by Christianity. It was, above all, in the changed perception of history that Christianity left its most significant mark on culture.

Bavinck highlights the difference between the Greek view of history found in writers such as Herodotus—whom Bavinck says is rightfully "called the father of history"—and the Christian view of history, and he uses a brilliant rhetorical strategy to point out the distinction and its warrant. For confirmation of this he appeals not to an established Christian source but to a source that even secular people in the Dutch Senate would have to acknowledge as informed and impartial, the German litterateur/

---

[18] *PofR*, 249–50.

philosopher Rudolf Christoph Eucken (1846–1926), the father of "practical idealism" or "activism." According to Eucken, "history meant far more to Christianity than it did to the Ancient World" because of the incarnation: "It was the Christian conviction that the divine had appeared in the domain of time, not as a pale reflection but in the fullness of its glory; hence as the dominating central force of the whole it must relate the whole past to itself and unfold the whole future out of itself."

> Christ could not come again and yet again to let himself be crucified; hence as the countless historical cycles of the Ancient World disappeared, there was no longer the old eternal recurrence of things. History ceased to be a uniform rhythmic repetition and became a comprehensive whole, a single drama.

Life was now much more dramatic, even "tense," because human beings themselves were now responsible for developing and transforming nature, whereas before "man had merely to unfold an already existing nature." As a result, Christianity brought forth "a higher valuation of history and of temporal life in general."[19]

Not only did Christianity place a higher value on history and life in the world; the changed attitude also produced historical *actors* and *agents*. Christians accepted responsibility to shape history, to redirect it, to fashion it in ways that they believed were more God-honoring and glorifying. Bavinck begins his ninth Stone Lecture, "Revelation and Culture," with a reference to the famous saying from Johann Christoph Blumhardt (1805–1880) that "man must be twice converted, first from the natural to the spiritual life, and then from the spiritual to the natural." Bavinck affirms the "truth" in Blumhardt's "somewhat paradoxical language, a truth which is confirmed by the religious experience of every Christian and by the history of Christian piety in all ages."[20] The first and highest desire and duty of human beings is to be in fellowship with God. As this volume has said numerous times already, we were created for fellowship with God, for Sabbath, and being reconciled with God and personally assured of our salvation is the first order of business for every living person on earth. But what I said in the preceding chapter about work—namely, that once we are reconciled with God, our "work begins then in dead earnest" and we "be-

---

[19] *ESSR*, 96–97; Bavinck is citing Rudolf Eucken, *Geistige Strömungen der Gegenwart* (Leipzig, 1904), 190.
[20] *PofR*, 242.

come co-workers with God"—receives an even wider scope when we call attention to history and culture. We are now thinking of work not merely in terms of basic survival but also in terms of taking responsibility for history, accepting a cultural, civilizing obligation with our work.

Clearly, this vision was beyond the ken of our Lord's disciples and the apostles in the New Testament era. "When Christianity entered into the world," Bavinck observes, "it was immediately called on to face a difficult problem. Christianity, which is based on revelation, appeared in a world which had long existed and led its own life."[21] A stable society and well-defined and flourishing culture with a long history already existed, and Christians were faced with difficult choices. All cultures have religious roots, and it is always difficult for Christians, especially new Christians, to discern what in their "old" way of life must be left behind and what can be kept and modified or reformed. Using the familiar categories of H. Richard Niebuhr's *Christ and Culture*,[22] should Christians significantly separate themselves from a dominant culture, accommodate themselves to it, live in tension with it, or seek to transform it? We need not rehearse Bavinck's several treatments of the history of Christianity's wrestling with this question, but may instead focus on the heart of his concern: *dualism*. Whether in reference to the classic monastic asceticism of Roman Catholicism or the radical discipleship emphasis of Anabaptism, Bavinck's most pointed rhetoric is usually directed against the separatist, sectarian tendency in Christianity.

In this concern Bavinck is undoubtedly addressing many in his own Secession community, as he does in the following critique of some Dutch Reformed emigrants to America. In his address "The Catholicity of Christianity and the Church," Bavinck finds fault with Reformed Christians who limit the struggle against sin to *individual* sins.

> The unbelieving results of science are rejected, but there is no inner reformation of the sciences on the basis of a different principle. Public life is ignored and rejected—often as intrinsically "worldly" while no effort is made to reform it according to the demands of God's Word. Satisfied with the ability to worship God in their own houses of worship, or to engage in evangelism, many left nation, state and society, art and science to their own devices.

---

[21] *PofR*, 242.
[22] H. Richard Niebuhr, *Christ and Culture* (New York: Harper and Row, 1951).

Then comes the comment on emigration: "Many withdrew completely from life, literally separated themselves from everything, and, in some cases, what was even worse, shipped off to America, abandoning the Fatherland as lost to unbelief." Bavinck appreciates the piety of such people but considers their vision incomplete and inadequate: "It needs to be noted that while this orientation has much about it that is Christian, it is missing the full truth of Christianity. It is a denial of the truth that God loves the world. It is dedicated to conflict with and even rejection of the world but not to 'the victory that overcomes it' in faith."[23]

Bavinck insists that he has "no intention, by calling attention to these negative aspects, to deny the benefits that even these forms of Christianity have provided to the Christian life." In fact,

> Jesus himself indeed calls us to the one thing that is necessary, namely, that we seek the kingdom of heaven above all and set aside concerns about everything else because our heavenly Father knows what we need. The life of communion with God has its own content and is not exhausted in our moral life or in the exercise of our earthly vocation.

Furthermore, as Christian persons we are all different, have our own passions and gifts, and become guilty of "one-sidedness." "None of us has our intellect, emotions and will, our head, heart and hand, equally governed by the Gospel."[24]

Bavinck loves to explain the relationship between Jesus's call to radical discipleship, to forsake all for his sake and for the sake of his kingdom, by drawing together two of our Lord's metaphors—on the one hand, the kingdom of God as a treasure, the pearl of great price, and on the other, the kingdom of God as a leaven. Bavinck treats the order of priority of these two sets of images in a twofold manner. At the most basic level, the kingdom is a pearl before anything else. The gospel of the kingdom creates a new society, a people whose origins and social status are different but who are united in Christ into a "spiritual and holy community," "an elect family, a holy nation, a people made [Christ's] own, a holy priesthood, one body with many members."[25] Bavinck follows this with a claim that startles us with its total indifference to practical results:

---

[23] "Catholicity," 246–47; see Bavinck's sermon on 1 John 5:4b, which concludes this volume.
[24] "Catholicity," 247.
[25] ERSS, 141.

> Even if Christianity had resulted in nothing more than this spiritual and holy community, even if it had not brought about any modification in earthly relationships, even if, for instance, it had done nothing for the abolition of slavery, it would still be and remain something of everlasting worth.

It is a mistake to rate the Christian faith in terms of its benefits for human civilization. "The significance of the Gospel does not depend on its influence on culture, its usefulness for life today; it is a treasure in itself, a pearl of great value, even if it might not be a leaven."[26]

Bavinck does, however, believe that "although the worth of Christianity is certainly not only and exclusively, and not even in the first place, determined by its influence on civilization, it nevertheless is undeniable that it indeed exerts such influence." To make this point he reintroduces the image of leaven: "The kingdom of heaven is not only a pearl, it is a leaven as well. Whoever seeks it is offered all kinds of other things. Godliness has a promise for the future, but also for life today." Bavinck understands this leavening blessing in terms of obedience to God's law: "In keeping God's commandments there is great reward. Christianity in its long and rich history has borne much valuable fruit for all of society in all its relationships, in spite of the unfaithfulness of its confessors."[27]

Bavinck's other angle on the pearl and leaven metaphors for Christian discipleship gives a certain priority or superiority to the life of cultural engagement over the life of cultural withdrawal. Radical forms of discipleship may have an immediate appeal, but Bavinck wonders whether avoiding the challenges of entering the world as a culturally engaged follower of Jesus Christ might indicate a lack of faith, a lack of confidence in Christ's lordship over all things.

> Faith appears to be great, indeed, when a person renounces all and shuts himself up in isolation. But even greater, it seems to me, is the faith of the person who, while keeping the kingdom of heaven as a treasure, at the same time brings it out into the world as a leaven, certain that He who is for us is greater than he who is against us and that He is able to preserve us from evil even in the midst of the world.[28]

To retreat is to play into the world's wishes: "The world would gladly banish Christianity and the church from its turf and force it to a private

---

[26] *ERSS*, 141.
[27] *ERSS*, 141.
[28] "Catholicity," 248.

inner chamber. We could give the world no greater satisfaction than to withdraw into solitude and leave the world peacefully to its own devices." To accept this is to deny the catholicity of the church.

> But the catholicity of Christianity and the church both forbid us to grant this wish. We may not be a sect, we ought not to want to be one, and we cannot be one, without denying the absolute character of truth. The kingdom of heaven may not be of this world, but it does demand that everything in the world be subservient to it.[29]

Like his Dutch Calvinist contemporary Abraham Kuyper and his oft-quoted "every square inch" conviction, Bavinck too opposed all notions of neutrality in life; the kingdom of God "is exclusivistic and refuses to accept an independent or neutral kingdom alongside of it." The discipleship that our Lord expects of us does not promise peace, quiet, and rest in this life. In fact, says Bavinck, "such a restful peace is not permitted us here." Why? Because God's creation is good, and "rejection of any one of His creatures would be ingratitude to God, a denial of His gifts. Our conflict is not with anything creaturely but against sin alone." Bavinck's challenge to Christians to be culturally engaged is uncompromising:

> No matter how complicated the relationships may be within which we as Christ-confessors find ourselves in our age, no matter how serious and difficult, perhaps even insoluble, the problems may seem in the areas of society, politics, and above all, in science, it would testify to unbelief and powerlessness for us to withdraw proudly from the fray and under the guise of Christianity to dismiss the whole of our age's culture as demonic.[30]

Instead, we must live out of the convicted assurance that "this is the victory that overcomes the world—our faith" (1 John 5:4).

Culture and Education

We can summarize our discussion about cultural discipleship thus far with three words: *nature, work,* and *history.* Human work creates culture, and purposive work shapes history. In all instances, culture and civilization are made possible by and reflect the spiritual or souled capacity that we hu-

---

[29] "Catholicity," 248–49.
[30] "Catholicity," 249.

mans have for transcending the strictly physical and material dimensions of nature. In this final section, we add a fourth term that is an essential component of all cultures and civilizations: *education.*

Questions of education, particularly pedagogy, were a major occupation for Bavinck in the last decade of his life. In no other area do we see as clearly the complete integration of his theoretical work and his practice. He wrote several major works on education,[31] helped organize Christian school societies, and was a fierce defender of Christian education in Dutch public life. In addition, many of his other writings during this time, notably his works on psychology,[32] had an immediate relevance to questions of pedagogy and institutions of education.

I cannot possibly do full justice to Bavinck's educational philosophy or practical pedagogy in one section of one chapter in this volume; it has been the subject of three full-length studies.[33] We will focus our attention on Bavinck's educational philosophy more broadly and conclude with a few summary statements about practical pedagogy. Our entry point into both areas will be two of Bavinck's essays that are readily available to English-only readers, "Trends in Pedagogy"[34] (1909) and "Classical Education"[35] (1918). Since these two essays reflect Bavinck's mature thought on education, taken together they will provide a useful summary of his key educational ideas.

Bavinck begins the first essay by observing that in his own time many were trying to sever pedagogy from any theological or philosophical foundation and make it a "completely independent subject." This was a fruitless and futile effort: "These attempts, however, will not succeed, because education always assumes an answer to questions about human origin, essence, and purpose, and this answer (if ever possible) cannot be supplied by any exact science, but only by religion or philosophy." Education is never reducible to practical skills because it is always "governed by worldviews and also by the cultural situation and social milieu."[36]

After observing that Christianity has played a significant role in

---

[31] *Paedagogische beginselen* (*Pedagogic Principles,* 1904; rev. 1917); *De opvoeding der rijpere jeugd* (*The Education of Adolescents,* 1916); *De nieuwe opvoeding* (*The New Education,* 1917).

[32] *Beginselen der psychologie* (*Principles of Psychology,* 1897; rev. 1923); *De overwinning der ziel* (*The Triumph of the Soul,* 1916); *Bijbelsche en religieuze psychologie* (*Biblical and Religious Psychology,* 1920).

[33] Fr. S. Rombouts, *Prof. Dr. H. Bavinck, gids bij de studie van zijn paedagogische werken* (1922); Jacob Brederveld, *Christian Education: A Summary and Critical Discussion of Bavinck's Pedagogical Principles,* trans. two members of the faculty of Calvin College (Grand Rapids: Smitter, 1928); C. Jaarsma, *The Educational Philosophy of Herman Bavinck* (Grand Rapids: Eerdmans, 1935).

[34] *ESSR,* 205–8.

[35] *ESSR,* 209–43.

[36] *ESSR,* 205.

shaping education, including educational reform movements in history, Bavinck calls attention to the crisis in European education brought about by what he calls broad-based "pessimistic complaints" and "unmerciful judgments" against schools. Flowing forth from the romanticism of Rousseau and Tolstoy,

> all of our culture was condemned and regarded as the cause of all our miseries. Our modern education was particularly considered an impenetrable thicket of foolishness, prejudices, and blunders. Education, it was said, destroyed all that was good in a child—desire for knowledge, capability of observation, independence and personality. Instead education filled children with fear and fright, brought about anemia and nervous breakdown, and often caused suicide. It would be desirable if a flood would come and obliterate education from the earth.

Though not all of the criticism was this shrill, Bavinck adds, "Nearly everyone became convinced that our system of schooling and education, which had for years been regarded as nearly perfect, was terribly deficient. Thus reformation had to come, not just here and there, on some issues, but completely and radically, in head and members."[37]

What strikes us in the twenty-first century, in North America, is how similar our own educational struggles and debates are to those of Bavinck's day. The burden of the criticism sketched in the preceding was directed against intellectualism in the schools and particularly against the belief that the flowering of science education would lead to a better society and that money—lots of money!—spent on schools would be well spent because it would lead to spending less on prisons. The results were massively disappointing. In Bavinck's day, as in ours, "the misery in the lowest classes increased dramatically."[38] We have vastly expanded budgets for prisons *at the same time* that we are spending more and more (and never enough!) on schools. With this historical parallel before us, we are better equipped to assess the key reform proposals that arise.

Bavinck divides the educational reformers among "the designers and builders of all civilized nations" into four groups. Contemporary readers will be startled with the first group he mentions only briefly. "The first group is formed by those who know no other firm foundation either for all

---

[37] *ESSR*, 206.
[38] *ESSR*, 207.

of our culture or for our school system than what Christianity offers in its ecclesiastical confessions." What is even more startling is his claim about this group:

> This group forms a broader phalanx, assumes a firmer position, and is more strongly armed than its opponents imagine. Moreover, this group inspires us with courage in the struggle in our country, encourages us to persevere, and even more than they have till now, can provide us with weapons, and equip us for both offense and defense.[39]

The date of Bavinck's observation—1909—is important here. Looking back at the nineteenth-century Dutch struggles to honor the consciences of Christian parents with respect to their children's education, combined with Bavinck's own membership in the Secession Christian Reformed Church, one might have expected Bavinck to accent the marginalized place of Christian-education supporters in Dutch life. Such a picture would have been true in 1880 and even 1890, but it was no longer the case in 1909. Abraham Kuyper and his Anti-Revolutionary Party initially came into being in large measure to fight precisely this battle for the soul of Dutch public education against those who wanted to secularize it completely. Kuyper and his party won the election of 1901 and Kuyper served as the prime minister of the Netherlands from 1901 to 1905. Though the ARP suffered a few electoral defeats in the first decade of the twentieth century, its strength was obviously increasing, and it came to be the dominant party in the Netherlands for the next sixty years.

In 1917, the government of the Netherlands constitutionally guaranteed freedom of education for all children and created a system whereby the state monopoly in education came to an end and all schools, now organized along religious lines, received funding from the state. Freedom of education in the Netherlands came into being thanks to the commitment to freedom of religion. Free education became the most important component of the sociologically distinct pattern known as "pillarization," in which most of the social aspects of Dutch life received their own religious or ideological imprint. Through the twentieth century this meant religiously distinct political parties, trade unions, business associations, professional groups, sports clubs, and so. In education, for those who did not

---

[39] *ESSR*, 206–7.

identify with any particular confessional tradition or ideology such as humanism, there were the so-called neutral (*openbare*) schools, unions, clubs, and so on. Though none of this was finally in place yet in 1909, Bavinck was on fairly solid ground when he expressed his confidence about the strength of his first, Christian, group and how it continued to inspire others to persevere. Bavinck's first response to the crisis in education, to which he was a witness, was to affirm a renewed and strengthened Christian education.

Bavinck does not name the second group he considers, except to say that they "want to place pedagogy on one of the idealistically tinted philosophies," and that though there is a wide variety of thinkers to whom people appeal,

> they all agree in that they connect the doctrine of evolution with and make it serve teleology. In nature everything proceeds mechanically and according to fixed laws, but finally nature produced in humans a being that is equipped with understanding or spirit or intuition, with moral consciousness or self-consciousness or will.

He describes this group as opposed to mechanistic and deterministic views of human nature, instead seeing humans as spiritual beings capable of transcending nature and ruling nature by their wills.

> Humanity is therefore open to education, and this education serves especially to strengthen body and soul, to exercise the will, to form the character, to enrich the emotions, and to develop personality. This process will be served not only by education and physical training, but also by art and religion and morality.[40]

Bavinck does not provide a single descriptive term for this group, but perhaps *progressive humanism* would be fitting. This is an evolutionary, progressive vision of human perfection achieved by humane education in the humanities.

The third group that comes under Bavinck's eye is captivated by a vision of *scientific pedagogy*, an approach that comes in either an *individualistic* form or a *social* form. Proponents of the former hurl "their anathemas at all of modern society and culture, in the schools they were busy with tremendous passion for the rights, freedom, independence—that is, the majesty of the child." Their

---

[40] *ESSR*, 207.

coat of arms, says Bavinck, is "Who trains least, trains the best." To state this in summary fashion: this is a child-centered pedagogy, buttressed by claims of social science about the nature of the child. In our contemporary setting, think of the "self-esteem" movement in modern education. The second branch of this tree seeks to educate children not in order to maximize the child's inner potential but as a useful member of society. Bavinck mentions here the important German educational theorist and director of Munich's public schools from 1895 to 1919, Georg Michael Kerschensteiner (1854–1932). Kerschensteiner developed a very pragmatic approach to education and established a network of vocational schools. Bavinck describes his approach as "one-sided national education" that "in the modern democratic, industrial state wants to achieve general education through vocational training and to create the ideal person as a useful person."[41] Within this social pedagogy group, Bavinck finds an even more radical version "in the pedagogy of Paul Bergemann, who completely disallows the rights of the individual and grossly exaggerates the importance of society." The goal here is the "socialization of all of education." Bavinck concludes, "Thus, no matter how many important differences there are in social pedagogy, as a whole the movement is characterized by the idea that it sees in schooling and education a *means* where only society (the state) is in control and where it can maintain itself and reach perfection."[42]

A Defense of a "Classical" Education

We will reserve our consideration of Bavinck's critique of this last approach until the next chapter, on discipleship in civil society, and conclude this one with a brief look at what he says about the *content* of a good and Christian education. In his essay on "classical education," Bavinck notes that "when Christianity gained entrance into the Greek-Roman world through the preaching of the apostles, it soon faced the serious question about its posture towards the existing, richly developed culture."[43] Though much of that world was hostile to the gospel, and Christians faced persecution and violence, they could not escape the world.

> They got married and were given in marriage, they had children and had to educate them for some kind of occupation. They themselves were involved in various jobs and had to work for their daily bread. Thus they

---

[41] *ESSR*, 207.
[42] *ESSR*, 208.
[43] *ESSR*, 210.

participated in manual labor and industry, in commerce and shipping, even in the service of army and state.

As Christians sought "learned professions" for themselves and their children, they were put in a quandary: "Where could one obtain such training apart from the pagan schools? After all, in the beginning the Christians themselves did not have their own institutions of education, except for the catechumens, and for a long time in many places lacked those institutions."[44] Strong differences of opinion arose in the early church, famously represented on the one side by Tertullian and on the other by the Alexandrians Clement and Origen. Tertullian wanted nothing to do with Greek philosophy: "What does Jerusalem have to do with Athens, the academy with the church? We no longer need philosophy since Jesus, and no scientific research since the gospel. The whole culture of the Roman empire is a *pompa diaboli* [diabolic procession], because whatever is not from God is of the devil." The Alexandrians, by contrast, "loved literature and sought a union of philosophy and theology, of culture and Christianity."[45]

The church as a whole avoided both extremes "and took a middle road." She affirmed the value of asceticism but "forced it into more narrow boundaries, assigned it an importance but not an exclusive place, and was able to absorb it and make it serve its own ends." As the church became more "respectable" in the empire, it also "steadily assumed a more positive attitude with regard to the world." The church not only "absorbed as much culture as was necessary to subject and guide it," but also "raised itself to be empire of culture, which soon governed all areas of secular life." Ordinary life became "sacred" to the degree that it was sacramentally blessed by the church.

Thus, on the one hand, the church acknowledged marriage, family, occupations, science, art, and so forth, as natural gifts that could be appreciated and enjoyed (as Augustine said, *magna haec et omnino humana* [this is great and wholly human]). On the other hand, all these gifts were of a lower rank, inferior to and in the service of the supernatural order, which had descended to earth in itself, and in its hierarchy, mysteries, and sacraments.[46]

---

[44] *ESSR*, 211.
[45] *ESSR*, 211; Bavinck is paraphrasing a passage from Tertullian, "The Prescription against Heretics," 7, in *Ante-Nicene Fathers*, 3:246.
[46] *ESSR*, 212.

Practically, this *via media* meant that Christians

> could thus make free use of the treasures that the Greek-Roman culture possessed. They were like the people of Israel who in their departure from Egypt had taken the gold and silver of their oppressors and decorated the tabernacle with it. Christians performed a God-pleasing work when they dedicated all human gifts and energies that had been revealed in ancient culture to its highest purpose. Thus the paintings in the catacombs already resembled the style of antiquity, the architecture of the churches was arranged according to the models of the basilica, and philosophy was used for the defense of the Christian faith.[47]

The church accepted Latin as the language of the church, preserved the art and literature of antiquity in its monasteries, and eventually established cathedral and monastery schools that became important vehicles for transmitting the learning of Greece and Rome, not the least thanks to "various learned men [who] did their utmost to collect the knowledge and wisdom gained in antiquity, and to provide brief summaries." Aristotle was made "available to the West through translation and commentary," adjusted to serve theology, and the "so-called seven liberal arts (*artes liberales*, divided into *trivium* and *quadrivium*) handed down the knowledge of antiquity to the Middle Ages."[48]

Bavinck's high regard for the development of education under the tutelage and sponsorship of the church is not unqualified. In particular he faults it for its excessively *bookish* nature.

> People did not read literary works to be shaped by them, but to obtain the knowledge that was found in them; scholasticism had no other sources of learning than books. In theology scholasticism derived its life from Scripture, and even more from the tradition of the Church Fathers. In scholarship and philosophy one did not consult nature and history, but the works that had been written about those fields in antiquity. And often people did not even consult these works, but were satisfied with handbooks and textbooks.

Bavinck summarizes this approach as "scholasticism" and observes that a "reaction against such an academic system" was inevitable and "came in

---

[47] *ESSR*, 212.
[48] *ESSR*, 213.

that peculiar cultural movement known as the Renaissance." He defines the Renaissance as "nothing other than the birth of that new spirit that over against the authority and objectivity of the mediaeval outlook again emphasized the subject, the individual, and gradually revived the thirst for freedom."[49] The Renaissance insisted on a return to the actual source texts of antiquity; its rallying cry was *ad fontes* ([back] to the sources). For Renaissance scholars "this study of the classics had a totally different goal in mind from that intended by scholasticism. Humanism was very interested in nurture and education, and thought that the purpose of education was to be sought in *humanitas*," which it understood to be more than "humanness, friendliness, love of people," but "a humane culture that supersedes nationality, and which must be acquired through education."[50] This return to the sources emphasized language and rhetoric of these texts in their own right rather than probing them for metaphysical and theological knowledge.

> When the humanists thus returned to the sources, and became absorbed in the writings of the ancients, their eyes were opened to the beauty that was revealed in literature and the arts. It was as if they, like Columbus, had discovered a new world. Antiquity appeared to them as a period of ideal humanity that one must now attempt to relive, or at least where one must attempt to lead all those who value human, real culture.[51]

The Renaissance had an ambivalent relation to the Christian faith. Bavinck notes that for some "this revering of the classics turned into enmity against the church, Christianity, and even against all religion," but that the influence of the Renaissance on the Protestant Reformation must not be forgotten. "In the beginning there was great agreement and a strong relationship between the two movements. The return to Holy Scripture in the Reformation had its analog in the humanist revival of classical antiquity." In addition,

> humanism is to be thanked for the rich development it gave to the study of languages and related subjects. The interest in Greek and Latin literature led to the discovery of a multitude of manuscripts, from unknown to famous authors, which had to be critically sifted, published, and provided with commentaries.[52]

---

[49] *ESSR*, 215.
[50] *ESSR*, 216.
[51] *ESSR*, 217.
[52] *ESSR*, 217.

Included among these texts, of course, were manuscripts of the New Testament, which over time gave the church a Bible that was closer to the original.

We will skip over Bavinck's extensive commentary on the history of classical education and the growth of the so-called Latin Schools or *gymnasia* in Europe, and bring the discussion into Bavinck's own time. He refers to two major challenges to classical studies and classical education that took place in the nineteenth century. The first was historical, notably archeological, discoveries that vastly increased our knowledge of ancient civilizations, including our understanding of the ancient Near Eastern context within which the Scriptures of the Old and New Testaments were formed. Archeological excavations and historical explorations

> enable us much better than before to know the milieu where Israel lived and they make it possible to give a clear account of the political relationships of Israel to Assyria and Babel, Media and Persia, Egypt and Phoenicia. They also throw light on the social situations, religious and moral life, learning and art among those ancient nations, and contribute to a better understanding of much of what we encounter in Israel.

This reality leads us to an enriched understanding of biblical revelation itself. "In spite of special revelation that was given to Israel, one finds fibers and threads everywhere that connect it with the surrounding nations."[53] Bavinck takes issue with an "older" view of revelation that was insensitive to these connections.

> The old theology construed revelation after a quite external and mechanical fashion, and too readily identified it with Scripture. Our eyes are nowadays being more and more opened to the fact that revelation in many ways is historically and psychologically "mediated." Not only is special revelation founded on general revelation, but it has taken over numerous elements from it. The Old and New Testaments are no longer kept isolated from their *milieu*: and the affinity between them and the religious representations and customs of other peoples is recognized. Israel stands in connection with the Semites, the Bible with Babel.[54]

This enriched understanding of biblical revelation has profound significance for Christian education. Any motives of isolation are directly

---

[53] *ESSR*, 222.
[54] *PofR*, 22.

challenged by the Bible's own testimony concerning its content. The Hellenistic world of the Intertestamental and New Testament eras was "the product of the coming together of East and West, of the Semitic and the Aryan races" and thus "prepared people for Christianity and laid the foundation for our modern culture."[55] Therefore, earlier motives for studying classical antiquity, where it was regarded "as a unique, elevated, unsurpassable example that must be followed by all who value true civilization; as the only true means for the nurture toward humanity,"[56] were no longer tenable. The chasm between us and the classical past is too great. At the same time, Bavinck notes,

> the significance of classical antiquity for our civilization has never been realized as clearly as today; next to Christianity, that is where the roots of our culture are to be found. Classical antiquity thus does not have only historical value, such as the history of China or Japan, but it has cultural-historical significance, and in that regard the study of antiquity today is even more necessary and significant than ever.[57]

Bavinck was committed to a Christian education that served the common good. Believing as he did that the Dutch common good could be realized only by a *national* attentiveness to God's ordinances, he saw Christian education as essential in nurturing good citizens for the kingdom of the Netherlands as well as the kingdom of God.

In conclusion, we need to consider an additional challenge to the ideal of classical education. The love of nature, already present in the Middle Ages, eventually led people like Roger Bacon (1214–1294) and his namesake Francis Bacon (1561–1626) to emphasize observation and experience as the path to knowledge and generated the empirical, experimental, inductive method of modern science. As a result, "a new learning had to arise that would be practiced according to a strictly empirical and experimental method, that would achieve power through knowledge, and would grant man dominion over nature." When this desire for mastery over nature was combined with the development of a modern industrial society, calls arose for "a different education, one that is derived from nature and that takes its position not in antiquity but in the present. Its purpose is to form a person

---

[55] *ESSR*, 227.
[56] *ESSR*, 228.
[57] *ESSR*, 229.

to be an independent being, with his or her own thoughts and judgments, to be a useful, helpful member of society."[58]

A second stream of secondary education, focusing on mathematics and the natural sciences and intended for those preparing for study at technical universities and going into such fields as medicine or engineering, became standard, first of all in Germany and then in other countries. And since not all children are suited for university preparatory education, European governments began to develop vocational training schools as well. The Dutch government too, in addition to vocational schools, created two streams of secondary education: the classical *gymnasium* and the *hoogere burgerscholen* ("higher-citizens schools," that is, schools between the vocational schools and the *gymnasium*).[59] Bavinck's detailed survey of developments in Dutch secondary education does not concern us here; we only need to take note of his conclusions.

Bavinck offers no arguments "from a Christian point of view against modern learning" including the emphasis on the natural sciences and vocational training. However, he objects to privileging the *hoogere burgerscholen* at the expense of the *gymnasium* and classical education. "Many scholars today would like to see classical studies abolished as soon as possible," he says.[60] Bavinck acknowledges that the *gymnasia* need reform, particularly with respect to "the nature, the method, the goal of classical education." Narrow antiquarian and philological study of texts is not enough.

> One can say without fear of contradiction that the one-sided grammatical-critical method that has long reigned in our country and other countries, has done much damage to the love for classical antiquity. If at the *gymnasium* or university one spends weeks and months reading Homer, Plato, Sophocles, and others, without any serious attempt to introduce the student to know the person and the time of the authors, to the content and the philosophical, aesthetic, cultural, historical value of their works, then one cannot expect that the student will feel interest or love for classical antiquity.

Fortunately, it does not have to stay this way; "new developments in philology" along with the explosion of historical knowledge about antiquity present opportunities for revitalized and exciting classical education.[61]

---

[58] *ESSR*, 231–32.
[59] *ESSR*, 234–37.
[60] *ESSR*, 237.
[61] *ESSR*, 241.

Classical education remains valuable for us because "the foundations of modern culture were laid in antiquity." But—Bavinck is writing as the First World War is drawing to a close—international crises and concerns require it. "The current world war estranges nations from each other—nations that belong to each other according to history, religion, and culture, but it appears that all unity and cooperation will go under in enmity and hate for a long, long time, perhaps forever."[62] Contemplating the belligerents of that war, Bavinck points to the growth of nationalism and chauvinism as a destabilizing force in the international order: "Germany, France, and England are busy with their own, national culture, and whatever was held in common up till now is pushed into the background." It is for that reason that international order needs to be built "on the foundations of modern culture which was itself shaped by the Christian religion."[63] Bavinck concludes:

> If there is one thing that is essential in these grave times, it is that Christian nations be reconciled to each other, close ranks, and to take to heart the call to conserve the treasure that has been entrusted to them in religion and culture. This is also true for religion, for the Christian religion. . . . How will these nations ever again become a power for mankind, if they do not possess an inner unity in Scripture and do not draw from one communal well?[64]

Can there be any doubt that we, in the early years of the twenty-first century, live in equally perilous times? As secular ideologies increasingly seek to marginalize public Christian voices, Bavinck's call to resist the temptation to flee from the battle and isolate ourselves remains a powerful reminder to Reformed Christians. We must be faithful in our discipleship, a discipleship that includes a sacrificial commitment to a Christian education that prepares its students for full-orbed discipleship in the world.

---

[62] *ESSR*, 242.
[63] *ESSR*, 242.
[64] *ESSR*, 243.

CHAPTER 10

CIVIL SOCIETY

Likely the most significant cultural achievement of human work is society itself. Starting with the basic family unit and branching out into group cultic activities, trade, and business, and developing the structures, laws, and policing of our life together, has always been and will remain the greatest challenge of our human life in community. All that we have considered thus far—our creation in God's image, the law, our union with Christ, life in marriage and family, our work, and our culture—comes to a culmination in the *polis*, the ordered social life of our various communities. In this concluding chapter of this third part of the book, on concrete Christian discipleship, we will examine Bavinck's biblical reflections on the social order.

Reflections of this sort today are included in the broad category of *public theology.* Public theology is more than merely spelling out social-ethical implications of important Christian doctrines; it is an attempt to think theologically about universal public life itself. The topics listed in the previous paragraph as an ordered set must be taken into account in any theology that takes the doctrine of creation as its starting point. Our reflection on who God is and what he is doing in the world cannot overlook the way God's redeemed people live in his creation in general and how they relate to other image bearers in particular. We must therefore understand Bavinck's own involvement in Dutch political life, briefly sketched in the sixth chapter, as a continuation of his theological vocation.

I have already touched on the topic of this chapter in previous chapters, directly or indirectly. Our consideration of the image of God in chapter 2 pointed to the Trinitarian character of the image, a foundation that directs us to the unity in diversity of the whole human race. Scripture clearly teaches a universal human solidarity; we are our brother's keeper. No one exists as an isolated creature: "We are born out of and in and unto a community, of family, race, nation, state, church and humanity, unto a community of diverse material and spiritual goods."[1] The human race is one in origin but also one in essence; we all share the same human nature. We are by nature social beings, created in the image of the triune God. Furthermore, our dual vocation, the first one "earthly" and the second "eternal," summarized in the Great Commandment to "love God above all and our neighbor as ourselves" (see Matt. 22:37–40), plainly teaches us that we were created for *fellowship*, for *community*, for *society*. We are created for fellowship with God and we exercise that fellowship in our social relationships and earthly vocations by intentionally following God's law.

The importance of God's law in shaping Christian discipleship has been the *leitmotif* of this volume. As Bavinck noted in his report to the 1891 Christian Social Congress in Amsterdam, "God's law—written on human hearts—was given as a rule and guide for our entire existence in its internal and external dimensions, covering our daily walk and our commerce. This law is summarized in the duty to love God and the neighbor."[2] The first resolution of that congress underscored this point: "Holy Scripture teaches that human society must not be ordered according to our own preferences but is bound to those laws that God himself has firmly established in Creation and His Word."[3] I concluded chapter 2 with some reflections on the Christian understanding of the image of God as the foundation for social and political orders that cherish and protect liberty and human dignity.

We considered Bavinck's report to the Social Congress briefly at the conclusion of chapter 3 and in somewhat greater detail in chapter 8, where I brought into view the historical and social context of the late nineteenth century, a world massively dislocated by the industrial revolution and large population shifts from rural areas to the cities of Europe. Generally referred to as the "social question," the wretched plight of large populations of urban poor was *the* burning issue on the hearts and minds of all European Christians during the second half of the nineteenth century. Dutch Reformed people were no exception, and in addition to Bavinck's report,

---

[1] Herman Bavinck, *Bijbelsche en religieuze psychologie* (Kampen: Kok, 1920), 77.
[2] "Gen. Prin.," 438–39.
[3] "Gen. Prin.," 445.

the congress was opened with an address by Abraham Kuyper, "The Social Question and the Christian Religion."[4] Our focus in chapter 8 was on work and vocation, particularly on the need for justice to establish the conditions of liberty and an opportunity for our labor.

In what follows we will consider Bavinck's report once more, looking now at social principles more broadly. We shall also take a look at what is arguably Bavinck's most important essay on Christian life in society, "Christian Principles and Social Relationships."[5]

Revolution and the "Social Question"

The First Christian Social Congress in the Netherlands met in 1891, a year that represents something of a high-water mark in the development of Christian social consciousness in the modern world. We have already taken note of Abraham Kuyper's famous essay on the topic, but the best-known and most influential treatment of the topic in that same year was Pope Leo XIII's important encyclical *Rerum Novarum*.[6] As already mentioned, European governments struggled with what needed to be done about the growing number of urbanized, working-class poor who struggled to meet basic necessities of life. As the forces of industrialization, driven by technological innovation in iron and steel production and textile manufacturing, pulled rural poor into Europe's cities, social upheaval and misery became so pronounced that denial or avoidance was impossible. Desperate conditions led to searches for solutions, and intellectuals such as Karl Marx produced global analyses along with radical proposals that encouraged dramatic political activism. In a single phrase, it was a time of *revolutionary* thought and action. Bavinck captured this in the first sentence of his only published sermon, on 1 John 5:4b (reproduced at the conclusion of this book): "The nineteenth century, which concluded only a few months ago, has been rightly called by many the age of unbelief and revolution."

Bavinck and his Dutch hearers had a firsthand acquaintance with the revolution in their national life. The revolutionary fervor that had seized France in 1789 swept into the Netherlands in 1795, overthrew the monar-

---

[4] Abraham Kuyper, *De sociale vraagstuk en de Christelijke religie* (Amsterdam: Wormser, 1891); ET *The Problem of Poverty*, ed. James W. Skillen (Washington, DC: Center for Public Justice; Grand Rapids: Baker, 1991). See above, pp. 175–80.
[5] *ESSR*, 119–44.
[6] The importance of Leo's encyclical is reflected in the fact that its publication year was commemorated by no fewer than five anniversary papal encyclicals in 1931 (*Quadragesimo Anno*), 1961 (*Mater et Magistra*), 1971 (*Octagesima Adveniens*), 1981 (*Laborem Exercens*), and 1991 (*Centesimus Annus*).

chy, established the profoundly anticlerical Batavian Republic, and turned all of Dutch life upside down. After the defeat of Napoleon at Waterloo in 1815, the Congress of Vienna restored the House of Orange, and William I became the monarch of a United Kingdom of the Netherlands. The unification included the seven southern provinces of what eventually became Belgium along with the Duchy of Luxembourg and was inherently instable. The clear, historically based division between a predominantly Protestant North and a Roman Catholic South that included a large French-speaking population should have served as a warning to the diplomats drawing a new European map at the Congress of Vienna. Though it flourished economically, especially in the South, owing to industrialization, the United Kingdom lasted only fifteen years. A revolt against the monarchy began in 1830 and included a declaration of Belgian independence. War between the southern provinces and the monarchy lasted until 1839, when the Treaty of London was signed between the two countries, guaranteeing Belgian independence and sovereignty.

In 1848 Europe's revolutionary spiral continued to unwind as working and middle-class people agitated for reform and took to the streets in country after country. Only a few countries and regions—notably Great Britain, the Netherlands, the Iberian Peninsula, and the Russian and Ottoman Empires—were spared from the revolutionary onslaught. But even a country such as the Netherlands, which did not experience significant unrest in 1848, was not left untouched by the spirit of revolution. In 1848 the Netherlands significantly revised its fifteen-year-old constitution and instituted a "liberal" parliamentary democracy that effectively neutered the monarch's power. Europe's revolution continued in the second half of the nineteenth century. On September 28, 1864, the world's workers formed the International Working Men's Association (IWMA; later the "First Internationale") in London, and on March 28, 1871, the Paris Commune momentarily seized power, establishing a brief "communist" rule until its bloody defeat two months later. General strikes and other forms of labor unrest remained common in Europe during the 1870s and 1880s. It truly was an "age of revolution."

Keeping the persistent revolutionary ferment in view is crucial for understanding the two distinct streams of Christian social thought and action that developed in the second half of the nineteenth century. One, borrowing language and conceptual frames from Karl Marx, called for a

"Christian socialism." Notable among its proponents were British Anglicans Charles Kingsley and F. D. Maurice, along with American Baptists Walter Rauschenbusch and Francis Julius Bellamy (1855–1931). The social-gospel theologians appealed to biblical themes such as the kingdom of God, which they interpreted as a brotherhood of cooperation and love. The gospel was understood as a matter of helping the poor, and the problems of the age were seen as arising from a class conflict between the rich and powerful, on one side, and the poor and marginalized, on the other. Tragically, the advocates of the social gospel said, the church throughout history has usually taken the wrong side and aligned itself with the powerful and rich. It must repent of this and change its course; this means, concretely, that the church and Christians must side with and fully support the social-democratic movements of our day (i.e., become socialists). Rauschenbusch, for example, spoke of Jesus as a "revolutionary," claiming that while "Plato dreamed of an ideal republic, Christ instituted it." In fact, he added, "the splendid principle of the French Revolution: 'Liberty, equality, fraternity,' contains the social principles of the church."[7] In short, Jesus preached and intended for his followers to practice socialism.

This combination of revolutionary ideas—even among well-known Christian theologians and preachers—with the political agitation that seemed ever present in the nineteenth century, is the necessary background for understanding the other stream of Christian response represented by Leo XIII's *Rerum Novarum*, Abraham Kuyper's *The Problem of Poverty*, and Herman Bavinck's social theology. Though each of these responses differs from the others in minor respects, what all three have in common is a fierce opposition to all forms of socialism.

The Problems with the "Social Gospel"

In order to understand Bavinck's constructive discussion about valid biblical principles for our social life, we need to summarize his objections to the "social gospel" and its Christian form of socialism. The following topics are all relevant to Bavinck's critique: biblical hermeneutics, gospel and law, the kingdom of God and the soteriological focus of Scripture, sin instead of inequality as the problem, and the need for both eschatological reserve and Christian mercy. Since I have already treated a number

---

[7] Walter Rauschenbusch, *The Righteousness of the Kingdom*, ed. Max Stackhouse (Nashville: Abingdon, 1968), 172–73.

of these issues in previous chapters, my remarks will be in the nature of summary.

Bavinck was keenly aware that Christian socialist visions were rooted in an appeal to the New Testament, particularly to the teaching of Jesus in the Sermon on the Mount and about the kingdom of God. And it is here that Bavinck set his opposition to all social-gospel appeals to Jesus's teaching, firmly resisting any use of the kingdom of God as a this-worldly political reality. "The kingdom of God is not an ethical communion nor a democratic society, but a religious fellowship."[8] Put in other words, "at its core, in the depths of its being, the Kingdom of God is spiritual, eternal, invisible. It does not come with outward form (Luke 17:20), does not consist in food and drink (Rom. 14:17), is invisible and intangible."[9] When Jesus and the apostles preached the "good news of the kingdom," what they had in mind were not earthly goods such as an improved society, but "spiritual goods . . . such as the vision of God and eternal life."[10] The kingdom of God is an eschatological reality regarded primarily in terms of future consummation. To the extent that it is also a present reality, it is spiritual and internal. Furthermore, it is crucial to distinguish the kingdom of God from the church. "The church *already exists*; the Kingdom of God *is becoming*. The church is an historical, visible organization; the Kingdom of God is invisible and spiritual."[11] To speak of the kingdom of God as "becoming, as unfolding, as awaiting its completion," is to call attention to the *spiritual* conflict in which its citizens are involved.[12] The kingdom of God will only be complete "when every opposition has been vanquished and the kingdom itself is completely sanctified[;] then Christ will return the sovereignty granted to him to the One who bestowed it, and will give the Kingdom without spot or wrinkle to his God and Father."[13]

Bavinck interprets the significance of Jesus's teaching about the kingdom of God in a nonethical, nonsocial manner because his hermeneutics (his principles of interpreting the Bible) are quite different from all social-gospel interpreters. As he takes note of the Old Testament prophets who "raise their voice against the religious and moral apostasy of the people,"

---

[8] *Handboekje*, 249.
[9] H. Bavinck, "The Kingdom of God: The Highest Good," trans. Nelson D. Kloosterman, *The Bavinck Review* 2 (2011): 140.
[10] *Handboekje*, 248–49.
[11] Bavinck, "Kingdom of God," 158.
[12] Ibid., 148.
[13] Ibid., 148–49.

he repeatedly insists that all their complaints about "robbery and intemperance, bribery and miserliness, hunger for money and pleasure, injustice and deceit in goods, measure, and weight, holding back wages, selling the righteous, oppressing the orphan and the widow," and so forth are always about the *spiritual* roots of such sins, about hearts turned away from God and toward idols.

> They never look for the reasons of the misery in the ordinances and laws, in the institutions and regulations, in the poor organization of state and society, in the inequality between rich and poor, for God made them both; but they always look into the hearts of the people, at their apostasy and their breaking of the covenant, at their idolatry and world conformity, at their abandoning God and his word.[14]

Similarly, for the remedy "they do not expect restoration [to come] from a political revolution or social legislation, but only from a true return to God and his service. They called the entire nation back to the law and the testimony, to justice and righteousness, and urged people to humility and repentance." The ultimate horizon of the prophets is profoundly eschatological.

> And if the present offers little or no hope for this, they look forward eagerly and with great longing to the future when God will write his law on the hearts of all people. Then the kingdom of the Anointed of David's house will flourish in righteousness and peace, and everyone in the Holy Land will receive an inalienable inheritance (Ezekiel 47:14; 46:18), and sit down under his own vine and fig tree in safety. There will be no more slaves, for men-servants and maid-servants will also receive the Spirit of the Lord, and even aliens will share in Israel's privileges.[15]

The Bible's concentration and focus is *soteriological*, not social and ethical; the latter two concerns are derivative and secondary. Social renewal is the fruit and byproduct of the regenerating work of the Holy Spirit starting in individuals but coming to expression in the redeemed community, the body of Christ.

Bavinck also holds to a radically different understanding of the human problem and sin than does the social gospel, which in turn fundamentally

---

[14] *ERSS*, 128–29.
[15] *ERSS*, 129.

alters the meaning of Christ's atoning death on the cross. For the social gospel, sin is seen primarily in social terms. According to Rauschenbusch:

> Jesus did not in any real sense bear the sin of some ancient Briton who beat up his wife in B.C. 56, or of some mountaineer in Tennessee who got drunk in A.D. 1917. But he did in a very real sense bear the weight of the public sins of organized society, and they in turn are causally connected with all private sins. [16]

It was *public sins* that led to Christ's crucifixion, and its saving effect is *solidarity* with humanity, not a "legal fiction" of imputation. The six *social sins* that Jesus bore on the cross, in Rauschenbusch's view, are

> religious bigotry, the combination of graft and political power, the corruption of justice, the mob spirit (being "the social group gone mad") and mob action, militarism, and class contempt—every student of history will recognize that these sum up constitutional forces in the Kingdom of Evil. Jesus bore these sins in no legal or artificial sense, but in their impact on his own body and soul. He had not contributed to them, as we have, and yet they were laid on him. They were not only the sins of Caiaphas, Pilate, or Judas, but the social sin of all mankind, to which all who ever lived have contributed, and under which all who ever lived have suffered. [17]

For Bavinck, this series of abstractions gets things completely backward. What Rauschenbusch calls "social sins"—the grave problems that he believes Christ came to save us from by establishing a new brotherhood of love—are in Bavinck's view only symptoms of a deeper flaw and not the flaw itself. Broken relationships among human beings are rooted in broken fellowship with God. The real, fundamental human problem is "unbelief, disobedience, and enmity against God." Because of this, "the right relation of humans to themselves was also disturbed." "Egoism replaces love in the human heart and as a result produces envy, deceit, hatred, murder, and so forth. Sin has thus become the basic given of human life, the motivating power of human conduct." It is this flaw in every human person that has transformed

> the entire social existence of human beings [into] a war of all against all. . . . Driven by egoism, everyone no longer thinks about that which they

---

[16] Walter Rauschenbusch, *A Theology for the Social Gospel* (New York: MacMillan, 1917), 247.
[17] Ibid., 257–58.

have but focuses on what belongs to someone else. Society becomes a stage-play about the struggle for existence, a world where one man acts as a wolf toward the others.[18]

Thankfully, God does not let this situation go unchecked. He sends "punishments and judgments that he links to sin." God also permits "a few weak remnants of his image and likeness to remain [after the fall]," such as "reason and conscience; some knowledge of his existence and character, a seed of religion; a moral sense of good and evil; and a consciousness of our eternal destiny." He also "awakens in the human heart a natural love between men and women, parents and children. He nurtures a variety of social virtues among people: a pull toward social relationships and a longing for affection and friendship." However, though this activity of God restrains human beings, it does not renew them.[19] For personal and social renewal to be possible, individual persons need to be saved. This order is crucial. "Sin, in the first place, breaks off fellowship with God, and then, in consequence, all genuine relationships that humans have with all other creatures. Thus, the first order of the day is restoring our proper relationship with God." In considering the cross, "the heart and mid-point of the Christian religion," Bavinck boldly states:

> Jesus did not come, first of all, to renew families and reform society but to save sinners and to redeem the world from the coming wrath of God. This salvation of our souls must be our ultimate concern for which we are willing to sacrifice everything: father and mother, house and field, even our own lives, in order to inherit the kingdom of heaven (Matt. 6:33; 16:26, etc.). This new, reconciled relationship to God that is effected through faith in Christ, is of such great significance and value that all our relationships and distinctions vanish because of it. In Christ, there is neither male nor female, Greek nor Jew, slave nor free (Gal. 3:28; Col. 3:11).[20]

It hardly needs to be mentioned here that *all people* are sinners, and that the social-gospel effort to locate sin in *structures* of power and wealth miserably fails as a diagnosis of the human problem. Most importantly, this means that *inequality* is not a sin and that socialist redistribution is

---

[18] "Gen. Prin.," 439.
[19] "Gen. Prin.," 440–41.
[20] "Gen. Prin.," 443.

not a remedy to the ills of humanity. This issue is sufficiently important to Bavinck that we need to devote a separate section of this chapter to it.

When Inequality Became a Sin

For advocates of the social gospel, inequality is the great sin to be challenged with prophetic preaching and overcome by social transformation. To this day, the rhetoric of politicians who favor redistributive programs and policies makes much of growing inequities between the richest 1 percent and the rest of society as if inequity itself were an intrinsic evil that required "social justice" as its remedy. This issue represents the fundamental fault line dividing the two streams of Christian social teaching we have identified. As Leo XIII took note of the lamentable conditions of people in industrializing and urbanizing Europe, he agreed "that some opportune remedy must be found quickly for the misery and wretchedness pressing so unjustly on the majority of the working class."[21] However, he also resolutely opposed the socialist answer because it would have made things worse rather than better and, besides that, unjustly taken someone's legitimate property in order to give it to another.

> They hold that by thus transferring property from private individuals to the community, the present mischievous state of things will be set to rights, inasmuch as each citizen will then get his fair share of whatever there is to enjoy. But their contentions are so clearly powerless to end the controversy that were they carried into effect the working man himself would be among the first to suffer. They are, moreover, emphatically unjust, for they would rob the lawful possessor, distort the functions of the State, and create utter confusion in the community.[22]

Bavinck's position is similar. It is clear from his report to the 1891 Social Congress that his survey of biblical principles was intentionally framed as a rejoinder to the challenge of Christian socialism.

Bavinck concluded his report with seven resolutions to be discussed, debated, and eventually adopted. His first resolution dealt explicitly with inequality: "The inequalities that exist in every respect among people are grounded in the Creation, that is to say, in God's will itself, and serve precisely to make possible humanity's earthly task." The two resolutions

---

[21] *Rerum Novarum*, par. 3.
[22] *Rerum Novarum*, par. 4.

that followed dealt with the consequences of sin on human inequality and the effects of redemption on sin's consequences. The congress's own final resolutions mirrored Bavinck's, though the congress also incorporated some changes, notably by adding a new introductory resolution: "Holy Scripture teaches that human society must not be ordered according to our own preferences but is bound to those laws that God himself has firmly established in Creation and His Word." The congress's third resolution tied Bavinck's second one on inequalities to its own introductory resolution and came up with the following statement on the consequences of sin:

> In general, the origin of all social ills and abuses comes from setting aside these ordinances and laws. Thanks to this, the differences that are present among creatures by virtue of creation, lost their unity, were changed into oppositions, and placed creatures in a relationship of enmity against God and to each other.

The social ills of the day, in other words, are to be attributed not to inequalities as such but to the sinful human heart that turns them into oppositions and conflicts between people. Class conflict, therefore, comes not from the simple fact of wealth disparity but from sinful human hearts. And, finally, the redemption that is provided to God's people in Christ does not eliminate differences and inequalities but puts them in a new framework: "Redemption does not set aside the differences that exist thanks to God's will but renews all relationships to their original form by bringing all of them into a reconciled relationship with God."[23]

Bavinck celebrated and championed the diversity and multiplicity of God's creation but was also keenly aware that, though "there is beauty in diversity," a down side is that variety may hide "a great many contradictions, for diversity is often a pseudonym for a mysterious struggle between clashing powers."[24] Because the fall brought about enmity between the seed of the woman and the seed of the Serpent, "there is no peace or harmony anywhere; instead dissonance and struggle are everywhere." Human beings do not live comfortably with dissonance and struggle and try again and again, without lasting success, to encompass diversity within a greater unity. Bavinck categorizes all such efforts into two main streams: (1) "pantheistic

---

[23] "Gen. Prin.," 445.
[24] *ESSR*, 145.

or monistic systems that have tried to reduce variety to an appearance of reality with the slogan 'variety is basically one reality'"; (2) "pluralistic systems that despair of ever finding one single reality and that do not go beyond accepting an original, eternal multitude of gods or spirits, of powers or matter." As representatives of the first view, he mentions Gnosticism, neo-Platonism, and the nineteenth-century philosophies of Spinoza, Hegel, and Spencer.[25] As Bavinck reflects on the thought currents of his own time, he observes, "It is quite remarkable that in our day, more so than ever before, this idea of diversity has become a *practical* problem. The great diversity in our world is seen by many people today, especially in the social realm, as inequality."[26]

Bavinck thus places the question of social and economic inequality within a larger philosophical framework, the problem of unity and diversity. We have already seen that Bavinck's own wrestling with this question finds resolution in his organic understanding of the triune God and his works. Whether we are considering the relations between God's sovereignty and our human responsibility to will and act, our earthly task and our heavenly destiny, justification and sanctification, the work of the Holy Spirit and the importance of the "means of grace," covenant fellowship and obedience to God's law, the Word (of Scripture) and the Holy Spirit, faith and works—and much more besides—Bavinck turns to the fundamental Christian confession of God's tri-unity: Father, Son, and Holy Spirit as three distinct persons in one substantial, essential unity. Here is the basis of the Christian worldview; here are the spectacles required to see reality as it truly is. In addition, thinking about the unity-in-diversity of the triune God as the foundation for creation's own oneness and multiplicity helped Bavinck to resist some of the ideological excesses of Abraham Kuyper and his followers. Bavinck realized that "principles" and "application" are both necessary even as we "remain bound to established, ethical" norms and the law of God.[27] In all of this we need revelation; only if God as Father, Son, and Holy Spirit *manifests* himself, *discloses* himself, and *displays* who he is can we come to a proper understanding of reality. "The world itself rests on revelation; revelation is the presupposition, the foundation, the secret of all that exists in all its forms. . . . The foundations of creation and

---

[25] *ESSR*, 146.
[26] *ESSR*, 146.
[27] Herman Bavinck, "Politieke rede 1918" (unpublished manuscript, n.d.), 11.

redemption are the same. The Logos who became flesh is the same by whom all things were made."[28]

The practical and operational consequence of this conviction is that Christians should oppose all forms of monistic or pantheistic thought in which God and world are absorbed into a oneness or sameness, as well as any pluralistic thought that acknowledges only chaotic diversity and recognizes no cosmos or unity at all. We saw how Bavinck's organic thinking influenced his understanding of marriage and family in chapter 7 and framed his understanding of work in chapter 8. We will now consider it further with respect to matters of wealth, poverty, and inequality.

Earlier we took note of Bavinck's observation that his contemporary age's obsession with diversity and inequality was "quite remarkable."[29] He acknowledges that the actual conditions of life in Europe made this practical preoccupation quite understandable; he speaks of "many highly deplorable disparities that exist in real life," where "a few may live in luxury" and have homes that "are furnished lavishly or comfortably," while others "have to endure living in stuffy rooms, narrow alleys, and dreary slums that lack light and fresh air."[30] The world, however, has known poverty and misery before the late nineteenth century. What, then, led an entire continent—and beyond!—to embrace this passionate objection to inequality with its corresponding zeal for equality? Bavinck attributes the revolutionary turn primarily to the personal revolution within the thought of one man: the second great Genevan shaper of world history, Jean-Jacques Rousseau (1712–1778).

Bavinck describes Rousseau's "conversion" in the summer of 1749 when the thirty-seven-year-old drifter who had "become accepted in the drawing rooms" of Paris but "had not yet found himself" came across "an announcement about an essay contest sponsored by the Academy of Dijon on the topic "Has the progress of the sciences and arts tended to corrupt or purify morals?" Rousseau's world was suddenly transformed. "At that very moment a tremendous change took place in him. Suddenly a light went on in his mind. He writes in his *Confessions*: 'At the moment of that reading I saw another universe and I became another man.'"[31] What was this momentous change

---

[28] *PofR*, 27.
[29] *ESSR*, 146.
[30] *ESSR*, 147.
[31] *ESSR*, 148; the reference is to Jean-Jacques Rousseau, *The Confessions and Correspondence, Including the Letters to Malesherbes*, in *The Collected Writings of Rousseau*, ed. Christopher Kelly, Roger D. Masters, and Peter G. Stillman, trans. Christopher Kelly, vol. 5 (Hanover, NH: University Press of New England, 1995), bk. 8, p. 294.

Rousseau experienced? Simply put, he renounced culture and embraced nature. Human learning and acquired wisdom, all customs and laws, he came to see, were all "faulty and foolish, and caused only oppression and misery in our social order." He came to regard his own learning—a product of "rationalized reason and a corrupt culture"—as something that had to be set aside for the beauty of nature. His own soul and nature were now in harmony and

> became for him something different and much more meaningful: nature without and his soul within now set free from the unnatural trappings imposed on them by reason and culture, suddenly turned into revelations of one and the same God, that is, a God who is pure goodness, and from whose hands nothing evil can come.

Whence, then, came the evil and misery of humanity?

> The multitude of wrongs and all the misery in our world can only find their origin in society and the culture it has created. And having understood the original relationship of soul and nature, of man and the world, of subject and object, of myself and not-myself, he became the powerful, influential fighter for the rights of naturalness.[32]

Having diagnosed society and culture to be the problem, Rousseau was confident that the remedy could be found in turning "from culture to nature, from a society that is complex and corrupt to the original natural state of innocence, from the deceptiveness of the mind to the pure dictates of feeling."[33] We can recognize the pattern that Bavinck describes here because the turn away from *reasoned* public discourse and careful argument to appeals to feeling—to personal, subjective desires and wants—is one of the hallmarks of our own day. But can this all be attributed to one man's personal odyssey? Bavinck notes that Rousseau's ideas were "by no means new or original, because most of them are found in his predecessors, especially the English deists, and were already more or less consciously part of the thinking of his contemporaries." He then quotes a voice from the generation after Rousseau: "Madam Staël put it well when she said, 'He has invented nothing new, yet he has set the whole world on flame.'"[34]

---

[32] *ESSR*, 151–52.
[33] *ESSR*, 151–52.
[34] *ESSR*, 152; Anne Louise Germaine de Staël (1766–1817) was a French-speaking Swiss litterateur, an enthusiast of Rousseau, and an influence on nineteenth-century Romanticism.

According to Bavinck, Rousseau "represented the thinking of his day. He spoke the language of his day. He gave voice to what people thought subconsciously, and he could do so because he was a man with a heart. That distinguished him from the men of the Enlightenment." Rousseau was not satisfied with the idolization of reason and science that the Encyclopedists used "to mock God and religion[;] Rousseau's heart was homesick for a return to the innocence of nature. Behind the arts and sciences, the riches and opulence that were the pride of the Enlightenment, Rousseau saw the misery of the masses, their spiritual poverty, and their empty hearts."[35] Rousseau put to word the feelings, longings, and desires of an entire age.

What Rousseau offered as an alternative was the *idea* of a natural state without differences and inequalities. Bavinck introduces an important caveat here:

> One must also remember that Rousseau never intended to introduce the natural state in its absolute sense; he understood quite well that this would be impossible. Nor did he portray the natural state as a situation that had really existed once upon a time. He only used this idea as a means to portray what he thought a desirable arrangement of society and the state should look like, with common interests for all and in which everything was to be done for the people and by the people. Contrary to the existing state of affairs of his day, he wanted a State that was based on freedom for all, in which no class or persons would enjoy privileges that had been obtained illegally or by force.[36]

Rousseau's "state of nature" was a product of his "unrestrained imagination." Nonetheless, his vision became a powerful force in late eighteenth- and especially nineteenth-century revolutionary social and political movements; his impact remains with us to this day because "this idea of the injustice of social inequality has become deeply rooted in the hearts of men and has found wide acceptance. It may be said that the basic thought patterns of our century oppose such inequality and want to get rid of it completely."[37]

Bavinck sees the opposition to inequality and variety on a broader front than only the economic. Philosophically, he sees it in "the evolutionistic mind-set [that] tries hard to destroy all basic differences," such as that

---

[35] *ESSR*, 152.
[36] *ESSR*, 153.
[37] *ESSR*, 154.

"between God and the world, between man and animal, soul and body, truth and lie, good and evil, Christianity and paganism, and so forth." The other attack comes, he says, "as though from below, by all those modern movements that seek to obliterate the differences between husband and wife, parents and children, the government and the governed, employers and employees, rich and poor etc."[38]

Inequality Is Not a Sin

Bavinck segues from his reflections on Rousseau to the first prominent and influential "citizen of Geneva . . . who lived and worked in Geneva two centuries earlier, namely, the powerful Reformer John Calvin." That Calvin is going to be Bavinck's own inspiration for his critique of Rousseau becomes apparent when he immediately adds, "But what a tremendous contrast arises the moment these two names are mentioned together." Both men

> experienced a transformation in their lives, but with Calvin it consisted of a turning away from the errors of the Roman Catholic Church and an embracing of the truth and the freedom of the Gospel, while with Rousseau it was no more than a breaking with all culture and a return to the instinctiveness of nature.

The heart of the difference between the two men, therefore, does not surprise us:

> Calvin sought the cause of all misery in sin which was a personal act consisting of disobedience of God's law. Rousseau blamed society and civilization, and was moved to tears when he thought of his own goodness; no one had ever existed who was as good and compassionate as he! Calvin did not expect anything from nature, but expected everything from God's grace in Christ. In one word, Calvin cast man and all creatures in the dust before the overwhelming majesty of God. Rousseau, on the other hand, put man on the throne, himself first of all, at the expense of God's justice and holiness.[39]

When he begins to unpack this key difference, Bavinck pulls what we might call a rhetorical *tour de force*; he continues with the theme of inequality:

---

[38] *ESSR*, 155.
[39] *ERSS*, 155–56.

> But the demolisher of the eighteenth century was not the only one to con-
> template the immense problem of inequality—the reformer of the six-
> teenth century did the same. However, he approached it from a different
> angle: it was not political and social inequality that struck him first of all,
> but religious inequality. How does one explain, when human nature in
> all men is equally polluted, the profound and ever continuing difference
> between those who accept the Gospel and those who reject it, between
> those who are saved and those who are lost?[40]

As Bavinck deals with the question of inequality, therefore, he makes the
problem more rather than less difficult from a human moral standpoint.
It is one thing to raise theodicy questions about a God who permits some
to live in the lap of decadent luxury while others are reduced to begging
and starving; it is quite another to wonder about a God who sovereignly
disposes the ultimate, eternal destiny of human beings in an inequitable
manner. If all are equally sinful, why are not all saved?

The answer given by Calvin and the Reformed tradition since him is
that this serious and mysterious, not to mention existentially troubling,
question can be attributed finally only to "the good pleasure of God, his
sovereign, omnipotent free will." And what is true for the eternal destiny
of the elect and the reprobate is manifestly also the case with respect to the
diversity and inequality in creation.

> God's preordaining was the final, most profound cause of all differences
> among creatures such as kind, gender, gifts, and in all that is and is just
> so. It is neither the free will of man, nor merit and worth, nor culture or
> even nature that is the source of all multiplicity in creation, but God's
> almighty and all-powerful will which is, at the same time, wise and holy,
> though inscrutable and inexplicable.

Bavinck even takes issue with attributing diversity to "nature": "Nature is
not the cause either, for it did not come into being and does not exist on
its own, but is carried by the Word of God's power from its beginning and
always. By his will all things are and have been created."[41]

I will say more on Bavinck's comparison of Rousseau's and Calvin's
social visions but turn first to his more constructive, biblically based treatment of social relationships in his essay "Christian Principles and Social

---

[40] *ERSS*, 156.
[41] *ERSS*, 156.

Relationships." This will provide for us a picture of how Bavinck construes a biblically informed portrait of a God-ordained social order in which diversity and inequality are not condemned but valued. This essay too has, as background, the reality of "the social question" and the response of the social gospel and Christian socialism as its twin challenges.

Bavinck observes what he calls the "remarkable" fact "that until today science, in spite of all its research, knows nothing for certain about the origin of things. Because it always takes a position on the basis of what exists, it cannot penetrate to the origin of things."[42] This presents us with a large problem when we want to go beyond description to prescription, beyond *is* to *ought*, to a normative pattern for social life.

> From a scientific point of view, we know nothing with certainty about the origin of heaven and earth, of plant and animal and human, of husband and wife, of marriage and family, of society and the state, of religion and morality and justice, of language, art, and science. All these institutions and phenomena exist everywhere already, and we examine them in the light of scientific research, even though that research is still in a primitive stage; but never and nowhere are we witnesses of the origin of these phenomena.

This does not mean, however, that we are held hostage to ignorance, that all we can do is guess and let those with the most power determine how we are to live together. "What science withholds from us, however, is given to us by special revelation that comes to us from Scripture. It gives us a story of the origin of creatures; this story has foundational significance for their existence and destination."[43]

Since I have already touched on some of the social relationships Bavinck discusses further in this essay, notably marriage and family, work, vocation, and rest, we will not consider those here but concentrate on the larger portrait of society as a whole. It all starts with marriage and the family according to Bavinck. Sex differences between men and women and marriage were instituted at creation. Bavinck adds:

> This marriage receives God's special blessing; it is for the multiplication of the human race. Implied in marriage is the family; in the family society; in society, unity, community, and cooperation of the human race. . . .

[42] *ERSS*, 121.
[43] *ERSS*, 121.

Marriage and family contain the point of departure and principles of all kinds of relationships that will later develop in society.[44]

Old Testament Israel models this development because "with no nation did the significance of the family, as foundation of all of society, feature so prominently as with Israel."[45] Israel's tribal structure, based on the lineage of Jacob's sons, was *patriarchal*, says Bavinck, not *hierarchical*; it was a *theocracy*.

> God was Israel's lawgiver, judge, and king; and Israel was God's people, his inheritance, his kingdom (Exod. 15:18; Num. 23:21; Deut. 33:5; Judg. 8:23; 1 Sam. 8:7; Isa. 33:22; etc.). The only thing required of Israel was to live according to the law that God had given, not only religiously but also morally, as well as civilly and as a society. Thus all power in Israel had a servant character; it was tied to God's law in every respect.[46]

Even the priests and Levites, "though they served in the temple," unlike those in the pagan world around Israel, "possessed no secret creed or art, and certainly had no hierarchical, conscience-binding power." They had no inheritance in Israel but "had to live from the donations of the people and thus were very dependent."[47] Bavinck even points out "that Church and State, however closely allied, were nevertheless also different, not only so far as members were concerned, but also in offices and administrations, in institutions and laws." In addition, "foreigners could participate in the spiritual privileges of Israel, and thus, so to speak, be members of the church, without being citizens."[48] And finally, though a theocracy,

> Israel, also religiously, enjoyed a great measure of freedom. Unbelief and heresy were not punished; there was no inquisition; restraint of conscience was totally unknown. And when the prophets testify against a turning away from God and resist kings and priests, they avail themselves of the word, call for a return to the law, but never insist on using force.[49]

It is not difficult to move from these biblical givens to imagining a sociopolitical order of liberty that is nonhierarchical and ruled by law that

---

[44] *ERSS*, 122.
[45] *ERSS*, 123.
[46] *ERSS*, 123–24.
[47] *ERSS*, 124–25.
[48] *ERSS*, 124.
[49] *ERSS*, 125.

binds the powerful as well as the weak, the rich as well as the poor, the healthy and productive as well as the infirm and disabled, the young as well as the old. And though Israel was a theocratic, religiously founded and bounded nation, it is also not difficult to let our imaginations run to a sociopolitical order where liberty of conscience is of highest importance; where influence is morally acceptable only as persuasion, and coercion is repudiated; where the nation's moral compass is by design left to voluntary religious, moral, and civic institutions. In short, it is not a long journey to move from Bavinck's summary to the ideal of the American experiment in ordered, constitutionally framed liberty.

Since this conclusion will strike many readers as unwarranted and perhaps even offensive—especially when combined with the emphasis, earlier in this chapter, on God's sovereign will and good pleasure as the antidote to complaints about diversity and inequality—I now need to return to Bavinck's portrait of John Calvin as a contrast to his fellow Genevan, Jean-Jacques Rousseau.

Justice and Mercy

We left off that discussion with the statement that the differences existing in nature and among people are caused not by culture or nature but by "God's almighty and all-powerful will which is, at the same time, wise and holy, though inscrutable and inexplicable." The standard response to this raises deep concerns about fairness and fatalism. That someone is born into a stable family in a prosperous American suburb at the exact moment another child is born to an unmarried teenager in a third-world slum just doesn't seem fair. Furthermore, for those who believe in God's sovereign, providential disposition of all things, doesn't this lead to resignation and despair? If this is just the way it is, there is nothing we can do to change things.

Bavinck acknowledges the difficulty of this conviction about God's sovereignty; "only a strong generation can accept" it, he says. His application of Calvin's thought only adds fuel to the fires of objection set ablaze against Reformed theology: "Through this confession . . . Calvin taught his followers first of all acceptance, submission, and contentment in times of struggle and oppression." Undoubtedly anticipating resistance to such a claim, Bavinck adds—with a slight smile, one might imagine—"however, few people today will thank him for this." What was going on in his day, and has not stopped yet in ours, is the exact opposite of "acceptance, submission, and contentment in times of struggle and oppression." Instead, "sowing discontent and systematically goading people to be hostile toward all prevailing conditions and arrangements are held in much higher esteem by many." This is the spirit inspired by Rousseau, "for he is the one who, blaming everything on society and culture, made people proud and rebellious." But unrest and disorder are not the only consequences of this posture. Rousseau "also caused them an endless series of disappointments, for revolution that runs counter to nature is a sword that always turns against the one brandishing it."[50]

Faced with the choice between passive resignation and ultimately disappointing activism, socially sensitive Christians might still take the second option. Such a choice is understandable for those of us who take seriously the Bible's instruction to love our neighbor, care for the poor, reach out to the marginalized, and stand up for justice for the weak and powerless. But even with respect to Calvin, says Bavinck,

> acquiescence is not nearly the only and most important thing that Calvin impressed upon his faithful followers. The will of God, according to Calvin's confession, may be absolutely sovereign, totally all-powerful, and inscrutable and therefore to be acknowledged with holy awe and deep reverence; yet it is for everyone who believes the will of a merciful and gracious Father, who loves all his children with an eternal love; his will may be hidden, but he always has wise and holy reasons for all the dark ways in which he often leads them. Such a will is not fate, in which a person acquiesces willy-nilly, but an object of childlike trust, an inexhaustible fountain of comfort, and the strong anchor of a firm and solid hope.

The heart of predestination for Calvin, we must never forget, is

> the abundant grace of God in Christ. For him this was the essence of Christianity through which God tells us how much he loves us. He saw the will of God revealed in all things, even in the iniquities of mankind. But basically and in essence this will is saving grace that leads the world and mankind through the darkness to the light and through death to eternal life.[51]

---

[50] *ERSS*, 156.
[51] *ERSS*, 157.

This comfort of the gospel is vitally important to those who suffer.

> Through the preaching about God's holy and gracious will Calvin fur-
> nished faith, heroism and inspiration to the least and simplest, to those
> persecuted for the sake of the Gospel, to prisoners in their jails, to mar-
> tyrs on scaffold and pyre, making them scorn all suffering and glory in
> oppression. And this kind of comfort we need just as much in our day.

Bavinck observes here that it is relatively easy to sow "discontent in the
hearts of men and to make them rebel against their own fate and society
at large." But this move might be nothing more than a "cruel flattery" of
the masses, "offering a stone and a serpent to someone who prays for a loaf
of bread or a fish." For Rousseau and his followers, the Christian hope for
a world that will be better than this one is exchanged for a utopian dream
of heaven on earth. Alas, it is a dream that will never be achieved, and the
failed journey is a path strewn with blood and corpses. This is an inevitable
result. "For when a person loses his faith in a higher, better world, life here
on earth begins to look more and more like a jail against whose walls he
butts his heads senselessly."[52]

What we are left with, then, is the necessary conclusion that full justice
will never be achieved to our satisfaction in this age. Only in the end, when
God the righteous Judge makes all things new and well, will his cause and
kingdom be fully vindicated. Does this lead Reformed people to defeatist
resignation in the face of injustice, tyranny, and oppression? Here Bavinck
calls attention to a third significant difference between Rousseau and Calvin.
Though Rousseau railed at society "and taught people to do the same, and in
keeping with the custom of the day turned the monarch into a scapegoat, and
made him responsible for their miserable condition, yet in the end he quietly
withdrew into seclusion without moving a finger to reform society." Then
the contrast: "Calvin, on the other hand, derived from the same will of God,
which he had come to know in Christ as a will of grace, the motive to strong,
energetic, and far-reaching actions." Bavinck acknowledges that the doctrine
of predestination, in the hands of the unskilled, did become an instrument
of fear leading to spiritual abuse and despair. But, he contends, this "is a
caricature of the Reformed confession." True reverence for God's will propels
us into action. He draws this contrast between the two citizens of Geneva:

---

[52] *ERSS*, 157.

If you believe, with Rousseau, that society is the cause of all evil, then you have pronounced its death sentence, and you have given man the right to execute people, and you have legitimized the revolution. But if you believe with Calvin that the will of God, his will of good pleasure, is the cause of all things, then that same will becomes his revealed will and the moving force and rule for our living. The words, "Your will be done," encompass and provide not only strength to acquiesce, but also strength to act.[53]

Justice and mercy are both important parts of that activity called for by the will and law of God. The fifth and seventh resolutions adopted by the Christian Social Congress in 1891 both address the need for justice. The fifth states:

According to Scripture the important general principle for a solution to the social question is that there be justice (*gerechtigheid*). This means that each person be assigned to the place where, in accord with their nature, they are able to live according to God's ordinances with respect to God and other creatures.[54]

We should note that this is not a complete and satisfying definition of justice, but its direction is clear. Justice should be defined not in terms of some abstraction like "equality" but procedurely, respecting the diversity of people, tasks, offices, roles, and gifts, all under the normative standard of God's will. The fact that justice does not entail a conservative maintenance of the status quo, but fully takes into account the needs of those who are marginalized, weak, and powerless, is evident in the concrete conclusions drawn from this resolution and articulated in the sixth resolution, which I cited in full at the end of chapter 3.[55] For our purposes here, it is important to note the religious character of the resolution, the concern for eternal and temporal well-being, the insistence that a just order is one that serves "not only [to] prepare people for their eternal destiny, but also to make it possible for them to fulfill their earthly calling." The seventh resolution calls on civil authority, "as God's servant called to maintain justice in society," to pay close attention to God's ordinances in administrating justice. The eighth and final resolution serves as a reminder that perfect

---

[53] *ERSS*, 158.
[54] "Gen. Prin.," 445.
[55] See above, p. 68.

justice will never be achieved in this dispensation: "There remains, in addition to this, a very large role for the ministry of mercy since, thanks to the working of sin and error, all kinds of miseries will always be with us, and in this earthly dwelling can never be removed by justice [alone]."

Bavinck wraps up his essay on Calvin and Rousseau by briefly pointing out Calvin's legacy as a social reformer and influential framer of laws, first in Geneva and then more broadly. Bavinck executes a masterful rhetorical pirouette by citing Rousseau's own praise for Calvin as Geneva's reformer of laws and civic life. Calvin's successes in Geneva, Bavinck adds, prove "that Calvin's religious philosophy of life, when applied, also contains a promise for today's society. Has it not often been shown that Protestantism to a large degree has benefitted civilization and the prosperity of nations?" According to Bavinck, Calvinist reform is not revolution because it operates with "a standard from above and beyond reality." Without it,

> we might easily seek our well-being in an unhistorical radicalism. However, when we believe in a higher order of things, namely, the holy and gracious will of God which comes to us not only through the facts of history, but also through the testimony of his Word, then we have found a norm with which to measure the present and change it. And the danger to condemn reality unconditionally or to justify it, is overcome then, at least in principle.[56]

Practically, "we will then refrain from condemning society in the way Rousseau and his superficial followers have made themselves guilty, and we will sooner learn to respect it as a wonderful artificial organism that developed under God's guidance and that has been a blessing for millions of people for centuries." At the same time, we ought to be grateful for "the new circumstances and new relationships [that] are constantly gaining ground in every area." That Bavinck has in mind the increasingly democratic and social egalitarian direction of modern society is clear from his distaste for any nostalgic longing for a class-ridden society.

> Nevertheless, who among us would wish for a return of the time in which the social classes were separated from each other almost like castes, and people were expected to praise whatever their masters decided, and the

---

[56] *ERSS*, 160–61.

practitioners of the sciences looked down upon everyone who had to earn his keep by manual labor?

He even directs special opprobrium against his own class of professors.

> The more we approach the middle of the seventeenth century, the more we notice how professors tend to avoid their fellow citizens and begin to constitute a separate caste. They did not participate, or very little, in social life, were very seldom seen in the circles of the unlearned, and demonstrated a formality and decorum that dismayed everyone, but that was quite in keeping with their dress, especially with their awful wigs that fell down from the head to their waist. Many wanted to be honored as deities. Their pride and conceit were often boundless, so that even learned people who associated with them complained about their conceit.[57]

That seems like a perfect segue to the final section of this chapter, where we will take a brief look at *Professor* Bavinck as a public figure in politics.

Bavinck the Statesman

Chapter 6 covered some of the biographical details of Bavinck's involvement with Abraham Kuyper's Anti-Revolutionary Party and its political activity, and I will not repeat them here. Instead, to sample Bavinck's work as a senator in the First Chamber of the Dutch Parliament, we will briefly consider his speech to Parliament, delivered on December 29, 1912, concerning the budget for the Dutch East Indies.[58] The speech is remarkable for its high tone and thoughtful, reasoned argument, showing Bavinck at his Christian professorial and statesmanlike best. In his active political life, too, Bavinck remained consistent with his own Christian principles as a follower of Jesus Christ.

The published speech was given the title, undoubtedly by Bavinck himself, "Christianity and Natural Science." While Bavinck's discourse about that topic is a linchpin in his argument, the bigger issue was summarized by a Dutch senator, C. Th. van Deventer, who is Bavinck's interlocutor: "What is to be the foundation of the education of the natives [in Indonesia]: is it to be based on religion or on general humanism; is it to be confessional or

---

[57] *ERSS*, 162.
[58] *ERSS*, 81–104.

neutral?"[59] Van Deventer's own view strongly favored a neutral, secular, humanistic education, one that would inculcate Western values but not offend the religious sensibilities of Muslims and introduce the Christian religion. Van Deventer did, however, favor the "Christianization of Java's Muslims," though he thought direct engagement would be counterproductive because "history shows that where Islam with its consequent monotheism has established itself, chances for Christianity are as good as nil." Van Deventer urged Christian missions in Indonesia to "concentrate its efforts on those regions of the Archipelago that have not been taken over by Islam as yet, where it could be active with a much better chance of success." In order to have a hope of bringing Muslims to Christianity, Van Deventer urged a policy of Westernizing Java's Muslims first, in the hope that an opening would present itself. Western humanism, so he argued, "will continue to awaken the spirits, placate the emotions, and ennoble morals. Maybe by following this pathway an attitude will be created among Muslims that will make them more receptive to the teachings of Christ."[60]

In a nutshell, Bavinck's reply reminds his fellow senators that modern culture, including the development of the natural sciences, cannot be divorced from Christianity. To make the case for this claim, he appeals to internationally recognized scientists such as physiologist Emil du Bois-Reymond (1818–1896), a professor at Berlin who, though an atheist himself, nonetheless contended that "natural science, however paradoxical it may sound, nevertheless owes its origin to Christianity." He adds to this the testimony of another German idealist philosopher and winner of the 1908 Nobel Prize in Literature, Rudolf Christoph Eucken (1846–1926), who stated that "the discipline of history, as we know it today, is intimately connected with Christianity both concerning its essence and its value." Bavinck concludes:

> Once again, it is Christianity that has made possible a uniform history and made it known to us as one mighty, gigantic drama that includes all peoples, the entire world, and all of humanity. On that basis I believe that we have to dispute the claim that culture without religion and without Christianity would definitely be adequate for the population in our colonies in order to give that population what it needs.[61]

---

[59] ERSS, 81.
[60] ESSR, 82–83.
[61] ERSS, 83–84.

This testimony before the Dutch Senate—of which we have provided only an inadequate synopsis—is sufficient to mark Bavinck as a committed and eloquent Christian statesman who argues at the highest levels and with the highest standards of reason and persuasion for applying "God's ordinances" in the land. What strikes me as even more telling is Bavinck's manner and tone in dealing with ill-treatment in public life. In the same speech he calls attention to the way in which a writer in a public journal has badly misquoted something he said in an earlier Senate speech on a similar subject. The essayist took Bavinck's quotation from Du Bois-Reymond, attributed it to Bavinck himself, and then proceeded to attack Bavinck for the content of the statement. Bavinck carefully lays out in detail how distorted this account was and rightly notes that when a speaker quotes someone in a speech, "it is mostly immaterial whether the person who made it part of his speech agreed with it or not."[62] The statement must be evaluated on its own merit. The essay author's argument was not with Bavinck but with Du Bois-Reymond, the source of the statement.

And then came the remarkable move in Bavinck's rejoinder. With Du Bois-Reymond's statement in his pocket Bavinck had a great deal of persuasive capital at his disposal; if he were merely trying to win a political argument, he could have let matters rest where they were. He had made his case and won. But, he did not leave it there; he softened the blow instead and indicated his ability to meet the author of the article "quite a way." "If I had wanted to speak about the relationship between Christianity and the natural sciences in my own words, I certainly would have expressed myself less dogmatically and less forcefully than Du Bois-Reymond." Bavinck's critic had attributed to him "the strange claim that Christianity is the only source of natural science and that there has never been anywhere else, neither in Greece, nor in Arabia, anything that resembled investigation of natural phenomena." Fortunately, Bavinck had his own *Reformed Dogmatics* in hand as evidence that he did not hold such an extreme view. Bavinck said that his own claims always countered critics who contended that Christianity was hostile to science. "It is not true that Christianity with its supernaturalism was hostile to the natural order and made science impossible." On the contrary, "Christianity made science—specifically natural science—possible and prepared the way for it." How? Christianity repudiated the deification of nature that in polytheistic and pagan contexts

---

[62] *ERSS*, 85.

ensured a resistance to all scientific inquiry of the natural world because it would be a desecration. "But Christianity distinguishes God and the world, and by its confession of God as the Creator of all things, separated God from the nexus of nature and lifted him far above it. The study of nature, therefore, is no longer a violation of Deity."[63]

The remainder of the speech is also remarkable in its erudition, its calm and careful reasoning, its clear testimony to the Christian gospel and a Christian worldview, and its persuasive overview of the gospel's influence and transforming effect for the well-being and flourishing of nations. Bavinck concludes with the expressed desire that all people in the world might enjoy the cultural, social, and political benefits with which Europeans have been blessed, thanks to the gospel. This too is a fruit of God's providential wisdom, not a matter of our deserving or earning. If we truly care about the world's poor, if their marginalization and misery trouble us—and they should!—we should not be satisfied with simply offering our culture, and not be content with providing for physical needs alone or even with redistribution schemes that might diminish inequality. How do we bring "the comfort of faith [to such people] in their dire struggle of life?"

> [We] tell them about God, the Father of our Lord Jesus Christ, who by his almighty and ever-present power upholds, as with his hand, heaven and earth and all creatures; who so rules them that leaf and blade, rain and drought, fruitful and lean years, food and drink, health and sickness, prosperity and poverty—all things, in fact, come to us not by chance but from his fatherly hand.

"Essentially, the church's mission has no other aim than this."[64]

As we face the big questions about humanity's many problems, miseries, and suffering, we need humility and patience. Bavinck concludes his essay on Rousseau and Calvin by acknowledging that much of this will remain a mystery to us; in the meantime we are to be faithful stewards of the gospel's riches and

> perhaps we will find the answer gradually, over time, in the same way in which the kingdom of God came about in the parable: "This is what the kingdom of God is like. A man scatters seed on the ground. Night and

---

[63] *RD*, 2:611.
[64] *ERSS*, 104.

day, whether he sleeps or gets up, the seed sprouts and grows, though he does not know how."[65]

Our concern is with obedience; the results are in God's hands.

That is the ultimate confidence in God's sovereignty; Christ's kingdom is not our work but his, and he alone guarantees the victory. On that note, we are ready to take in Bavinck's sermon "The World-Conquering Power of Faith."

---

[65] *ERSS*, 163.

"THE WORLD-CONQUERING POWER OF FAITH"

A SERMON ON I JOHN 5:4B DELIVERED IN THE BURGWALKERK, KAMPEN, JUNE 30, 1901

Dr. H. Bavinck[1]

[Note to reader: Paralleling the structure of this book's ten chapters, I origi-nally intended to produce here a concluding "homily" on hopeful Christian discipleship, drawing primarily from two sources: Bavinck's essay "The Kingdom of God: The Highest Good," and his only published sermon, on 1 John 5:4b, "The World-Conquering Power of Faith." Excerpts from these would have been supplemented by key selections from Bavinck's treat-ment of eschatology in the fourth volume of his *Reformed Dogmatics* and the concluding chapter of *Our Reasonable Faith*, titled "Eternal Life." As in the rest of the book before you, my own narrative would have provided

---

[1] H. Bavinck, *De wereldverwinnende kracht des geloofs* (Kampen: Zalsman, 1901). Bavinck provided the following explanation at the head of the published work: "This sermon was delivered on the occasion that President Kruger [of South Africa] and his entourage, during his visit to Kampen on Sunday, June 30, 1901, was present in the congregation. Many who heard the sermon expressed the desire of having it available in print. Though I was not able to reproduce it word-for-word, I nevertheless did not object to honoring that friendly request. This written sermon is entirely in substantive agreement with the message delivered at that time." My heartfelt thanks here to two colleagues and friends, Arie Leder and Nelson Kloosterman, who carefully read my first-draft translation and offered numerous suggestions for correction and improvement that I was glad to incorporate in the final version.

the structure for an eclectic gathering of Bavinck quotations. As I came to the end of writing, however, two or three considerations led me to change course.

First, as I indicated in the preface, I wanted to let Bavinck's own voice be heard as much as possible and let my voice be subordinated to his, even if that presented some stylistic challenges. But I became dissatisfied with my plan to combine two voices in the homiletic genre I intended for the conclusion. Multiauthored sermons just don't seem right and, above all— the documentary hypothesis of the Pentateuch notwithstanding—aside from Holy Scripture itself, good sermons should not be riddled with source footnotes! And, since Bavinck's own delivered and published sermon was going to be a primary source anyway, why not feature it as a whole instead? I saw no gain in excerpting parts of it and thus decided to provide a full translation below.

A second consideration tipped the balance. My other envisioned source, "The Kingdom of God: The Highest Good," was already available in English translation,[2] while the sermon was not. By simply translating the sermon and using it as the concluding homily, I could achieve two goals: let Bavinck's full authentic voice close this volume, and provide a real service to the many Bavinck fans who do not read Dutch.

Finally, as I went over this sermon carefully again, it struck me how prescient and relevant it is for the social circumstances in which we find ourselves today. I will make only three comments about it.

(1) Though Bavinck's historical examples are clearly dated and some are even debatable—such as the references to the Boers of South Africa—his powerful appeal to the gospel received in faith as the only way to overcome the world remains timely. This is especially so, I might add, when Christians and churches today are again tempted to look to social-activist distractions as ways to transform the world. Bavinck challenges us directly, telling us that won't work. (2) The sermon is entirely consistent with the portrait I have sketched throughout of Bavinck's understanding of Christian discipleship. It shows how his vision of grace restoring us to our true humanity so that we could flourish as renewed image bearers in God's world was grounded in the text of Scripture itself. (3) Bavinck clearly preached what he practiced.

---

[2] H. Bavinck, "The Kingdom of God: The Highest Good," trans. Nelson D. Kloosterman, *The Bavinck Review* 2 (2011): 133–70.

Therefore, *tolle lege*: be edified, encouraged, and challenged as followers of our Lord Jesus Christ. *Ad maiorem Dei gloriam.*[3]]

The Sermon

The nineteenth century, which concluded only a few months ago, has been rightly called by many the age of unbelief and revolution.[4] Yet, no sooner have we entered the twentieth century than we feel the question involuntarily welling up within us: Could this new era perhaps give us an opportunity to see a return of the Christian faith and an application of the principles of the Reformation to all areas of life?[5]

Three signs in particular give rise to this thought in our hearts. In the first place, along with the turn of the century we perceive a turn in the current of thinking and striving among the nations. The revolution did not deliver on its expectations; hardly any of its promises have come to fruition. To this day, the paradise that it held before humanity has not been established on earth. Rather, disappointment and disillusion reign everywhere. On the one hand, there are the exhaustion of living and the insatiability of culture; on the other hand, there are dissatisfaction and bitter complaint about the misery of social circumstances. And while many, such as the radicals and socialists, expect deliverance only from applying the principles of the revolution more strictly and broadly, there has also arisen an increasing number of those who are retreating from the practical consequences of dogmatic unbelief, who again desire to make room for religion in the various areas of human life. It is evident that many children of our generation experience an interest in religion. Instead of the most insolent denial has come an acknowledgment and consideration of those things that we do not see. One can even notice a striving, along impenetrable routes, to penetrate the appearance of things to get to their essence, to penetrate the visible world to reach the invisible background that sustains it. Whatever errors exist in this new spiritual current, there also exists a great deal that warrants our joy and gratitude. The tyranny of reason has come to an end, and the heart has reassumed

---

[3] *Tolle lege*: "take up and read." *Ad maiorem Dei gloriam*: "for the greater glory of God."
[4] Bavinck is alluding here to the famous work of historian-statesman Guillaume Groen van Prinsterer, *Unbelief and Revolution*, originally published in 1847.
[5] A knowledge of the immediate context of Dutch history is essential for understanding a key source of Bavinck's hope here; for details, see the next note.

its rights; faith has obtained its initial victory over the idolatry of the material and the worship of the senses.

The second event that deserves our attention and occasions the preceding question is the war in South Africa. Many wars were fought throughout the last century and at its close, but among them all, none has awakened the interest of so many people as profoundly as the struggle of both South African Republics for their freedom and independence. No doubt the primary reason for this can be found in the telling fact that in no war in recent times have right and might been so sharply set against each other as in this struggle of a small nation against a powerful state. That all nations with virtual unanimity allied themselves through sympathy, gifts, and prayers with the oppressed Afrikaners is due to the heinous way in which England has violated the sense of justice. But the interest that was awakened by the violation of justice was matched by amazement at the simple, powerful faith exhibited in this struggle as the core of the courageous Boer warriors. While unbelief was gaining the upper hand in the civilized world, suddenly there arose a people in South Africa, small in number, weak in power, untrained for major warfare, but strong in faith, filled with passion for justice, and prepared for every sacrifice, no matter how severe, for the sake of freedom. That faith astonished the world and proved its strength superior to worldly power and might.

Finally, the third event that points us to the power of faith is the outcome of the general elections in our fatherland.[6] Without a doubt, strange fire has been placed on the altar in connection with this service that we as citizens had to render for the glory of God. Not nearly all who participated in this work let their choice be determined by the requirement of Christian principles. Nonetheless, we may be grateful and rejoice at the outcome of the election, albeit with trepidation. Whoever compares the beginning of this century with that of the previous one sees our boldest expectations exceeded. Beyond our prayers and thoughts, God has done good for his people in these lands, increased them and established them day after day. And now with the results of

---

[6] The general election for the House of Representatives in the Dutch Parliament had been held only two weeks earlier, on June 14, 1901, with the Anti-Revolutionary Party led by Abraham Kuyper coming in a very close second to the Liberal Party (27.4 percent versus 27.6 percent). Though the ARP had received larger percentages in the elections of 1888 and 1891, the 1901 election marked the first time the party was in a position of practical equality with the previously dominant Liberal Party. Abraham Kuyper was asked to form a coalition government and took office as prime minister on August 1, 1901, a position he held until August 17, 1905.

the elections, the majority of Dutch voters have made it clear that they do not want to continue along the path of unbelief and revolution. We desire that the government of this nation also take Christian principles into consideration. At the voting both, our nation has given a beautiful testimony, and in that testimony a triumph over the world was achieved through faith.

These three events have led me today, when the president of the South African Republic and his entourage are gathered with the congregation of Christ in the house of prayer in this place, to speak to you about the "world-conquering power of faith." Before doing so, however, let us in thanksgiving and prayer come before the face of God and seek his blessing for our gathering.

1 John 5:4b
"And this is the victory that overcomes the world, (namely) our faith."

It is not without reason that the apostle John is usually referred to as the apostle of love. But this does not in the least rule out his ongoing concern with faith. In the first five verses of this chapter, he even testifies about three glorious features of faith.

First, he tells us that faith implants a new beginning of life within a person: Whoever believes that Jesus is the Christ is born of God. Through faith he has passed from death into life; he is no longer from below but from above; he no longer belongs to the world but is a child of God, a citizen of heaven, an heir of eternal life. For as many as have received Christ, to them he has given the power to become children of God, that is to say, those who believe in his name and have been born not of blood, nor of the flesh, nor of the will of man, but of God.

In addition John testifies that faith in Jesus as the Christ is a mighty power for the love and obedience to God's commands. Whoever believes that Jesus is the Christ, the Son of God, has thereby experienced the great love that God revealed in sending his Son and in reconciling us to himself through his blood. And the experience of this unbounded love compels him to love with all his soul and mind and strength the One who gave him birth. For God is the First One. This is love: not that we loved God, but that he loved us and sent his Son as an atoning sacrifice for our sins. Nonetheless, after this we have also loved him, because he has first loved us. And whoever loves God with grateful reciprocal love will automatically love all those who along with him have been born of God and belong to the same family of the Father. Indeed, through faith he receives an inner desire to walk in righteousness not only according to some but according to all God's commandments.[7] And those commandments are not burdensome. The commandments of the world are burdensome and serving the world is harsh. But those who love God find his commandments a delight all day long. The yoke of Jesus is gentle for his disciples, and his burden is light for them.

In the third place, John assures us in the fourth and fifth verses of this chapter that faith is a power, a power that conquers even the world. For all who are born of God overcome the world, and overcome that world by faith; that is, the faith that Jesus is the Son of God. This world-conquering power of faith will become apparent to us, we trust, when we consider in turn

> the *opposition* that this faith encounters
> the *character* that this faith displays
> the *triumph* that is promised to this faith.

I.

Everything that opposes faith, all the resistance it encounters, the entire power of the enmity against which it must do battle, is captured by John with the term "world." The Greek word that is translated by "world" actually means "adornment," "adorning," and points to the fact that the people who spoke this language saw the world primarily in terms of its beautiful side. On account of the richness of her forms and colors, on account of its harmonious order and regularity, the "world" was admired by the Greeks as a creation of art, as a work of beauty.

Holy Scripture also manifests a keen eye for this beauty of the world. Scripture tells us about something concerning which the Greek philosophers had not the slightest clue, namely, that the almighty and eternal God, who called into being those things that did not exist, created the entire world by his word. Then, at the conclusion of his work of creation, he saw all that he had made, and, behold! It was very good. But even after the fall, Scripture still frequently sings about the beauty of the world in powerful,

---

[7] The language here resonates so strongly with that of 1 John 4 and 5 that one might easily overlook the seamless manner in which Bavinck has also included language from Lord's Day 44, answer 114 of the Heidelberg Catechism.

devotional language. The heavens declare the glory of God, the firmament the work of his hands. God's voice is upon the great waters; his breath renews the face of the earth; his paths drip with fatness. Even human beings are made a little less than the angels and crowned with honor and glory. The Lord alone is good; his name is glorious over the entire earth; his mercies are over all his works.

Nonetheless, Scripture does not stop with this aesthetic worldview. Here Scripture differs as widely as the heavens themselves from the nature idolatry of the pagans, though they do admire God's work and extol his virtues in all of creation. However, it is not enough for Scripture to praise the beauty of the world. Scripture applies to the created world an additional, higher, ethical standard and measures everything by the requirement of divine righteousness. Then, using this measuring stick, Scripture declares that this world is not what it is supposed to be; it is fallen and has failed to reach its ideal. Creation has become a world opposed to God, having placed itself in the service of sin.

The fallen angels, who in spite of gloriously gathering at the foot of God's throne, nonetheless did not retain their position; they are included in the "world" understood in this sense. Included also are people, all of whom fell in their representative head and are therefore conceived and born in sin, daily increasing their guilt before God. The human mind that is darkened, the human will that is inclined to evil, the human heart from which come forth all evil thoughts, the human soul that has turned away from God and cleaves to the dust, the human body that turns all its members into weapons of unrighteousness—all of this belongs to the "world."

To the "world" belongs everything set up and established by human beings: the institutions of family and society, the state, professions and trades, science and art, business and commerce. To the "world" belongs the sum total of all humanity, from the first human being to the very last one, all of whose births proceeded from a single woman. The "world" includes all generations and tribes and languages and nations throughout all the periods of history throughout its development and expansion, its times of struggle and prosperity, its times of civilizing and times of degeneration. The "world" consists of the states that human beings have established and the empires they have set up.

To the "world" belongs the irrational and nonliving creation as well, for the earth has been cursed on account of human beings; the entire creation groans in labor pains together until now. For creation has been subjected to futility, not of its own will but by the will of him who subjected it.

The entire composition of created reality, all the meshing gears of God's creation, that enclosed totality of visible and invisible things, insofar and to the extent that it is an instrument of unrighteousness, is summarized by the apostle John by the term "world." And he is able to designate it with one name, in one word, because sin has affected the whole world and caused it in its totality to live from one principle, caused it to be enlivened with one spirit, and caused it to be directed to one goal: namely, enmity and opposition against God, its Creator and Lord.

True, people may assert and thoughtlessly declare that God is love. And it is indeed the case that he is eternal love and boundless mercy: for God so loved even that guilty and lost world that he gave his only-begotten Son, that whosoever believes in him might not perish but have eternal life [John 3:16]. Yet, outside of Christ, who dares to glory in God's love? Does not all of nature, does not our own heart and conscience proclaim to us that God's favor does not rest upon his creatures, that God has a quarrel with what he has made, that all creatures perish by his wrath and are terrified by his anger?

Is that not a terrible situation? God and the world at odds with each other because of sin! A state of enmity and hatred, of conflict and war between the Creator and his creature, between the Maker and that which he made, between the almighty, eternal God and the powerless creature who is nothing but dust and ashes and has no existence in himself. For that entire world does not rest on its own foundation but is sustained by the word of God's power moment by moment. From him the world derives all its being and life, all its gifts and strength, all that it is and all that it has. Even Satan would have no power unless it were given him from above. Nevertheless, sin organizes the entire universe, with all its creatures and powers, into an instrument against God and his kingdom. It turns the universe into a world whose ruler is the Prince of Darkness, who lies in the grip of evil, who operates in a state of injustice, who forms a kingdom of sin and unrighteousness, and who by means of violence and guile seeks to triumph over God, his name, and his kingdom.

And precisely by means of sin placing all God's creatures and gifts into its service, that world constitutes such a virtually unlimited power. Who is capable of resisting its domination or escaping its influence? Would a creature who is surrounded on every side by the world and lies imprisoned in its snares be able to do that? Would a person who belongs to the world in body, soul, thought, and desire, be able to do it? After all, not only is that world outside of us, but it dwells within the most important part of us, in our heart, in our mind, in our will, and in our affections. That is why the world has such power over us, leads us astray by the lusts of our flesh and the desires of our eyes and the grandeur of life. All of these things are not from the Father but from the world. For everyone who commits sin is a slave of sin.

No, we do not serve the world willy-nilly. In the core of our being we do not stand against the world and on God's side, although we sometimes willingly delude ourselves into thinking so. By nature we are all children of wrath, without God, without Christ, without hope in the world. As human beings we are the most prominent part of that fallen world. The world has its strongest foothold in us; we are its fiercest warriors. We serve the world willingly and willfully, with all the gifts God has bestowed on us, with all the abilities he has bequeathed to us. We follow the world's track without any resistance. Along with the entire world we are guilty, impure, stained, and damnable before God's face. That is why the world always drags us farther and farther away from God and toward our destruction. For whoever belongs to the world will also pass away along with the world and all its desires. The world is an irresistible force within us and around us, and extends the scepter of its dominion over all creatures.

Oh, wretched people that we are, who shall deliver us from the power of this world? Who will set us free from the guilt of sin, from the stain of impurity, from the servitude of destruction, from the power of the grave? Who will restore to us the dominion over the world and crown us as its conquerors?

II.

See, beloved, when we humans are clueless and search in vain among other creatures for deliverance, John the apostle of the Lord Jesus Christ comes to us and holds God's Word before our eyes: this is the victory that overcomes the world, even our faith.

Faith, the victory over the world!

When we take note of this word for the first time, we could easily sense the notion rising within us that John is mocking our misery, that he has no understanding of the world's power and has formed a scientifically inadequate understanding of faith.

Because faith, so it is often said, even if it is something more than opinion, is still much less than knowledge and never brings us any further than a certain degree of probability. And would such a faith, which is nothing more than an uncertain and unstable opinion, really be a victory over the world? A victory, not over a few ideas or desires, but over the whole world and over every power that it exerts within us and outside of us?

Would it not be more reasonable for us to act as Naaman the Syrian did when he responded angrily to Elisha's command to wash himself seven times in the Jordan in order to be healed? "Are not Abana and Pharpar, the rivers of Damascus, better than any of the waters of Israel? Couldn't I wash in them and be cleansed?" In the same way we run the risk of thinking that in the conflict with the world, John knows of no other weapon to place in our hands than faith, and we then react in anger and say: Are not the states and empires, the arts and the sciences, the discoveries and inventions that humans have brought forth better weapons in this battle than the simple faith that John commends to his readers and to us? If he wanted to equip us for battle against the world, why does he not mention the sciences by which human beings exercise dominion over all the works of God's hands? Why does he not mention art, a powerful ability that incarnates the highest and most beautiful human thoughts in the recalcitrant world of matter? Why does he not mention the state that tames the wild animal within human beings and compels them to walk in the way of righteousness? Why does he not mention the world's empires that provide the violent with victory over the peoples and force all peoples into one nation? Why does he say nothing about the glory and greatness of human beings, and speak only about faith, shared by only a few?

Before we angrily turn away from John's word, however, let us examine more closely what he has in mind with this faith and why he ascribes such world-conquering power to it. Serious, unbiased examination forbids us from letting ourselves be deceived by the appearance of things. And if we simply think about the conflict that is present here, the character of the issue changes immediately. For it is a world of sin and unrighteousness, of destruction and death, that must be overcome. And whatever laurels science may have won in its own terrain, it has never delivered a single person from guilt and made someone appear without terror before the face of God. Whatever pleasantness art may have introduced into human life, it has never furnished any creature with the only comfort that can lead to blessed living and dying. And whatever victories that states and world empires have registered over people and nations, they have never changed human hearts and subjected them in voluntary obedience to the will of the King of kings. All these weapons made by human hands are borrowed from the world, are taken from the world, and will all pass away with that world. Conceived and born in sin, they have frequently been used in the service of the world, promoted its power, and expanded its dominion.

The faith of which John speaks, however, can speak of other victories. Behind it lies an entire history, a history that begins with a lost paradise and continues from generation to generation. Allow some of the heroes of faith to pass before your spirit for a moment. By faith Noah, being warned by a divine message concerning things not yet seen, prepared the ark for the salvation of his family; and by means of that ark he condemned the world and became an heir of the righteousness that is according to faith. By faith Abraham was obedient when he was called to go out to the place he would receive as an inheritance; and he went out not knowing where he would end up. By faith Moses, when he had grown up, refused to be called a son of Pharaoh's daughter, choosing to be ill-treated with God's people rather than to enjoy the pleasures of sin for a short while. He considered the reproach of Christ greater riches than the treasures of Egypt because he looked to the recompense of the reward. By faith the children of Israel passed through the Red Sea as on dry land while the Egyptians, trying the same, were drowned. By faith the walls of Jericho fell after they had been encircled for seven days. By faith Paul entered the pagan world and planted the banner of the gospel of the cross at the crossroads of civilization. By faith the early church withstood the Roman world imperial power and led the peoples of Europe to the obedience of Christ. By faith Luther raised his voice against the corruptions of the Roman church and placed the pure light of the gospel once again on the candlestick. By faith our forefathers strived eighty years long against Roman idolatry and Spanish oppression, and gained the victory of freedom over both. By faith the heroes of South Africa took up arms on behalf of freedom and justice against English su-premacy and, to the amazement of observers, have remained standing to the present day. By faith—but whom else shall I mention of all those thousands upon thousands more, who through the course of the ages by faith have conquered kingdoms, exercised justice, received the promises, stopped the mouths of lions, quenched the raging fires, escaped the edge of the sword, received strength out of weakness, become mighty in war, put foreign armies to flight?

Acknowledge this history therefore as witness to the world-conquering power of faith! But history does not bear this kind of testimony to every kind of faith—not to the faith that is only a psychological phenomenon without reference to its object, its origin, its essence. For there are many kinds of faith. There is a faith that proceeds only from within a person, that belongs to the world, that bends the knee to an idol, that is nothing more than unbelief or superstition. Such a faith does not fight or conquer the world, but supports and establishes it. John, the apostle of the Lord, ascribes world-conquering power only to that faith that he shares with his brothers and sisters, the faith that Jesus is the Christ, the Son of the living God. Only this specific faith, this well-defined faith alone, is capable of victory. For this faith believes that *Jesus* is the Son of God, the Christ. *Jesus*—that is to say: that historical person, that man born of a woman who lived nineteen centuries ago in Palestine; who was like us in every way, sin excepted; who traveled through the land preaching, doing good, healing all kinds of diseases among the people; who gave his life on the shameful and scandalous cross. Such faith believes that this Jesus, who, when he came among us, would not be recognized by anyone using only the human eye as anything more than a man, that this Jesus, who had no form or comeliness that we should desire him, notwithstanding all this is the Son of God, the only begotten of the Father, full of grace and truth, truly human according to the flesh, but nonetheless true God, to be praised beyond all else for eternity. Such faith believes that this Jesus is the Christ—and neither our virtues nor our good works, neither art nor science, neither any state nor potentate, nor any creature in heaven or on earth, but he and he alone is the Christ—the Lord's Servant, God's Anointed, the Atonement for sins, the Redeemer of the world, our highest Prophet, our only High Priest, our eternal King.

By this means, namely, by means of faith's content and object, faith is such a world-conquering power. Such faith is not simply an activity of the lips or an intellectual affirmation of a historical truth. Rather, faith is a firm certainty, an unshakable conviction, an ineradicable trust, that comes not from blood nor the will of the flesh, not from human will but from God and his Spirit who implants it in our hearts. This is the bond that binds our soul to the Mediator and holds fast to him as though it is beholding the Invisible.

This is the power that transfers one out of darkness into the kingdom of the Son of God's love. This is the power that supplies the believer with a place to stand and a resting place in the world of immovable realities. This is the firm foundation for what the believer hopes, and the irrefutable proof for those things he does not see. This is the courage that enables him to defy the whole world and to rejoice: if God is for us, who shall be against us? This is the comfort that leads him to sing psalms in the night and in the most frightening persecution to lift up this song:[8]

> The Lord has become my help and strength,
>   He is my song, my psalmody;
> He it was who performed my salvation;
>   Therefore, I will praise him all my life.
> Glad songs resound in the tents of the godly
>   for our deliverance and salvation.
> There they sing joyously, with psalms of thanksgiving;
>   God's right hand does mighty deeds!

III.

Only because it is *this* faith in Jesus as the Christ is that world conquest promised and guaranteed to believers.

Even in its core and essence, faith is already the victory over the world. Faith enjoys such a victory not only as its result and fruit, but from its earliest beginnings faith is already a victory over the world. After all, believing that Jesus is the Christ is the most elementary thing imaginable; it is the only route, the fresh and living way for a guilty human being, out of sheer grace, to enjoy peace with God, eternal life, and heaven's salvation.

But this does not contradict the fact that in order for someone to receive and exercise that faith, so much is required that no one can personally grant it or acquire it on their own. For to truly believe that Jesus is the Christ requires that we deny ourselves, crucify our flesh with its desires, submit our minds and all our thoughts in captivity unto obedience, consider all our righteousness as a garment to be thrown away, accuse ourselves of having transgressed all the commandments, let go of our hope in every creature, fully acknowledge God's justice, and plead upon his grace

---

[8] What follows here in the original is Bavinck's quotation of Psalm 118, stanza 7 in the metrical psalter used in the Dutch Reformed churches of his day. I am providing my own free translation of this stanza.

alone! Oh, what arises to oppose such believing! Everything opposes it, everything within us and outside of us. Our mind and our heart, our will and our inclinations, our flesh and our blood, our name and our status, our money and our possessions, our circumstances and our society, the entire world within us and outside us, and above all, Satan who is the ruler of this world, the god of this age who blinds our senses. In order to believe, we must be crucified to the world and the world to us.

But that is exactly the reason why, already in its origin and essence, faith is the victory over the world. For whoever believes has received a new life. We have become new creations, called out of darkness into God's marvelous light; no longer citizens and subjects of the world, but born from above, from God, born of his Spirit. Our citizenship is in heaven. Our unrighteousness has been forgiven, our diseases healed; our lives are delivered from destruction, and we are crowned with mercy and compassions. Who shall bring any charge against God's elect? It is God who justifies. Who is it that condemns? It is Christ who died, yes, who was raised from the dead, who is at the right hand of God, who indeed intercedes for us. Who shall separate us from the love of Christ? Shall tribulation, or distress, or persecution, or famine, or danger, or sword? But in all these things we are more than conquerors through him who loved us.

Through faith the believer has first of all been rescued from the violence of the world, but in addition, through faith the believer rules over that world with prophetic, priestly, and kingly power. For the faith that Jesus is the Christ is not a musty tranquility; it does not withdraw into quiet solitude. Instead, this faith is living and powerful and courageously ventures out into the world. Faith not only enjoys, but it also works; faith says something and does something. It bears witness and it delivers. It speaks and it acts. It attacks with the power of the Word and ventures forth in a demonstration of Spirit and power. One who believes cannot be silent. In the midst of the world they sound the testimony that Jesus is the Christ. Believers do not proclaim their own wisdom, but preach the wisdom that comes from above, even though it may appear foolish in the eyes of the world. They testify that Jesus is the Christ; nothing else, nothing less, nothing more. Jesus is the Christ, not gold or power, not violence or coercion, not prestige or virtue, not science or art. None of these but only Jesus is the Savior of the world, the only, the perfect, the all-sufficient Savior, and nobody or nothing alongside him or below him or with him.

Through that testimony, faith is once again a world-conquering power. For the world has nothing about which to testify. It does not believe and therefore cannot confess. The world does not know the power of the word. As soon as the church takes its confession into the world, the world reaches for the weapons of repression and coercion, of abuse and persecution. These are the weapons that the world has at its disposal in its battle against the church of Christ. Faith, by contrast, is powerful only through its testimony. Faith does not mock, does not rage, and does not persecute. Faith only bears witness, firmly, confidently, unshakably, unceasingly, all the way to the hour of death, even to the fiery stake. Faith is like a rock, standing solid in the rolling surf. Bring on the world with its clatter of weapons and display of might! No violence or force, no scaffold or stake, can withstand rock-solid faith. Faith glories in oppression. Faith triumphs in its defeat. Faith is revived in death. Even the blood of martyrs is the seed of the church.

Faith not only bears witness; it also works and acts, through love. Love is the fruit, the ripe, glorious, precious fruit of faith. Whoever believes that Jesus is the Christ has experienced God's love, and therefore whoever loves the parent loves the child. Whoever does not love does not know God, for God is love. All who believe love everyone who with them is born of God and believes in the name of Jesus, for we know that when we love our brothers, we have passed from death to life. Whoever does not love his brother remains in death. Whoever believes also loves God's commandments; for this is the love of God, that we keep his commandments. And his commandments are not burdensome, they are all fulfilled by love.

Through this love, faith becomes a power that conquers the world. For the world does not know the secret of love, it hates both Jesus and his Father, and it hates all to whom Christ has given the Father's word, because they are not of the world. But the church of Christ is mighty when, according to the command and precept of her Master, she loves her enemies, blesses those who curse her, does well toward those who hate her, and prays for those who commit violence against her and persecute her. That love is stronger than death, it drives out all fear; it covers and believes and hopes and bears all things, and it never perishes.

Faith obtains all of this world-conquering power not from itself, however, but only from Christ. That is why, in the final analysis, faith is the complete victory over the world, because faith is in Christ, the Father's Anointed. Everything is from him. Everything depends on him. He is both the content and object of faith; he gives faith and sustains it; he is the pioneer and perfecter of our faith. In believing, we confess simply that he and he alone overcomes the world. He has overcome. Already before his death he told his disciples, "In the world you will have tribulation; be of good cheer, I have overcome the world." He overcame the world through his suffering and death; in dying he triumphed over it. Through the cross Christ triumphed over the principalities and powers. And he goes forth conquering and to conquer. He is now fighting against the world from heaven where he is seated at the Father's right hand, and he does that through the faith of his church, his mighty army to whom he furnishes gifts and powers from above. These gifts include the belt of truth, the breastplate of righteousness, the shield of faith, the helmet of salvation, and the sword of the Spirit. And he will triumph finally at the end of time, for he must reign as King until all his enemies are put under his feet. Then, near the end of the ages, when he will find hardly any faith on earth, he will come himself to deliver the final blow and overthrow all his enemies. In that hour, every knee will bow before him and every tongue confess that he is Lord, to the glory of God the Father.

Brothers and sisters, do you have that faith? Do you know that faith in its wonderful, world-conquering power? You bear the name of believer, but are you true to the name by which you are called? Paul admonished the church of Corinth: examine yourselves whether or not you believe; test yourselves! Or do you not know that Jesus Christ is in you? Unless you are in some sense unworthy. Everyone who lives in peace with the world and has not yet embarked on the battle of faith is unworthy, fit only to be rejected. For whoever loves the world does not have the love of the Father in him. Whoever is a friend of the world is called an enemy of God.

This struggle against the world is indeed frightening and serious because it pits us against flesh and blood, against thoughts and inclinations. But, it is, nonetheless, a good and noble struggle. There have been many wars waged on earth between peoples and nations. Some of them—not all of them by a long shot; in fact, not most of them, but nonetheless some of them—are still to be considered noble and great, notwithstanding the misery and distress they produce. Noble and great are battles on behalf of wife and children, for hearth and home, for fatherland and king, for freedom and for justice. Noble and great was the struggle of our fathers. Noble and great is that of both South African Republics; may God bless their weapons and lead them onward to triumph! But no matter how noble and great some wars may have been, they were nonetheless always on behalf of a different justice, on behalf of a sacred justice, to be sure, but were nevertheless waged merely on behalf of a restricted portion of justice and freedom.

But this battle is for nothing less than justice, for God's justice, for righteousness itself in its principle and essence, for perfect freedom, for the highest and holiest good that humans can ever enjoy. It is the noblest, most beautiful, most glorious battle in which a human being can ever engage. It is a struggle against the world, against everything that is from and of the world, against ourselves, against out money and possessions, against all the desires of the flesh and the lusts of the eyes and the pride of life.

But it is at the same time a struggle for our own salvation, for the salvation of our souls, for the heavenly inheritance, for the crown of righteousness that the righteous Judge will give to all who fight the good fight and finish the course. It is a battle for what is right, for truth, for liberty, for Christ and his kingdom, for the glory of God's name and the glory of all his attributes.

Let us take on this battle, push forward and persevere in it to the end, in the strength of the Lord, in the power of faith. For no other weapon equips and strengthens us in this battle except faith alone, the faith that Jesus is the Christ. There is no strength in us or in any creature in heaven or on earth. But Jesus, the Son of Mary, the only begotten of the Father—he is the hero from the tribe of Judah who conquered the world through his cross! Let us enter into his service, let us rest in his victory, let us appropriate his merits unto ourselves.

Then the victory will be ours. For this is the victory that overcomes the world, even our faith. Many wars have been fought on earth for the sake of freedom and justice. Nonetheless, they ended in defeat and subjugation. But this is a battle whose victory is certain in advance. Christ, who is exalted at the Father's right hand, is the guarantor of this victory. He has been anointed as King over Zion, the mountain of God's holiness. The pagan nations have been given to him as his inheritance, the ends of the earth as his possession. Soon he will return with flaming fire of wrath against those who do not know God and are disobedient to the gospel of our Lord Jesus Christ. In that return he will also be glorified in his saints and adored by all who believe. Come then Lord Jesus; yes, come quickly!

Amen.

GENERAL INDEX

SCRIPTURE INDEX

100:3f.	62	5:39–44	115
103:13	148	5:45	48, 67
104:30	49	5:48	16
118	247n	6:19	178
139:2	49	6:33	178, 213
		7:20	16
Ecclesiastes		9:12	149
2:21	162	10:10	178
3:19	49	11:10	114
12:7	182	11:27	73, 139
		15:4–6	153
Isaiah		16:24	15, 104
1:21	153	16:26	178, 213
6:1	72n7	17:14–20	153
33:22	223	18:3	151
45:18	147	19:4–6	153
49:15	148	19:23	178
53:11	162	20:25	115
57:15	60	20:26–28	115
61:10	153	21:13	114
62:5	153	22:37–40	206
66:13	148	26:28	91
		26:41	182
Jeremiah		28:18–20	100
2:32	153		
3:1	153	**Mark**	
		2:8	182
Ezekiel		7:10–12	153
3:14	182	7:15ff.	178
16	153	8:34	111
16:32	153		
46:18	211	**Luke**	
47:14	211	1:47	182
		4:4	95
Hosea		7:11–15	153
1–3	153	8:41–56	153
		9:23	111
Zechariah		9:62	111
12:1	182	17:10	61
		17:20	210
Matthew		23:46	182
4:4	95, 114		
4:7	114	**John**	
4:10	114	1	134
5:11–12	106	1:9	49
5:16	115	1:14	73
5:21–26	115	2	153
5:27–28	153	3	86
5:27–32	115	3:3	92
5:29–42	117		

WISDOM FROM THE PAST
FOR LIFE IN THE PRESENT

Other volumes in the Theologians on the Christian Life series

AUGUSTINE

BAVINCK

BONHOEFFER

CALVIN

EDWARDS

LUTHER

NEWTON

OWEN

PACKER

SCHAEFFER

WARFIELD

WESLEY

Visit crossway.org/TOCL for more information.